Combatting Child Abuse

CHILD WELFARE
A series in child welfare practice, policy, and research
Duncan Lindsey, General Editor

The Welfare of Children
Duncan Lindsey

The Politics of Child Abuse in America
Lela B. Costin, Howard Jacob Karger, and David Stoesz

Combatting Child Abuse:
International Perspectives and Trends
Edited by Neil Gilbert

Combatting Child Abuse

International Perspectives and Trends

Edited by
Neil Gilbert

New York   Oxford
OXFORD UNIVERSITY PRESS
1997

Oxford University Press

Oxford   New York
Athens   Auckland   Bangkok   Bogota   Bombay   Buenos Aires
Calcutta   Cape Town   Dar es Salaam   Delhi   Florence   Hong Kong
Istanbul   Karachi   Kuala Lumpur   Madras   Madrid   Melbourne
Mexico City   Nairobi   Paris   Singapore   Taipei   Tokyo   Toronto

and associated companies in
Berlin   Ibadan

Library of Congress Cataloging-in-Publication Data
Combatting child abuse : international perspectives and trends /
edited by Neil Gilbert.
p.   cm.
Includes bibliographical references and index.
ISBN 0-19-510009-3
1. Child abuse — Reporting — Cross-cultural studies.   2. Abused
children — Services for — Cross-cultural studies.   3. Child abuse —
Prevention — Cross-cultural studies.   I. Gilbert, Neil, 1940-   .
HV8079.C46C66   1997
362.7′663 — DC20   96-16327

1 3 5 7 9 8 6 4 2

Printed in the United States of America
on acid-free paper

for Harry Specht

Acknowledgments

This book is the result of a comparative investigation of child abuse reporting systems that took shape over three years, an effort sustained by generous assistance from several sources. Once again, I am indebted to the family members who established the Milton and Gertrude Chernin Chair in Social Services and Social Welfare at the University of California, Berkeley, which permitted me the time and resources to plan this project and to begin work on the initial phase. I owe special gratitude to the Conrad Hilton Foundation for providing the support needed to facilitate the research efforts of the international study team. Toward the end of this project I was fortunate to receive a foundation grant to organize a final meeting with the research team—a lively gathering at which findings were shared as we grappled with some of the philosophical differences that animated the design and functioning of child abuse reporting systems.

My thinking on the difficult issues of identifying and treating child abuse has benefited from the works of many scholars in this area, but none more than those of Douglas Besharov and Duncan Lindsey. Rick Barth and Jill Duerr Berrick, along with other colleagues and students at the Family Welfare Research Group, are a constant source of critical insight and good advice. During the last two years of this comparative project, I was privileged to be a participant in the Executive Session on New Paradigms for Child Protective Services conducted at the John F. Kennedy School of Government, Harvard University. Led by Frank Hartmann and Mark Moore, we engaged in a series of probing discussions about how to address the crisis of child abuse reporting in the United States, which honed my interests in comparative analysis.

Special thanks are owed to Lissa Roos Parker, who kept me organized and helped in the preparation of the manuscript with meticulous care and a winning smile. In the last stages of this project, I served as the Acting Dean of the School of Social Welfare and was immensely fortunate to have Jim Steele, the Assistant Dean for Administration, as a stalwart partner to help manage the bureaucratic demands of university life. Finally, over the years much of what I did not understand about social welfare policy was brought to my attention (and frequently rectified) with habitual glee by my dear friend Harry Specht to whose memory this book is dedicated. His wise counsel is sorely missed.

Berkeley, California
May 1996

N.G.

Contents

Contributors

HERMAN BAARTMAN is a professor at the Free University, Amsterdam. He is the author of numerous publications on child abuse issues.

DAVID BERRIDGE is a professor of child and family welfare at the University of Luton. Dr. Berridge previously served as director of research for the National Children's Bureau; he has written several books, including *Children's Homes* and numerous articles on child welfare issues.

PATRICK BROOS is a special educationalist at the Confidential Doctor Center, Department of Child Psychiatry, at the University Children's Hospital in Brussels. He is executive counselor for the European Youth Care Exchange.

NEIL GILBERT is the Chernin Professor of Social Welfare at the University of California, Berkeley. His most recent book is *Welfare Justice: Restoring Social Equity*.

SVEN OLSSON HORT is past president of the Scandinavian Sociological Association and vice president of the Swedish Sociological Association. Dr. Olsson Hort is currently an assistant professor of sociology at Stockholm University; he is the author of *Social Policy and the Welfare State in Sweden*, which went into its second English edition in 1992.

RUTH LAWRENCE-KARSKI, MSW, is a doctoral candidate at the School of Social Welfare, University of California, Berkeley, and a research associate in the Family Welfare Research Group.

CATHERINE MARNEFFE is a doctor of medicine and a Ph.D. in Child Psychiatry; in 1986 she founded the Confidential Doctor Center at the Free University of Brussels. Dr. Marneffe has published numerous articles, is associate editor of *Child Abuse and Neglect: The International Journal*, and is widely recognized as one of Europe's foremost experts on child abuse and neglect.

TARJA PÖSÖ, Ph.D., is an assistant professor of social work at the University of Tampere, where she does research and lectures on child welfare. Her most recent publications are about family discourses and residential care.

VITA BERING PRUZAN holds a law degree from the University of Copenhagen; she is head of the Research Unit on Children and Families for the Danish National Institute of Social Research and has published widely on family policy and child welfare.

MARIAN ROELOFS has an M.A. in social science from Utrecht University and is working on her Ph.D. under a grant from the Dutch Organization for Scientific Research; she has authored several publications, including a study of child abuse and social services in the *Journal of Child Abuse and Neglect*.

KAREN SWIFT, Ph.D., is an assistant professor of social work at McGill University; she has considerable experience as a practitioner in child protective services and as a researcher on child welfare policy issues; her most recent book is *Manufacturing "Bad Mother": A Critical Perspective on Child Neglect*.

REINHART WOLFF is a professor of sociology and education at the Alice Salomon-Fachhochschule, Berlin School of Social Work, and an adjunct professor at the Free University of Berlin; he served as special vice president of the International Society for the Prevention of Child Abuse and Neglect; his publications include nine books and over 90 articles. In 1975 he founded the Berlin Child Protection Center.

Combatting Child Abuse

Introduction

The problem of child abuse has become increasingly evident in North America and Western Europe. Between 1980 and 1993, for example, the number of children reported one or more times to the public authorities for maltreatment more than doubled from 1.1 to 2.3 million cases in the United States (U.S. Department of Health and Human Services, 1995); child abuse reports to confidential doctors climbed from 3,179 to 13,220 in the Netherlands between 1983 and 1993 (Roelofs and Baartman, chapter 8), in Belgium the number of reports increased by 70% between 1986 and 1992 (Marneffe and Broos, chapter 7), and in Quebec, Canada, the number of reports jumped by 100% from 1982 to 1989 (Swift, chapter 2). This increase in reports has produced acute strains on child welfare service systems and has raised compelling questions about how best to detect and respond to child abuse (Besharov, 1990a, 1990b; Giovannoni and Meezan, 1995; Pelton, 1991).

The most extreme pressures are conspicuous in the United States, where an enormous surge in the number of child abuse reports has transformed the system of child welfare services; here, an increasing amount of resources are devoted to investigation of the problem, steadily diminishing the resources left to provide services to children and families at risk. As Kamerman and Kahn (1990) observe: "Depending on the terms used public social service administrators state either that 'Child protection is child welfare,' or that 'The increased demand for child protection has driven out all other child welfare services'" (p. 9).

In response to this development, a vigorous debate has emerged in the United States as some experts claim that too many reports and investigations are being made, while others charge that many cases of abuse go unreported. Those who view the net as being cast too wide point to the fact that most child abuse reports are unfounded; in 1993, for example, 38% of the child abuse reports investigated were substantiated or indicated (i.e., not fully confirmed, but sufficient reason to suspect maltreatment) (U.S. Department of Health and Human Services, 1995). "The current flood of unfounded reports," Besharov (1987) declares, "is overwhelming the limited resources of child protective agencies" (p. 7). Not only are most allegations of child abuse unsubstantiated, but the vast majority consist of cases that involve neither serious harm nor immediate threat of physical injury to the child. Lindsey (1994) estimates that 2% of child abuse reports involve cases of severe physical child abuse.

From this perspective much of the problem is attributed to the expansion

3

of mandatory reporting laws and the broadened definition of child abuse, which includes conditions of neglect that often derive from poverty-related circumstances (Hutchison, 1994; Lindsey, 1994; Pelton, 1989). Robin (1991) suggests that mandatory reporting and vague definitions of child abuse have contributed to the emergence of false allegations as a social problem. These criticisms of the child welfare system have prompted a number of proposals to modify reporting laws, narrow definitions of abuse, and refine evaluative procedures (Besharov, 1988, 1990b; Crenshaw, Bartell, & Lichetenberg, 1994; Kalichman & Brosig, 1992).

Other experts, however, argue that despite the increasing rate of reports, a large amount of child abuse remains undetected and that most substantiated cases involve threats of serious harm to children, if not the occurrence of physical injury (Finkelhor, 1990, 1993). At the same time, the experts maintain that unsubstantiated reports have information value that may help to avoid later abuse and that the negative effects of unwarranted intrusions into family life are usually negligible and accepted by the public as necessary to protect children (Barth, 1994; Finkelhor, 1993).

With the increasing recognition of child abuse, many countries are now struggling with issues similar to those being debated in the United States. What criteria define child maltreatment? Who is responsible for reporting suspected cases of maltreatment? What are the processes for inquiring into these reports? How are allegations of maltreatment substantiated, and what is the state's response? The initial answers to these questions vary considerably as governments have begun to develop diverse systems for identifying the problem and delivering services to abused children and their families.

This book is about the social policies and professional practices that inform alternative designs of child abuse reporting systems in nine countries: Belgium, Canada, Denmark, England, Finland, Germany, the Netherlands, Sweden, and the United States. In developing case studies on these countries, the researchers applied a common framework to guide their examination of basic features of child abuse reporting systems — legal definitions of abuse, reporting mandates, screening of reports, and investigative procedures — as well as reporting and placement trends. After drafts of the country studies were completed, the research group met for several days to review and clarify the findings on each country. In the course of this meeting a number of broader of categories emerged that served to highlight important similarities and differences in the way child abuse reporting systems are organized and function. Efforts to conceptualize broad dimensions for comparative purposes, of course, simplify reality somewhat. That is the price we must pay to cull and distill essential features of these systems.

Although the reporting systems in these countries cannot be fully sorted into neat classes, the chapters in this book are divided according to reporting systems that have a child protective orientation, which emphasizes legalistic interventions, and a family service orientation, which emphasizes therapeutic interventions. The family-service-oriented systems are further divided between those with mandatory and those with nonmandatory reporting standards. Under this classification the countries are grouped into three categories as follows:

1. *Child protection*
   United States
   Canada
   England
2. *Family service – mandatory reporting*
   Denmark
   Sweden
   Finland
3. *Family service – nonmandatory reporting*
   Belgium
   Netherlands
   Germany

In analyzing how their systems operate, the studies of these countries allow us to compare several approaches to reporting and dispensation of child abuse cases and to distinguish differences as well as common problems and policy responses currently emerging in this area. The purpose of this book is to help researchers and decision makers deepen their understanding of the social policies and institutional arrangements that frame societal responses to problems of child abuse in different countries – so that we might benefit from each other's experiences.

References

Barth, R. (1994). Should current laws regarding sexual and physical abuse of children be sharply limited to discourage overreporting? No. In M. A. Mason & E. Gambrill (Eds.), *Debating Children's Lives* (pp. 292-295). Newbury Park, CA: Sage Publications.

Besharov, D. (1987). Contending with overblown expectations: CPS cannot be all things to all people. *Public Welfare, 45,* 7-12.

Besharov, D. (Ed.). (1988). *Protecting children from abuse and neglect.* Springfield, IL: Charles Thomas.

Besharov, D. (1990a). Gaining control over child abuse reports. *Public Welfare, 48*(2), 34-40.

Besharov, D. (1990b). *Recognizing child abuse: A guide for the concerned.* New York: Free Press.

Crenshaw, W., Bartell, P., & Lichetenberg, J. (1994). Proposed revisions to mandatory reporting laws: An exploratory survey of child protective service agencies. *Child Welfare, 73,* 15-27.

Finkelhor, D. (1990). Is child abuse overreported? *Public Welfare, 48,* 22-29.

Finkelhor, D. (1993). The main problem is still underreporting, not overreporting. In R. Gelles & D. Loseke (Eds.), *Current controversies on family violence* (pp. 273-289). Newbury Park, CA: Sage Publications.

Giovannoni, J., & Meezan, W. (1995). Rethinking supply and demand in child welfare. *Children and Youth Services Review, 17*(4), 465-470.

Hutchison, E. (1994). Child maltreatment: Can it be defined? In R. Barth, J. Duerr Berrick, & N. Gilbert (Eds.), *Child welfare research review* (Vol. 1, pp. 5–27). New York: Columbia University Press.

Kalichman, S., & Brosig, C. (1992). Mandatory child abuse reporting laws: Issues and implications. *Law and Policy, 14.*

Kamerman, S., & Kahn, A. (1990, Winter). If CPS is driving child welfare — Where do we go from here? *Public Welfare, 48,* 9–13.

Lindsey, D. (1994). *The welfare of children.* New York: Oxford University Press.

Pelton, L. (1989). *For reasons of poverty: A critical analysis of the public child welfare system in the United States.* New York: Praeger.

Pelton, L. (1991). Beyond permanency planning: Restructuring the public child welfare system. *Social Work, 36*(4), 337–43.

Robin, M. (1991). The social construction of child abuse and false allegations. In M. Robin (Ed.), *Assessing child maltreatment reports: The problem of false allegations* (pp. 1–34). New York: Haworth Press.

U.S. Department of Health and Human Services. (1995). *Child maltreatment 1993: Reports from the states to the National Center on Child Abuse and Neglect.* Washington, DC: Government Printing Office.

I

Child Protective Orientation

1

United States

California's Reporting System

RUTH LAWRENCE-KARSKI

Defining the Problem: What Constitutes Child Maltreatment?

The maltreatment, misuse, and neglect of children are recognized as a serious social problem in the United States. Although children have been the subject of various types of maltreatment in different historical periods, concern for maltreated children now prompts action from private citizens and the government. As Nelson (1984) notes, a specific definition of this problem has been recognized, adopted, promoted, and maintained by the federal bureaucracy, state legislatures, and Congress.

The definition of child abuse that has been the focus of social concern and public services takes a medical-legal approach to the maltreatment of children by their parents or primary caretakers — that is, maltreatment of children within their families. This conceptualization of child maltreatment in California and in U.S. social policy in general, starts from the individual and family level, rather than a structural, institutional, or societal approach to the problem (Pecora, Whittaker, & Maluccio, 1992). Social conditions including poverty and a lack of housing and child care have not been the focus of government child welfare services.

The current conception of child abuse and neglect in the United States has its roots in the recognition of cases of parent's physical cruelty to children at the turn of the century. At this time the child had become emotionally "priceless" in American culture (Zelizer, 1985), and childhood was seen as a protected state. Against this backdrop, social workers and volunteers from humane societies were dealing with situations of cruelty to children. The conception of maltreatment focused on physical abuse of the child, and by the 1930s the expressions "physical abuse of children" and "cruelty to children" were used interchangably (Anderson, 1989, p. 241). It was not until the 1960s,

9

however, that the problem attracted widespread public concern and a national response to the problem was initiated. Following the work of radiologists Caffey, Woolley, and Evans from the 1940s (Nelson, 1984), C. Henry Kempe and his medical colleagues provided scientific evidence of child maltreatment. Pediatric X rays documented the results of parent's deliberate infliction of physical injuries on young children. Kempe and his colleagues coined the phrase "battered child syndrome" to describe their findings (Anderson, 1989; Kempe, Silverman, Steele, Droegemueller, & Silver, 1962). With the aid of the media and Kempe's data, Senator Walter Mondale succeeded in getting child abuse on the Congressional agenda in 1973 (Nelson, 1984).

Child abuse in the 1960s was seen as a problem of physical battering and the deliberate intention to harm the child, mainly by parents. Since that time the meaning of the term *child abuse* has expanded (Bourne & Newberger, 1979) to include not only physical harm of the child, but also sexual or emotional maltreatment by parents or caretakers. Abuse does not have to be deliberate infliction, but can also take the form of omission to act resulting in neglect of the child's needs. Depending on what the child's needs are seen to be, the definition of child neglect can be very broad.

In severe cases, there is general community and professional consensus in the United States as to what constitutes abuse or neglect of a child. For example, there is agreement that a child with fractured bones from repeated beatings is "abused," while a child who is not given the minimum amount of food, clothing, or attention necessary for survival (such as a young child left unfed in a room) is "neglected." Between these extreme cases, however, there is a wide range of situations on which there is often disagreement about what constitutes maltreatment. There are also different cultural and class perspectives on maltreatment, although there has been little research in this area. Alvy (1987, in Noh Ahn, 1994) found, for example, high rates of the use of physical punishment in low-income African American and Caucasian parents (99% and 95%, respectively), compared to 85% of high-income Caucasian parents. Noh Ahn (1994) reports that a bruise inflicted by a parent on a nine year old was not considered physical abuse by 90% of the Vietnamese sampled, although it was for 100% of the Cambodians in the study.

Measuring the Scope of the Problem

Estimates of the scope of child maltreatment vary according to the definitions used, the measures employed, and the populations studied. Studies by the American Association for Protecting Children (1989) and the National Center on Child Abuse and Neglect (NCCAN, 1993, 1994) use legal definitions of maltreatment as measured by the numbers of official reports of child abuse and neglect made to state departments of child protective services (CPS). Children reported to state CPS agencies constitute the population studied. Using these study parameters, the National Center on Child Abuse and Neglect estimated that 2,695,308 children, or 4.14% of children under 18 years of age in the United States, were reported as abused or neglected in 1991 (NCCAN, 1993).

In contrast to studies using official legal definitions of child abuse and neglect, other studies create their own definitions of maltreatment and include recognition of child maltreatment by professionals. The second national incidence study, for example, defines six different types of maltreatment (physical, sexual, and emotional abuse, and physical, emotional, and educational neglect) and produces categories classifying the severity of abuse (including demonstrable harm experienced and endangerment). The study measures the number of maltreated children known to CPS and to professionals in a national probability sample drawn from 26 counties (Westat Associates Inc., 1987). Using stringent criteria of "identifiable harm," the study reports a rate of child abuse of 14.5 children per 1,000 children in the population in 1986. In the broader definition of maltreatment in the study that includes children who are "endangered," the rate is 22.6 children per 1,000 children in the population in 1986 (Westat Associates Inc., 1987).

In contrast to the NCCAN and Westat studies, which define different types of abuse, Straus and Gelles (1986) concentrate on one type of maltreatment: physical violence directed toward children. Defining physical abuse to include striking a child with an object, Strauss and Gelles report a prevalence rate of 140 children aged 3–17 years per 1,000 children in 1975. In a second study conducted 10 years later they found a prevalence rate of 107 children per 1,000 children, adjusting for the differences in sampling. The statistically significant decrease in the rate of severe violence toward children is open to interpretation. Either the rate of severe violence actually decreased from 1975 to 1985, or the finding is a result of the study design. Abuse is self-reported with no independent corroboration. It is possible that in a climate of increasing social condemnation for abuse, parents are less comfortable admitting abuse of their children.

Although a lack of consensus remains in measuring child abuse and neglect, with the exception of Straus and Gelles (1986), estimates point to an increase in the number and rate of child maltreatment nationally. As reflected in Figure 1-1, the incidence rate of reports has also more than doubled, from 20 children per 1,000 children in the population reported in 1982 to 43 children per 1,000 children in the population reported in 1992 (NCCAN, 1993). As there are no standardized independent measures of abuse, it is not clear whether the rate of abuse has increased or whether the increase is the result of changes in the reporting system. Increased precision in definitions of abuse categories may in part be responsible for the increase in the number of reports (Rose & Meezan, 1993).

Some researchers believe that numbers of official reports merely capture the "tip of the iceberg" and severely underestimate the true size and scope of the problem as many situations of maltreatment of children by parents and caretakers are unreported (Pecora et al., 1992; Westat Associates Inc., 1987). Even studies with expanded definitions of abuse and neglect (Westat Associates Inc., 1987, for example), although more comprehensive, still rely on

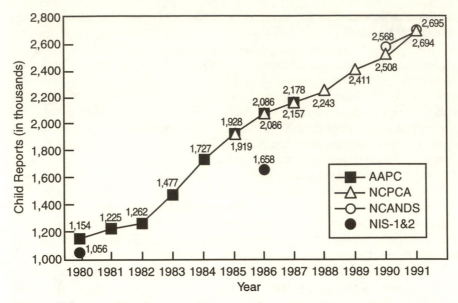

Fig. 1-1. National estimates of children reported. Data are from *Highlights of Official Aggregate Child Neglect and Abuse Reporting, 1987,* American Association for Protecting Children (AAPC), 1989; *Highlights of Official Aggregate Child Neglect and Abuse Reporting, 1986,* AAPC, 1988; *National Incidence and Prevalence of Child Abuse and Neglect: 1988 Revised Report (NIS-2),* Westat, 1991; *Current Trends in Child Abuse Reporting and Fatalities: The Results of the 1991 Annual Fifty State Survey,* National Committee for the Prevention of Child Abuse (NCPCA), 1992. *Source:* National Center on Child Abuse and Neglect, Washington, D.C., 1993.

professional recognition of the abuse. In contrast to proponents of underreporting, other researchers believe that the official reporting figures overestimate the problem as many cases that are reported are unfounded (Besharov, 1990). To gauge the amount of both underestimation and overestimation in official reporting figures, three questions must be addressed: (i) How many cases never are reported? (ii) How many unsubstantiated cases reflect instances in which abuse occurred but could not be proven? and (iii) How many substantiated cases reflect situations of abuse or neglect that do not seriously jeopardize the child's well-being?

Attempts have been made to estimate the answers to some of these questions. Schene (1987) calculates from NCCAN and Westat figures that for every child reported there are seven abused children who are not reported. As professionals do not report many cases of abuse and other cases never come to official attention, it is likely that the number of substantiated cases given in official reporting figures underestimates the number of children abused. This position is supported by Westat Associates Inc. (1987), Costin, Bell, and

Downs (1991), Pecora et al. (1992), and the National Research Council (1993). It is unknown what proportion of cases reported as unsubstantiated actually occurred but could not be proven. What is regarded as abuse that "does not seriously endanger the child" is not clear-cut. The second national incidence study records detailed categories of severity of abuse and endangerment to the child. The study finds that most (60%) cases that fit the definitions for inclusion in the study were moderate injuries (i.e., injuries persisting in observable form for at least 48 hrs). There were serious injuries in 10% of cases, there were probable injuries in 11%, children were believed to be seriously endangered in 19%, and there were fatalities in 0.1% (Westat Associates Inc., 1987). These findings suggest that there is some overreporting of abuse as some cases are not serious and other cases are not substantiated. Even so, this does not change the fact that there is an underestimation of the scope of the problem in reported figures.

Taking into account measurement problems, a possible schema for the scope of the problem is illustrated in Figure 1-2. As shown, estimates exist for the total number of reported cases (4% of all U.S. children), the percentage of reported cases substantiated (39.3%) and unsubstantiated (58%) (NCCAN, 1993), and the percentage of each level of severity of injuries among cases (Westat Associates Inc., 1987). What is not known is the exact size of the subcategories, the number of reports unsubstantiated or substantiated for which abuse actually did or did not occur. Until further research is undertaken, these categories remain open to speculation. Even though the exact size of the problem of child abuse is not known, the broad dimensions of this problem are large enough to have elicited a strong response by state and federal governments.

With the establishment of the Children's Bureau at the turn of the century the federal government acknowledged the problems of children. Each state, however, is responsible for designing and implementing its own child protection laws and services. As with other social problems, federal legislation and regulations strongly influence state programs through funding mechanisms; that is, for a state to obtain federal funding for a specific program, federal guidelines must be followed (see, e.g., Lawrence & Barth, 1993). After the mobilization of public opinion in the early 1960s, federal funding was used to encourage states to develop their own laws relating to child abuse. By 1967, every state had established laws concerning the maltreatment of children. Although there are minor variations among the states, each state has developed child abuse reporting systems (run by state departments of social services) in which certain classes of professionals are legally mandated to report abuse. States vary in the specificity of their legislation: Alaska and Colorado, for example, in contrast to most states, simply specify child abuse and neglect and do not detail categories such as mental injury or educational neglect. States also vary in who is required by law to report child abuse: Idaho, New Mexico, and Texas require the public to report child abuse, while states such as Illinois and Nevada have more than 40 detailed categories of mandatory

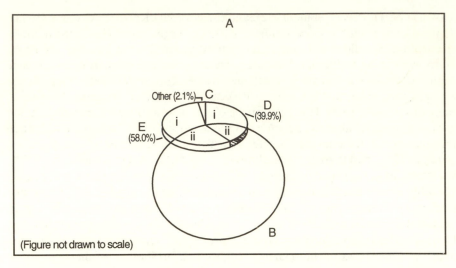

Fig. 1-2. A schema for measuring the size of the problem of child maltreatment in the United States. A: U.S. child population; B: Children in the population maltreated = ?; C: Children reported as abused = 4% of child population (National Center on Child Abuse and Neglect [NCCAN], 1993), ratio of children reported as abused : children in the population maltreated = 1 : 7 (Schene, 1987, calculated from NCCAN and National Incidence and Prevalence of Child Abuse and Neglect NIS-1 and NIS-2 data); D: Reports of abuse that are substantiated = 39.9% of reports nationwide (NCCAN, 1993) (i) proportion of reports that are false or nonserious and are mistakenly substantiated (false positives) = ? (ii) proportion of reports in which abuse occurred = ? (60% of substantiated reports involve moderate injuries, 10% involve serious injuries of the child, NIS-2); E: Reports of abuse that are not substantiated = 58% of reports nationwide (i) proportion of unfounded reports for which no abuse occurred = ? (ii) proportion of unfounded reports for which abuse occurred but could not be proven (false negatives) = ?

reporters. To explore in detail the basic features of state response to the problem of child abuse and neglect, we will examine the official reporting system in California, which is among the largest such system in the United States.

Responses to Child Maltreatment in California

Two years after a New York society adopted child abuse in its charter, the California Society for the Prevention of Cruelty to Children was established in San Francisco in 1876. The society dealt with all cases involving children referred by the San Francisco police. Many cases of neglect and abuse would be "privately arranged," while serious cases would be taken by the society before the police court, the juvenile court, or the superior court (Slingerland, 1916, p. 172). The duty of the society was to "present the facts which bring the case within the law . . . and then leave the disposition of the case to the officers of the law" (Gerry, 1883, p. 129). In 1881, the society received 409 complaints, examined 681 cases, and secured convictions in 81 cases. By 1906, there were three California humane societies (one in Fresno and two in San Francisco) that specialized in the "legal and protective relations of children" (Slingerland, 1916, p. 171), and by 1910 there were seven societies (Bureau of the Census, 1913). By 1913, the work of the societies had expanded. After "rescuing" cruelly abused and neglected children and often taking them before the court, these societies would place the children in institutional care or foster homes. The San Francisco society investigated 2,434 complaints (involving 4,472 children); the society brought 863 cases in the juvenile court and placed 124 children in institutions and 34 in families and assigned 371 to home-finding services.[1]

Besides rescuing children directly, the humane societies throughout the United States campaigned for legislation to cover various situations of child maltreatment. Laws in the states varied. In California the 1913 juvenile court laws were extensive and clearly defined dependency and neglect. A neglected person was a person under 21 years of age whose home was unfit for any of a variety of reasons including parental neglect, cruelty, or depravity, or whose father was dead or a "habitual drunkard" (Slingerland, 1916, p. 220).

Services for abused and neglected children in the late 1800s had different consequences for different social classes. Children in the system came from working-class homes where dependency was created by unfortunate circumstances and a lack of savings and insurance (Tiffin, 1982). The death of the father caused destitution of the family. Most single parent mothers occupied unskilled jobs and had lower wages than their male counterparts. Thus 50% of the children in care were "half-orphans," and 17% were orphans and foundlings (Bureau of the Census, 1913). Even some children with both parents living were given up to children's asylums; in cases of unemployment, sickness, or an accident, some families had no resources to fall back on and no other alternatives. Of the recorded classified cases of children in care in 1910, 50% were therefore children who were brought to institutions by relatives or friends (Bureau of the Census, 1913). Given these social conditions, many children considered "neglected" entered care because of poverty, rather than actual abuse of the child. Without detailed analysis of court records, it is not possible to discern the proportion of cases that were cases of maltreatment and what proportion were cases of neglect, poverty, or unacceptable working-class behavior.

Child Protection in California in the 1990s

In tracing the origins of "child-saving" work it is evident that some aspects of this work have not changed since the 1880s, while other aspects have taken quite a different course of development. In contrast to the origin of the system in California, where the responsibility for child protective work lay with non-governmental humane societies, maltreatment of children by parents and caretakers is now officially handled by government services (including the state's Department of Social Services and the California Department of Justice). Nongovernmental agencies still provide much-needed services for children and families, advocate for children in general, and work in concert with state agencies, but these nongovernmental agencies are not the prime agent of child protection. The scope, organization, and structure of state intervention have vastly changed.

In California, the child abuse reporting system is one program within the system of Child Welfare Services (CWS) run by the state's Department of Social Services (which is administered by the state's 58 counties). The organization of the department's CWS is oriented toward child abuse reporting and providing services to families who have been reported rather than directed toward voluntary clients who may come forward requesting services. The only entry point to CWS is an allegation of child abuse (except for voluntary adoptions, which is not part of the four programs described below). Reporting is the intake phase of the service system providing the point of entry to other CWS programs. The following programs were introduced in 1982 as a response to federal legislation, the Adoption Assistance and Child Welfare Act (Hill, 1991):

1. The Emergency Response (ER) Program provides social worker response (crisis intervention and referral) to allegations of child abuse and neglect.
2. Family Maintenance (FM) provides services for up to one year to families who have already been identified through the ER program to prevent removal of the children to foster care.
3. Family Reunification (FR) provides services to children in foster care and their families, with the aim to reunite the child and family within an 18-month period.
4. Permanent Placement (PP) Program provides services to children who cannot be safely returned to their families, with adoption being preferred to long-term foster care.

In 1993, legislation (S.B. 1125) redefined CWS as a continuum of services rather than four distinct programs; this legislation is currently being implemented.

In 1929, California was the first state to legislate the mandatory reporting by hospitals and physicians of intentionally inflicted injuries on any person (*California Penal Code [C.P.C.] Annotated*, n.d., 11160–11161, originally in *Statutes of 1929*, chap. 417, p. 739, §1). By 1963 the law related to children in particular (C.P.C. 11161.5). Current child abuse reporting law is contained in the C.P.C., whereas law relating to the removal of children from their families is contained in the Welfare and Institution's Code (W. & I.C.). The jurisdiction of current legislation relates to children under 18 years of age (although initially child abuse legislation in California set the age limit for a child who could be reported at 12 years [C.P.C. 11161.5, Supp. 1970]). The Department of Social Services is responsible for handling abuse by parents or caretakers, while the Department of Justice handles abuse of children by others.

The California Child Abuse Reporting Law (C.P.C. 11164–11174.5) is specific in the types of maltreatment that must be reported. The categories of abuse cover five basic areas.

1. Sexual abuse, sexual assault, sexual exploitation. Sexual abuse includes direct acts such as sexual assault and indirect acts such as sexual exploitation of the child and pornographic materials (C.P.C. 11165.1).
2. Neglect. Neglect of the child, either "severe" or "general," including acts and omissions resulting in harm or threatening to harm the child's health or welfare (C.P.C. 11165.2), must be reported. Severe neglect refers to the negligent failure of a person to protect the child from severe malnutrition or medically diagnosed nonorganic failure to thrive.
3. Emotional abuse: Willful cruelty or unjustified punishment. This section is defined as the direct infliction of, or permitting of a child to suffer, unjustifiable physical pain or mental suffering (C.P.C. 11165.3). Mental suffering or endangerment of the child's emotional well-being is not by itself required to be reported, but may be reported (C.P.C. 11166[b]).
4. Unlawful corporal punishment or injury. This is defined as any cruel or inhuman corporal punishment or injury resulting in a traumatic condition (C.P.C. 11165.4).
5. Child abuse (physical abuse). Physical abuse is seen as injury that is inflicted by other than accidental means on the child (C.P.C. 11165.6).

Despite these broad categories, some types of child abuse and neglect are not mandated to be reported. Although recognized as grounds for removal of a child from the home (W. & I.C., Section 300), emotional abuse does not have to be reported. Children who are not made to go to school (children who suffer educational neglect) and very young children who are not supervised by a caretaker after-school ("latchkey kids") are not covered by legislation. Since 1990, perinatal substance abuse alone is also not sufficient grounds for a report of child abuse (S.B. 2669, the Presley Bill, 1990; C.P.C. 11165.13). The law has set priorities for what is considered to be the most severe forms of maltreatment of children. The categories fall into two main domains: physical maltreatment (including sexual maltreatment) and neglect.

Legislation regarding reporting does not give detailed guidelines on indicators of abuse or guidelines on the severity of cases. As shown in Table 1-1, although severe neglect is medically defined, general neglect occurs when the child lacks food, clothing, and medical care. Guidelines for the standard of what is considered adequate care are not given, so the interpretation is left to county guidelines and individual professional judgment.

Table 1-1. Child Abuse and Neglect Definitions in California Legislation: Grounds for Reporting Child Abuse

Type of Abuse	Subcategories	Indicators
Sexual abuse	Sexual assault Sexual exploitation	(Adult's actions such as touching, fondling, photographing, rather than the observed results of these actions on the child are specified)
Neglect	Severe	Severe malnutrition, non-organic failure to thrive
	General	Lack of food, clothing, medical care
Willful cruelty, unjustifiable punishment		Physical pain, mental suffering
Unlawful corporal punishment or injury		Traumatic condition
Physical abuse	Intentional infliction	

Source: California Penal Code, Sections 11165–11174.5.

In contrast, legislation in 1989 (S.B. 243, 1989) contains detailed indicators of maltreatment that are grounds for children to be removed from their parent's care. Children can, for example, be removed on the basis of physical abuse resulting in "permanent physical disfigurement or disability." (W. & I.C., Section 300) (Further indicators are listed in Table 1-2.) Through detailed specification, this legislation narrowed the categories that are grounds for removal of the child. The exception to this narrowing effect is emotional damage, which is specified for the first time as a category of abuse that is grounds for removal.

It is not clear whether reporting legislation (like removal legislation) should

Table 1-2. Child Abuse and Neglect Definitions in California Legislation: Grounds for Removal of Children from Their Parents

Grounds for Removal of a Child Less than 5 Years of Age	Indicators
Single act of severe physical abuse	Permanent physical disfigurement, disability, or death if left untreated
Single act of sexual abuse	Significant bleeding, deep bruising, significant internal or external swelling
Multiple acts of physical abuse	Bleeding, swelling, bone fracture, deep bruising, bone fracture, or unconsciousness
The parent is convicted of causing the death of another child through abuse or neglect	

Source: California Welfare and Institutions Code, Section 300 (as amended by S.B. 243).

be more specific in its definitions and indicators of abuse. With broad categories, the legislation leaves room for state regulations, county guidelines, and professional judgment. Flexibility is appropriate when dealing with the variety of human situations that are encountered. This flexibility, if misused, can however have a number of negative consequences. There can be varying interpretations of the law and different treatment of families in different regions.[2]

Mandatory Reporting: Who Reports

In the 1880s concerned citizens would intervene in private family situations and bring the matter to court. Now trained and specialized state child welfare workers (in most cases social workers) are legally mandated to report child abuse. There are agreed-upon procedures for these workers that reflect the growth of public regulation of the field. With the dramatic increase of federal and state regulation and funding of services over the century, the religious dimension in much of the work in the 1880s has disappeared. The overt religious motivation and fervor of workers (see Gerry, 1883) and the religious view of the child, the family, and the need to rescue have been replaced by regulation and professionalization.

There has been an increasing number of categories of professionals for whom it is mandatory to report suspected child abuse. Initially, reporting laws in California in 1963 made it mandatory for physicians to report child abuse. Currently there are numerous categories of workers who are legally mandated to report: licensed clinical social workers, counselors, licensed nurses, dental hygienists, surgeons, podiatrists, chiropractors, teachers, foster parents, group home personnel, police and county probation workers, and workers who develop photographic films (C.P.C. 11165.8, 11165.9, 11165.10, 11166.5).

Professionals must report known abuse or an "objectively reasonable suspicion of child abuse." (C.P.C. 11166) A *reasonable suspicion* is defined as when

> it is objectively reasonable for a person to entertain such a suspicion, based upon facts that could cause a reasonable person in a like position, drawing when appropriate on his or her training and experience, to suspect child abuse. (C.P.C. 11166)

The criterion of reasonable suspicion for mandated workers has been criticized as it varies from the standard used by the CPS workers. Mandated reporters are required to notify on the basis of suspicion, but CPS workers can only act to remove children according to a much higher standard. Once a report is made, it is determined to be either "unfounded" (determined to be improbable or not to constitute abuse), "substantiated" (determined to constitute child abuse or neglect), or "unsubstantiated" (determined to be not unfounded, but with insufficient evidence and inconclusive findings) (C.P.C. 11165.12).

Screening Cases

Child abuse and neglect units receive a variety of phone calls: inappropriate referrals (e.g., family law cases, school truancy cases, and unfounded complaints designed to harass) and appropriate referrals, which vary in severity and seriousness.[3] In 1988, legislation (S.B. 1912) stated that not all cases require an in-person response. California counties adopted varying approaches to the screening of incoming cases. In response to this variability, legislation (Assembly Bill [A.B.] 60) in 1991 introduced a standardized statewide protocol and accompanying training for telephone screening of Emergency Response referrals. California's Emergency Response Protocol bases the first level of screening on legal definitions of child abuse and neglect with an emphasis on inappropriate referrals being referred to other agencies (Tabbert, Sullivan, & Whittaker, 1992).

Liability

In designing the child abuse reporting system, legislation tries to "encourage the reporting of child abuse to the greatest extent possible to prevent further abuse" (C.P.C. 11172, Notes on Decisions). To facilitate this, mandatory reporters are given immunity from civil and criminal liability for making a report of suspected child abuse to a child protective agency. As reporting laws are vague in their definitions of abuse and as to the type of immunity allowed, absolute immunity has been granted to reporters. Workers who make negligent, reckless, or even intentionally false reports are protected (see *McMartin v. Children's Institute International,* 1989; *Thomas v. Chadwick,* 1990). Others making a report have qualified immunity—they are not liable unless it can be proved a purposely false report was made. In 1984 legislation provided for the state to reimburse for legal expenses (to $50,000) incurred by mandatory reporters sued for making a report. For failing to make a report, mandatory reporters may be fined up to $1,000 dollars, confined in jail up to six months, or both (C.P.C. 11172).

The absolute immunity clause has been criticized on two major grounds: first, the state should not support negligent, reckless, or intentionally false reports; and second, it is unconstitutional for the state to grant immunity as under the Supremacy Clause only federal law can grant immunity (March, 1992). Examination of allegations of negligent reports could be used as one avenue to monitor workers. Instead, the granting of absolute immunity contributes to a worker's power in the system, with no recourse for victims of genuinely negligent reports.

Trends in Child Abuse Reporting in California

Prevalence of Child Abuse Reports

The number of child abuse reports in California has dramatically increased since the 1970s from 119,000 reports per year in 1976 to 475,000 per year in 1988 (Barth, Duerr Berrick, Courtney, and Pizzini, 1990). This reflects a nationwide trend. The prevalence of child abuse reports (the average number of reports per year) has increased (Fig. 1-3) from reports involving 41 children per 1,000 children in California in 1985 to reports involving 70 children per 1,000 children in 1990.[4] The large jump in prevalence of reports between 1987 and 1989 has in part been attributed to changes in the budgeting of services. Allocation of funds changed from being based on a demographic formula to being based on a caseload-driven formula (see Albert & Barth, 1994; Pizzini, 1994).

As regards the increase in the total number of child abuse reports, more detailed analysis shows that the increase has occurred in every category of child abuse. Figure 1-4a shows the monthly number of reports in each category of abuse from 1985 to 1993. The average monthly number of reports displayed in Figure 1-4b (and detailed in Table 1-3) shows that the different types of child abuse per 1,000 children have increased over the time period 1985 to 1990. Every category increased every year except exploitation, which remained at a fairly constant small rate.

The relative contribution of each type of abuse to the overall rate of child abuse is shown in Figure 1-5. The highest prevalence to the lowest prevalence of type of abuse in 1992 was neglect (36.01% total, with 28.85% general and 7.16% severe neglect reports), physical abuse (32.54%), sexual abuse (18.20%), caretaker absence or incompetence (9.08%), emotional abuse (3.87%), and exploitation (0.31%). This follows the national pattern for prevalence rates of

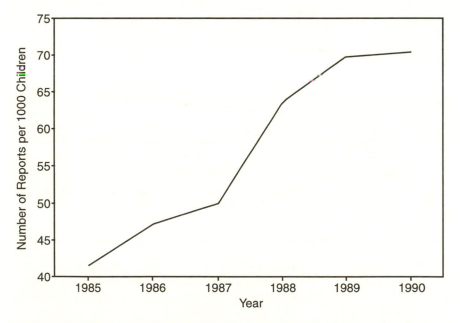

Fig. 1-3. California child abuse reports average yearly prevalence 1985–1990. *Sources:* Child abuse reports from DSS, Soc. 291 form; demographic data from U.S. Department of Finance Census.

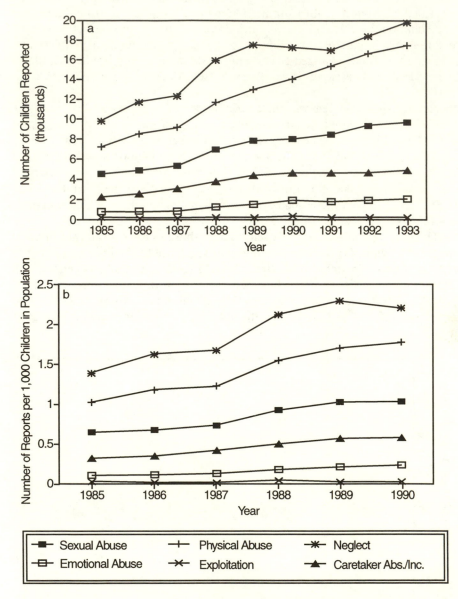

Fig. 1-4. California child abuse reports by category of abuse. a, Number per month. b, Monthly prevalence. *Sources:* child abuse reports from DSS, Soc. 291 form; demographic data from U.S. Department of Finance.

Table 1-3. Monthly Prevalence of Child Abuse Reports by Category of Abuse Per 1,000 Children in California

	Sexual Abuse	Physical Abuse	Severe Neglect	General Neglect	Total Neglect	Emotional Abuse	Exploitation	Caretaker Absence	Total Per Month	Total Per Year
1985	0.64	1.02	0.22	1.15	1.37	0.11	0.02	0.31	3.47	41.66
1986	0.67	1.17	0.35	1.26	1.61	0.11	0.02	0.35	3.92	47.06
1987	0.72	1.23	0.43	1.24	1.66	0.12	0.01	0.42	4.17	50.00
1988	0.92	1.55	0.51	1.61	2.12	0.17	0.03	0.50	5.29	63.53
1989	1.02	1.69	0.49	1.80	2.30	0.21	0.02	0.57	5.82	69.85
1990	1.02	1.78	0.42	1.79	2.20	0.24	0.03	0.59	5.87	70.37

Sources: child abuse reports from DSS, Soc. 291 form; demographic data from U.S. Department of Finance Census.

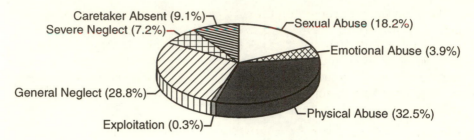

Fig. 1-5. California child abuse reports: type of abuse 1992. *Sources:* Child abuse reports from DSS, Soc. 291 form.

types of abuse (NCCAN, 1994). As Barth, Courtney, Duerr Berrick, and Albert (1994c) have noted, it is not possible to identify from these data whether general neglect, physical abuse, and sexual abuse are actually more prevalent or whether it is easier for reporters to identify these types of abuse.

Data on child abuse reports are not accurate in California before 1985. Data since 1985 are collected monthly from each county via a reporting form (Soc. 291). The calculations are based on reported numbers of dispositions, that is, cases that were judged to warrant face-to-face contact and investigation. Reports that are incomplete or insufficient are not included. Dispositions consist of unduplicated counts, that is, one report per child per incident in each one-month period. The number of reports does not therefore give an indication of how many families are involved. Dispositions that are averaged over the year may include children who reenter CWS during the year. Yearly averages thus reflect the number of dispositions and may include counts of the same children who are reported for different incidences of abuse during the year. Calculations of prevalence per 1,000 children in the population are not calculated beyond 1990 as extrapolation of census data is not accurate past this time.

Regarding the characteristics of children reported, Department of Justice information (NCCAN, 1993) for 1991 indicates that

- There were considerably more girls than boys reported; 57.48% of reports for which the sex was recorded involved girls compared to 42.5% involving boys.
- There were 100 known cases of children who died from abuse and neglect in California in 1991; that is, 1 child died per 81,630 children in the population.

Racial groups are not represented in child abuse reports according to their proportion in the population. In California there is evidence that African American children are two to three times more likely to be referred for abuse or neglect than other racial groups (Barth, Duerr Berrick, Needell, & Jonson-Reid, 1995).

Without further data on how the child abuse system in California is operating, it is difficult to draw any conclusions from the above figures. These figures raise several questions. Are girls' behaviors more stigmatized or are girls suffering more abuse? Is institutional racism operating within the child welfare system? To what extent do cultural differences in definitions of abuse account for ethnic minority groups being overrepresented in the number of reports received?

Placement Trends and Characteristics of Children in Care

Although there is an increasing number of children and families coming to the attention of child protective services, there is evidence to suggest that fewer and fewer families receive services beyond the initial investigation. In 1976, 70% of reports investigated received in-home or out-of-home services beyond initial screening and referral, whereas in 1992 only 6% of reports received these services (calculated from Soc 291 DSS figures). Despite emphasis in policy to keep children in their homes and to reunify children with their families whenever possible, there is a large and growing number of California's children in foster care. In 1986, 5.7 children per 1,000 children and in 1991 9.3 children per 1,000 children in the population were in foster care (Barth et al., 1994a), which in 1991 was almost 1% of California's children. This high rate of foster care leads to most funds in California being spent on the maintenance of children removed from their families, rather than just child protective work. (It was estimated that 36% of CWS funds were spent on the Emergency Response Program in Fiscal Year [FY] 1989–1990.)

Once children are in foster care in California, they tend to stay longer than in other states in the United States. Since 1988, only 50% of children in care are no longer in care within 2.5 years (Barth et al., 1994a). Analysis of the average length of stay must be interpreted cautiously. As Friedman, Baron, Lardiere, and Quick (1982) already noted 11 years ago, examination must be made of the reasons for exiting care. For example, a child may exit care through running away, living independently, death, adoption, or returning to his or her family. These reasons are all qualitatively different. The rate of reentry into care must also be taken into account. For example, children who stay in care longer may have a lower rate of reentering care and higher rates of reunification and permanent placement. There is a substantial rate of recidivism (the rate of the sample who were in foster care, were returned to their family, and again entered substitute care) for children in California (see Courtney, 1992). Analysis of a recent sample of 8,753 children reunified with their families showed that the rate of recidivism increased from 8% after 6 months to 13% after 1 year and increased to 17% after 2 years (Barth, Courtney, Needell, & Jonson-Reid, 1994b). Different rates of recidivism have also been found for different ethnic groups, with African American children having higher recidivism rates (10%, 15%, and 19% after 6, 12, and 24 months, respectively).

There have been definite trends in certain types of placements during the last 10 years. Kinship care — placement of a child with relatives — has increased dramatically. This growth can be attributed to an emphasis in policy to place children in the least restrictive familylike placements and to funding policies that have provided financial support to relative foster parents. Of 79,034 children in care in California in 1992, 44.57% (35,226 children) were placed with kin, while 41.04% (32,432 children) were in nonrelative foster care (Children Now, 1992). The dynamics of kinship placements are different from those of nonrelative foster care. In California, children of minority groups are more likely to be in kinship care, and the rates of return of these children to their families are much lower (see Barth et al., 1994a). There has also been a recent trend in California to place children in specialized foster care. In 1990, 3,422 children were in this type of care.

Group homes in California vary in size; care is provided for from 6 to over 100 children at a time. In 1992, 12.01% (9,439) of children in care in California were in group homes (State of California, 1992). The exact number of children in each size facility is not known. Contrary to good child welfare practice, the number of infants placed in group homes has increased. During the period 1988–1991, over half of the infants placed in a group home remained there for more than four months, a significant amount of time for an infant (Barth et al., 1994a). Of the children in the state CWS who are removed from their family's care, less than 10% of children who are not reunified with their families are adopted (Barth et al., 1994a). As in other countries, younger children are more likely to be adopted than older children. There are also racial differences in the system: African American children have a smaller likelihood of being adopted than Caucasian or Hispanic children (Barth et al., 1994a). In summary, there is a large and increasing number and rate of California's children in out-of-home care, and these children stay there for considerable periods of time. African American children are overrepresented in this group. Most children in out-of-home care (85.6% in 1993) are in foster care, and almost half of these children are in relative/kinship foster care. The rise in the rate of foster care can be attributed to several different trends: the rise in kinship care, the long duration of foster care periods, and the rise in the rate of young children coming into the substitute care system.

Regarding the characteristics of children in care, in 1990 approximately four of five children in foster care were from single-parent families, and approximately two of three children were from families on public assistance (Aid to Families with Dependent Children). A study of random samples of children in foster care reveals that a significant number of the children have special medical needs (34%) and developmental disabilities (30%) (Barth, Duerr Berrick, & Courtney, 1990). A growing medical problem of children in foster care is HIV. Other health and emotional problems of children reported to CWS and in care are related to drug exposure. There are many drug-exposed infants in California. It is estimated that approximately 11% of all births in California are born substance-exposed (California Department of Alcohol and Drug Programs [CDADP], 1990). In 1988 this rate was estimated as between 59,000 and 72,000 infants (CDADP, 1990).

In summary, foster care is associated with very young children (less than three years of age) with significant medical and developmental problems who come from single-parent African American families on public assistance; a substance abuse problem may exist in those families.

Critical Perspectives on the Child Abuse Reporting System

The child abuse reporting system in California is a large-scale, complex operation consuming federal, state, and county dollars. In FY 1989–1990, $462 million was spent on CWS. With an average rate of 36,700 allegations of abuse and neglect investigated each month in 1989–1990 (Hill, 1991), the reporting system affects the lives of hundreds of thousands of children and families. Similar reporting systems operate in all states.

In assessing how well it functions, the child abuse reporting system tends to be viewed from three perspectives:

1. The first perspective uncritically accepts the form and operation of the reporting system.
2. The second perspective is critical of the form and operation of the system and suggests minor reforms.
3. The third perspective questions the entire rationale on which the system is based. This perspective has alternative definitions of the problem and suggests a major reform of the system.

Perspectives on the reporting system vary according to the different vantage points of participants (children, families, social workers, lawyers, and the public) and academic theoreticians (of different ideological and political viewpoints). Participants have varying interests at stake in the current system. Each of the three conceptualizations above will be examined, as far as data allow, with reference to these vantage points.

Acceptance of the Current System

The first perspective accepts the form and operation of the system and fails to examine whether the stated goals of the system are being achieved in practice: Does the system in fact protect children from abuse and neglect? The outcome and consequences of the system are not examined and, as will be outlined, many troubling aspects of the current system are ignored.

As mentioned in the sections on trends in child abuse reporting, an overview of the current system reveals that there has been an enormous increase in child abuse reports since the 1970s. One explanation for the increase is that changes in the reporting system have created more reports. A second explanation is that the actual incidence of abuse has increased. There have been a number of changes in the reporting system that could account for part of the increase: more categories of mandated reporters, an increase in the categories and forms of child abuse, and heightened community awareness of child abuse. There is some evidence of an increase in both mandated and public reports. Another explanation for the growing number of reports is that there is an actual increase in the incidence of child abuse and neglect in the community related to rising rates of homelessness, poverty, unemployment, drug dependency, and domestic violence. (Some of these social indicators for California are shown in Table 1-4.) Whatever the cause, the increased number of reports in the system has had a dramatic impact on the child welfare system.

CWS now focuses resources on children and families in which maltreatment has already occurred and offers little in the way of services to these families. Since 1985 when 23% of the subjects of reports received services in California, there has been a steady decrease in the proportion of abuse report subjects that receive services (see Fig. 1-6). In 1992, only 6% of reports result in receipt of services. An abuse report, even if substantiated, will in the vast majority of cases result in little more than an investigation and recording of the incident.

Viewing investigations from the service recipients' point of view, Gordon (1985) has suggested that historically in situations of child maltreatment that occurred in the context of domestic violence, women welcomed intervention from an outside party. A positive view on intervention is also supported by Steinberg's (1994) recent study. Despite complicating the therapeutic relation-

Table 1-4. California State Profile

Characteristic	Number, Rate, or Percentage	State's Rank in United States	National Average
Population under 18 years, 1990	7,750,725 26% of population		
Minority population under the age of 18 years	4,168,861 53.8%		
Children ages 5–17 years who do not speak English at home	1,878,957 35%		
Percentage of children without health insurance	17.8%		
Child ages 1–14 years death rate in 1990 per 100,000 children	30.3 (1,873 deaths)	28	30.5
Percentage of all births that are to single teens, 1990	7.7% (46,983 births)	20	8.7
Juvenile violent crime arrest rate, 1991, ages 0-17 years per 100,000 youths	645 (20,607 arrests)	47	466
Teens ages 15–19 violent death rate per 100,000 teens, 1990	72.4 (1,487 deaths)	23	70.9
Percentage graduating from high school in 1990	63.1%	43	68.7%
Percentage of children in poverty, 1989[a]	21.2%	35	19.8%
Percentage of children in single-parent families, 1990	23.6%	30	24.7%

[a]Live in families with incomes below the U.S. poverty threshold ($12,675) defined by the Bureau of Census in 1989 for a family of four persons.

Source: Center for the Study of Social Policy, 1993.

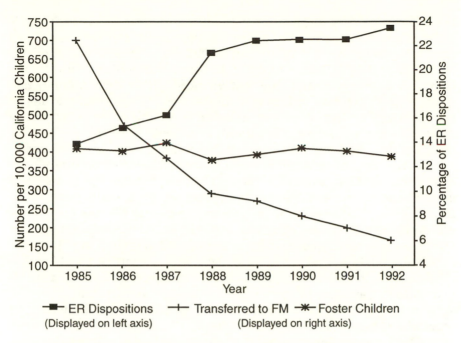

Fig. 1-6. Emergency response for the state of California per 10,000 children and family maintenance and total foster care per Emergency Response dispositions, 1985–1992. *Source:* Barth, 1994b, p. 177.

ship, only 27% of clients dropped out of therapy shortly after a report was made by the therapist. The majority of families continued with therapy after the report was made, with 59% of families being relieved when a report was made. Apart from these isolated studies, we are not aware of the service recipients' point of view.[5]

There are data suggesting that many mandated reporters are unhappy with their role and with the operation of the reporting system. Professionals working in therapeutic relationships often experience conflict between their roles as helpers and as police agents; they believe that mandated reporting breeches professional confidentiality (Levine & Doueck, 1995; Steinberg, 1994). Despite this finding, 80% of psychologists still are in favor of mandatory reporting laws (Steinberg, 1994). There is also evidence suggesting that mandated workers are frustrated by the increases in child abuse reports and the lack of resources to deal with these reports (Brosig & Kalichman, 1992). Zellman and Antler (1990), for example, found that 40% of mandated reporters had at some time not reported suspected cases of abuse.

Another feature of the operation of the current reporting system is the rates of reports that cannot be proved to constitute child abuse or neglect under the state's legal criteria, that is, are not substantiated. (As noted, NCCAN's 1993 data show a national average of 58% of reports that are not substantiated.) There is much conceptual confusion in the literature about this aspect of reports. Reports are substantiated if it can be proved that the maltreatment of the child fits the state's legal definition. Unsubstantiated reports cannot be proved to fit the state's definition of abuse. Unsubstantiated reports may (i) be deliberately false, deliberately malicious, or both; (ii) not constitute maltreatment; (iii) show maltreatment, but the child or family cannot be located; (iv) show maltreatment of the child, but the abuse may not be severe enough to warrant state intervention under the state's definitions of maltreatment; and (v) show maltreatment of the child under the state's definitions, but there may not be sufficient legal evidence to warrant intervention.

The high rates of reports that are not substantiated are troubling for opposing reasons. First, children may be maltreated, but the state is unable to protect these children as the maltreatment does not fit the state's guidelines or there is a lack of evidence in the case. Second, there may be many reports that are either false or do not constitute maltreatment or severe maltreatment. Most theorists have concentrated on this second position, with Besharov (1990) and Lindsey (1994) contending there is overreporting and Finkelhor (1990) and Barth (1994a) contending that the current rates are an acceptable unavoidable by-product of any investigative system. Reports that do not involve serious cases of maltreatment are seen to utilize resources needed for genuinely maltreated children. Also, some families may find the accusation and official investigation emotionally upsetting and socially stigmatizing.

Minor Reform to the System: Is the Current System the Most Appropriate Response to the Problem?

Those who argue for minor reform to the reporting system suggest that the system should be restricted to the most serious cases and there should be a dual reporting system, one system for professionals and another for other reporters. From this point of view, the reporting system is seen to be out of control and having taken on a self-perpetuating expansive life of its own. Resources are seen to be diverted toward "unnecessary" reports rather than more serious cases of neglect and abuse (Besharov, 1990). Critics propose that the focus of the current system should be changed so resources are used for the most serious cases. The literature often cites this option as a narrowing of the definitions of child abuse and neglect. This reform would, however, still use the current definitions and refocus resources for the most serious cases. Thus cases that do not warrant investigation would be screened out using techniques such as risk assessment instruments (Downing, Wells, & Fluke, 1990). There has been a substantial move in this direction in California with statewide training in screening of cases. Many states have adopted risk assessment practices to help screen the large number of incoming reports. In Florida, however, screening has also been accompanied by a service delivery system designed to help provide services for families. Severe cases of child abuse and neglect are investigated, while other families in need who are reported are offered services in a nonadversarial manner (Howard, 1994).

In view of the reluctance of many mandated professionals to report child abuse, some critics have suggested minor reforms of the reporting system that would legitimize reporting practices that are currently covert (Levine & Doueck, 1995). One such reform is to establish reporting guidelines for a dual reporting system, one system for registered child abuse reporters and one for the public (Finkelhor & Zellman, 1991). This dual system would create "flexible reporting options" for child abuse professionals who are registered as such with CWS. Reporting options would include deferred reporting and reporting without CWS intervention. Professionals could then support child abuse reporting laws more closely, and current practices would be more carefully monitored (Finkelhor, 1990).

Major Reform to the System: Is Child Abuse and Neglect the Real Problem?

More fundamental criticism of the reporting system challenges the entire focus and form of services in the current system. From this perspective, overlapping models reconceptualize the problem by focusing on the societal or institutional causes of the problem, rather than on the individual or familial level causes. Pelton (1990) and others (e.g., Besharov, 1990, and Kamerman & Kahn, 1990), for example, reconceptualize the fundamental problem as a lack of support services to families, rather than the maltreatment of children. Historically there have been two competing uses for child welfare resources: the investigative function in child protection work and the provision of family services. With increased reporting and finite child welfare budgets, resources are now used for child protection work at the expense of provision of services to families. Not only has a child abuse report become the "passport" to CWS, but only the most serious cases are served by the system, with other cases receiving at most a referral to other agencies (Barth, 1994a).[6] The imbalance in provision of services reflects the political decision to use resources to respond to a situation of "moral panic" (Robin, 1991) rather than considering a broader structural or long-term response to the problem. Under the current situation, a mother who requests services is refused until the child is actively abused. The system does not encourage or respond favorably to parents who recognize that they need support in their parenting role and who would like help. Because of the police nature of social services and the lack of services, parents know that the likely outcome of seeking help is an abuse report, in some instances followed by removal of the child. Clearly, there needs to be a different approach to service provision.

Another unintended consequence of the current social policy toward child maltreatment that has not as yet been explored in the literature is the effect of the reporting system on parents' confidence and perception of their role. The strong cultural message that has arisen is that everyone, including you, may be a child abuser, and many parents are worried about being accused as such. Sensational stories in the media about children unjustly being removed from their parents' care (suffering from a bruise from an accident, for example) have in some instances eroded parents' confidence and authority in the home. As Solnit (1982, p. 502) notes:

> There may have been a change in the community's social-psychological climate in regard to parent-child relationships. . . . Such changes . . . weaken the presumption that parents are competent to raise their children as they feel best and heightens the suspicion that parents are likely to neglect and abuse their children.

Clearly, this unintended consequence must be redressed. A different approach to this situation is suggested by the structural approach to social change. From this perspective, the lack of services for families is seen as a logical result of the "residual" model of service provision that operates in the United States. In the residual model, limited government services are provided as a "safety net" for those who are temporarily unable to participate in the market economy. As Lindsey (1994, p. 157) notes:

> Child abuse represents the extreme logical focus of the residual paradigm. If the residual model seeks to help the socially excluded—the outcasts, the abandoned, the less fortunate—the abused child is the perfect client since he or she is excluded in a way that no one else can be.

From this perspective, the focus and use of resources for child maltreatment not only inhibit the growth of services for families in general, but draw attention away from structural inequalities. Thus the preoccupation with the size of the maltreatment problem, the high rates of unsubstantiated cases, the specificity of the laws, and the media obsession with the horror of the most extreme cases distracts attention away from the inequalities in the system. The association of abuse with poverty (especially in neglect cases), women in poverty, and the overrepresentation of minority racial groups goes unnoticed.

Major reform of the child abuse reporting system would involve a radical reconceptualization of this social problem and the role of government in provision of services. If parenting was conceptualized in a community framework, large-scale "institutionalized" social services would provide supportive services for all parents. Although this approach would radically change the orientation of service provision, there still needs to be some sort of state intervention in situations in which children have already been abused. Lindsey (1994) proposes a model for this situation that extends the position of Pelton (1990), Kamerman and Kahn (1990), and Besharov (1990) by not only focusing on the lack of service provision, but also reconceptualizing child maltreatment as a criminal justice issue. Lindsey contends that besides failing to provide social services, public child welfare does not ensure a legal due process for families because of the agency's mixed legal role. Acts of violence that would be regarded as criminal assault outside the family are not dealt with as such within the child welfare system. As was argued when the first children's courts were established (Bruno, 1957), Lindsey proposes a clear separation of functions, with social service agencies providing assistance to troubled families and the criminal justice system dealing with criminal offenses (prosecuting offenders, ensuring due process for offenders, and protecting children as victims of assault). Fundamental reform to the system would therefore separate the criminal justice issue of assault to children from the social services issue of provision of services to children in troubled families.

The need for increased provision of social services for families is not in contention, and the preventive and ameliorative aspects of these services on child maltreatment remain to be seen. As Lindsey notes, there are sound arguments for prosecuting criminal assault that occurs within the family. However, the protective service role should not only be limited to criminal standards and rules of evidence. As seen in the arguments for the establishment of the juvenile court, criminal standards would result in many children not being protected by the state. Lindsey's position, if slightly modified, would allow for a more lenient standard of proof than in criminal justice matters (while following all other due process procedures) to allow for protection of these children. At the same time, a clearer division would be provided between social services and criminal justice issues. An approach that adopts some of Lindsey's suggestions is being pioneered in Florida. Calls are screened and actions then follow two tracks: if the child is in danger, an investigation is initiated; otherwise, assessments are carried out with the purpose of offering services for families in a nonadversarial, supportive way (Howard, 1994). Missouri has also adopted the Florida model.

With the medicolegal definition of abuse focusing on the individual, the current reporting system responds to individual situations rather than the social structural dimensions of the problem. The reporting system is crisis orientated and limited, providing services to parents once they have abused their child. Intervention is limited to the most serious cases when situations have become chronic. A major reconceptualization of the system would recognize the common social characteristics of clients in the system. Services would be offered for all parents to support them in their parenting role. Rather than undermining parents' confidence as in the present investigative system, these services would be orientated to reinforcing parents' capacities and could include housing, day care, and drug-related services. Support services would be clearly separated from services that investigate abuse of children.

The second aspect of changing the orientation of the reporting system is to redefine severe abuse of children as a criminal rather than social service matter. Physical violence within the family would be redefined as assault. Parents would have due process rights ensured by the court. Criminal standards of proof would however result in many children not being protected. A more lenient standard of proof, while maintaining due process rights, would allow protection of these children. If support services were offered to all families, it is hoped that the reporting system would become a small component of social services for children. This reorientation would radically change the experience of many children and families in California.

Notes

1. California was a proponent of the private asylum system. By 1910, although an agricultural state, California had the second highest rate (after New York) of children

in institutional care: 381 children per 100,000 inhabitants (Bureau of the Census, 1913). The state also had the second highest spending rate for children in institutions: $75,000 per year for each 100,000 inhabitants ($159 per child per year for dependent children plus overheads) (Bureau of the Census, 1913). The heavy state subsidization of the 79 private institutions at the time resulted in institutions being the preferred mode of care as opposed to placing children in foster care (which was more popular in the eastern states).

2. It is widely known among social workers that the interpretation of each category varies among individual workers and counties (personal communication from Alameda county workers, July 23, 1993).

3. In 1993, one large, urban California county, for example, received on average 2,941 phone calls per month (over an 8-month period) in the child abuse and neglect response unit. Of these calls, only 1,130 per month were child abuse and neglect related.

4. Data are not available on whether the increase in reports in California is due to mandated reporters, nonmandated reporters, or both. One national study, however, has found that there has been more reporting by both mandated and nonmandated reporters nationwide (although the increase was not statistically significant from 1980 to 1986) (Westat Associates Inc., 1987).

5. There is evidence that not all parents are content with the current child abuse reporting and child welfare system. In California, a national group, Victims of Child Abuse Legislation (VOCAL), voices the views of parents who think they have been wrongly treated or falsely accused in the system. (There is no organized group to express children's points of view on the system.) The theme of false allegations has been taken up by a number of writers (see, e.g., Eberle & Eberle, 1986; Robin, 1991) and has been especially prominent in child sexual abuse cases. Gardner (1991) devotes a whole book to the subject of false allegations in sexual abuse cases, but is careful to point out that he believes 95% of sexual abuse cases are genuine and "sexual abuse hysteria" with accompanying false allegations only occurs in 5% of cases.

6. In California, there is a considerable move to introduce new legislation to provide more family preservation services and wraparound services (Lawrence & Barth, 1993). In family-focused services, preventive services (such as family preservation), and what are called wraparound services, the family's needs determine the form of service provision rather than the service structure determining the services the family is offered. Serious moves toward client-sensitive services in California would need to employ a larger contingent of ethnically diverse CWS staff. Again, these family preservation services are fiscally constrained and will only be offered to families once they have entered the child abuse system.

References

Albert, V. N., & Barth, R. P. (1994). *Explaining growth in number of Emergency Response dispositions for 18 California counties.* Berkeley: University of California at Berkeley, Child Welfare Research Center.

Alvy, K. (1987). *Black parenting: Strategies for training.* New York: Irvington.

American Association for Protecting Children. (1989). Highlights of official aggregate child neglect and abuse reporting 1988. Denver, CO: American Humane Association.

Anderson, P. G. (1989). The origin, emergence, and professional recognition of child protection. *Social Service Review, 63*(2), 223–244.

Assembly Bill 60. Sacramento: Government Printing Office. (1991).

Barth, R. P. (1994a). Limiting child abuse reporting laws: No. In M. A. Mason & E. Gambrill (Eds.), *Debating children's lives: Current controversies on children and adolescents* (pp. 285–299). Thousand Oaks, CA: Sage.

Barth, R. P. (1994b). Long-term in-home services. In D. Besharov (Ed.), *When drug users have children: Reorienting child welfare's response* (pp. 175–194). Washington, DC: Child Welfare League of America.

Barth, R. P., Courtney, M., Duerr Berrick, J., & Albert, V. (1994a). *From child abuse to permanency planning: Child welfare services pathways and placements.* New York: Aldine de Gruyter.

Barth, R. P., Courtney, M., Needell, B., & Jonson-Reid, M. (1994b). *Performance indicators for child welfare services in California. Executive Summary.* Berkeley: University of California at Berkeley, Child Welfare Research Center.

Barth, R. P., Duerr Berrick, J., & Courtney, M. (1990). *A second snapshot of families, children and child welfare services in California.* Berkeley: University of California at Berkeley, Family Welfare Research Group, School of Social Welfare and California Child Welfare Strategic Planning Commission.

Barth, R. P., Duerr Berrick, J., Courtney, M., & Pizzini, S. (1990). *A snapshot of California's families and children: Pursuant to the child welfare reforms of the 1980s* (No. 1). Berkeley: University of California at Berkeley, Family Welfare Research Group, School of Social Welfare and California Child Welfare Strategic Planning Commission.

Barth, R. P., Duerr Berrick, J., Needell, B., & Jonson-Reid, M. (1995). *Child welfare services for very young children interim report.* Berkeley: University of California at Berkeley, Child Welfare Research Center.

Besharov, D. J. (1990). Gaining control over child abuse reports; Public agencies must address both underreporting and overreporting. *Public Welfare, 48*(2), 34–40.

Bourne, R., & Newberger, E. H. (Eds.). (1979). *Critical perspectives on child abuse.* Lexington, KY: Lexington Books.

Brosig, C. L., & Kalichman, S. C. (1992). Clinician's reporting of suspected child abuse: A review of the empirical literature. *Clinical Psychology Review, 12,* 155–168.

Bruno, F. J. (1957). *Trends in social work: 1874–1956* (2nd ed.). New York: Columbia University Press.

Bureau of the Census. (1913). *Benevolent institutions 1910.* Washington, DC: U.S. Government Printing Office.

California Department of Alcohol and Drug Programs. (1990). *Preliminary fact sheet on perinatal drug and alcohol use.* Sacramento, CA: Department of Alcohol and Drug Programs, California.

California Penal Code Annotated. Sacramento, CA: Government Printing Office. (n.d.).

Center for the Study of Social Policy & the Anne E. Casey Foundation. (1993). *Kids count data book: State profiles of child well-being.* Washington, DC: Center for the Study of Social Policy.

Children Now. (1992). *California State 1992 Report Card: Data Supplement.* Oakland, CA.

Costin, J. B., Bell, J. B., & Downs, S. W. (1991). *Child welfare: Policies and practice* (4th ed.). White Plains, NY: Longman.

Courtney, M. E. (1992). *Reunification of foster children with their families: The case of California's children.* Unpublished doctoral dissertation, University of California at Berkeley, Berkeley, California.

Downing, J. D., Wells, S. J., & Fluke, J. (1990). Gatekeeping in child protective services: A survey of screening policies. *Child Welfare, 69*(4), 357–368.

Eberle, P., & Eberle, S. (1986). *The politics of child abuse.* Secaucus, NJ: Lyle Stuart.

Finkelhor, D. (1990, Winter). Is child abuse overreported? The data rebut arguments for less intervention. *Public Welfare,* 22–29, 46.

Finkelhor, D., & Zellman, G. L. (1991). Flexible reporting options for skilled child abuse professionals. *Child Abuse and Neglect, 15,* 335–341.

Friedman, R. M., Baron, A., Lardieri, S., & Quick, J. (1982). Length of time in foster care: A measure in need of analysis. *Social Work, 27*(1), 499–503.

Gardner, R. A. (1991). *Sex abuse hysteria: Salem witch trials revisited.* Cresskill, N.J.: Creative Therapeutics.

Gerry, E. T. (1883). The relation of societies for the prevention of cruelty to children to child-saving work. In R. H. Bremner (Ed.), *Care of dependent children in the late 19th and early 20th centuries.* New York: Arno Press.

Gordon, L. (1985). Child abuse, gender, and the myth of family independence: A historical critique. *Child Welfare, 64*(3), 213–224.

Hill, E. (1991). *Child abuse and neglect in California.* Sacramento, CA: Legislative Office.

Howard, B. (1994). Can "broken" child protection system be fixed? *Youth Today,* 20–21.

Kamerman, S. B., & Kahn, A. (1990, Winter). If CPS is driving child welfare—Where do we go from here? *Public Welfare,* 9–13, 46.

Kempe, C. H., Silverman, F. N., Steele, B. F., Droegemueller, W., & Silver, H. K. (1962). The battered-child syndrome. *Journal of the American Medical Association, 181*(1), 17–24.

Lawrence, R., & Barth, R. P. (1993). *Funding strategies in child welfare services, a survey of selected states: Title IV—A funding for family preservation services.* Berkeley: University of California at Berkeley, Child Welfare Research Center.

Levine, M., & Doueck, H. J. (with Anderson, E. M., et al.). (1995). *The impact of mandated reporting on the therapeutic process: Picking up the pieces.* Thousand Oaks, CA: Sage.

Lindsey, D. (1994). *The welfare of children.* New York: Oxford University Press.

March, D. K. (1992, Winter). Over-extension of immunity in the child abuse and neglect reporting act. *Beverly Hills Bar Association Journal,* 9–17.

McMartin v. Children's Institute International, 261 Cal. Reporter (2nd Dist. 212 Cal. App. 3d 1393, 1989).

National Center on Child Abuse and Neglect. (1993). *National child abuse and neglect data system: Working paper 2—1991 summary data component.* Washington, DC: U.S. Government Printing Office.

National Center on Child Abuse and Neglect. (1994). *Child maltreatment 1992: Reports from the states to the National Center on Child Abuse and Neglect.* Washington, DC: U.S. Government Printing Office.

National Research Council. (1993). *Understanding child abuse and neglect.* Washington, DC: National Academy Press.

Nelson, B. J. (1984). *Making an issue of child abuse: Political agenda setting for social problems.* Chicago: University of Chicago Press.

Noh Ahn, H. (1994). Cultural diversity and the definition of child abuse. In R. Barth,

J. Duerr Berrick, & N. Gilbert (Eds.), *Child welfare research review* (pp. 28–55). New York: Columbia University Press.

Pecora, P. J., Whittaker, J. K., & Maluccio, A. N. (1992). *The child welfare challenge: Policy, practice, and research.* New York: Aldine de Gruyter.

Pelton, L. H. (1990, Fall). Resolving the crisis in child welfare. *Public Welfare,* 20–25, 45.

Pizzini, S. (1994) *Responses of child welfare services to changing economic incentives.* Unpublished doctoral dissertation, School of Public Administration, University of Southern California, Los Angeles, California.

Robin, M. (1991). The social construction of child abuse and "false allegations." In M. Robin (Ed.), *Assessing child maltreatment reports: The problem of false allegations* (pp. 1–34). Binghamton, NY: Haworth Press.

Rose, S., & Meezan, W. (1993, June). Defining child neglect: Evolution, influences and issues. *Social Service Review, 67*(2), 279–293.

Schene, P. (1987). Is child abuse decreasing? *Journal of Interpersonal Violence, 2*(2), 225–227.

Senate Bill 1912. Sacramento, CA: Government Printing Office. (1988).

Senate Bill 243. Sacramento, CA: Government Printing Office. (1989).

Senate Bill 2669, the Presley Bill. Sacramento, CA: Government Printing Office. (1990).

Senate Bill 1125, Sacramento, CA: Government Printing Office. (1993).

Slingerland, W. H. (1916). *Child welfare work in California: A study in agencies and institutions.* Concord, N.H.: Rumford Press.

Solnit, A. J. (1982). Children, parents and the state. *American Journal of Orthopsychiatry, 52*(3), 496–505.

Steinberg, K. (1994). *In the service of two masters: Psychotherapists struggle with child maltreatment reporting laws.* Buffalo: State University of New York at Buffalo, Department of Psychology.

Straus, M. A., & Gelles, R. J. (1986). Societal change and change in family violence from 1975–1985 as revealed by two national surveys. *Journal of Marriage and the Family, 48,* 465–479.

Tabbert, W., Sullivan, P., & Whittaker, R. E. (1992). *California Emergency Response Protocol for child welfare services: Executive summary.* Fresno: California State University, School of Health and Social Work.

Thomas v. Chadwick, 274 Cal. Reporter 128 (4th Dist. 224 Cal. App. 3d, 1990).

Tiffin, S. (1982). *In whose best interest?* Westport, CT: Greenwood Press.

Westat Associates Inc. (1987). *Study findings: Study of national incidence and prevalence of child abuse and neglect: 1988.* Washington, DC: U.S. Department of Health and Human Services, National Center on Child Abuse and Neglect.

Zelizer, V. A. (1985). *Pricing the priceless child: The changing social value of children.* New York: Basic Books.

Zellman, G. L., & Antler, S. (1990, Winter). Mandated reporters and CPS: A study in frustration. *Public Welfare,* 30–37, 46.

2

Canada

Trends and Issues in Child Welfare

KAREN J. SWIFT

The Canadian child welfare system is not one system but many. Each of the 10 provinces and the two territories (Yukon and Northwest Territories) has its own legislation. Further, Aboriginal peoples are in the process of developing agreements with government concerning the way child welfare is funded and delivered. Also, differences between the two founding cultures of Canada, French and English, have resulted in the development of somewhat different approaches to child welfare.

Nevertheless, it is quite possible to discuss Canadian child welfare as a single entity; that is, the system in this country does express more or less common characteristics throughout. It is a system premised on the belief that parents bear the primary responsibility for the welfare of their children and a concomitant right to raise their children in accordance with their own wishes. It is a residual system, one that deals with the most serious problems of care and generally intervenes with the most vulnerable of families. It is a system that provides more investigation than preventive or treatment service, and it is an underfunded system, one that requires service providers to respond to the greatest crises while overlooking or postponing attention to other serious, high-risk situations.

Defining Child Abuse

Historical and Legislative Context

Harris and Melichercik (1986, p. 160) describe the origins of child welfare in Canada as a gradually evolving response to social and economic conditions of the 19th century. Two traditions were drawn on, they maintain, as the basis for child welfare provisions. One was the idea held by some ancient societies

38

that children are the property of their parents. The other tradition v
patriae, or the state as parent of the nation, the British doctrine a
intervention into the private family for the protection of children. Legi
developed in English Canada has tended to emphasize the second tradit
involving government intervention for the protection of children, while Qu
bec has focused more strongly on the parental rights tradition.

In 1891 the first Children's Aid Society was established in Toronto, and in 1893 Ontario passed An Act for the Prevention of Cruelty to and Better Protection of Children. Other Canadian provinces soon followed suit, and within a few years other provinces (except Quebec) developed similar legislation, which forms the basic framework for child welfare legislation today. To the present, child welfare remains primarily within the jurisdiction of the 10 Canadian provinces and two territories, with the federal government involved in a funding role and in criminal prosecutions via the Canadian Criminal Code.

In Quebec, the Catholic church exerted considerable influence on child welfare and other social welfare activity to the early 1960s. French Civil Law, which was the governing tradition in Quebec, placed the church in a paramount position with respect to social welfare, including a strong reliance on the church to step in when parents failed. Quebec did not initiate the study of child protection as a separate service until 1933. After this, various child protection societies, bureaus, and legislation were developed alongside church involvement in child protection, but it was not until 1977 that the Youth Protection Act came into force. This legislation, essentially similar to other Canadian acts, recognized children as "legal subjects" and brought under one act authority for protection of children in Quebec.

Legislation in most provinces originally focused on child neglect, although cruelty to children was also stressed. In Ontario's legislation, punishment in the form of a fine or imprisonment for cruelty, including both abuse and neglect, could be imposed. The family was viewed as the proper source of nurturing children of a dependent age, and foster care was seen as the best form of alternate care. Changes in legislation evolved gradually over the first half of the century. However, Ontario and other provinces retained the language of the protection mandate much as it was articulated in the original legislation until midcentury, when changes in legislation began to focus attention on the "best interests of the child." In Canada as elsewhere, changes in legislation were introduced to respond to the "discovery" of the battered child in the 1960s (Kempe, Silverman, Brandt, Droegemueller, & Silver, 1962); the most notable of the changes was the addition of reporting laws in all jurisdictions except the Yukon.

Related legislation has affected child welfare activity significantly. In 1984, the proclamation of the federal Young Offenders Act relieved child welfare authorities of direct responsibility for delinquent youth. In 1982, the Canadian Charter of Rights and Freedoms was introduced; it is a constitutional document that profoundly affects many aspects of Canadian society, including child welfare. According to Bala, Hornick, and Vogl (1991, p. 5), the charter

as parens
llowing
ation
ion.

ɔ restrict the authority of child protection workers to
ɔut warrants. It has also been used to ensure parental
g within a reasonable time after children have been
ʾhe charter has increased emphasis on the enforce-
process. Child protection work procedures as well
ɹy have been significantly altered as a result, a
ɹɛrred to as the "legalization" of child welfare. The intro-
ɹɪı C-15, which amends the sexual assault provisions in the Crimi-
ↄode of Canada and certain aspects of the Canada Evidence Act, have
also affected child welfare practice. This legislation facilitates the pressing of
charges and the giving of evidence by children in cases of sexual abuse.
Changes introduced by this bill mean that child protection workers are more
often involved in criminal court proceedings and work closely with police on a
regular basis.

Child welfare work before the 1960s involved considerable attention to
juvenile delinquency and behavior management, work with unmarried mothers, and adoption (Wharf, 1993, p. 123) and "fairly obvious" cases of abuse
and neglect (Bala et al., 1991, p. 3). Publicity accompanying the identification
of the battered child syndrome during and after the 1960s moved the issue of
abuse to the center of child welfare attention. Child neglect, which had been
the original impetus behind child protection legislation, has moved to the
distant background, although neglect cases have continued to the present to
constitute the largest single category of cases handled by child protection
agencies (Federal-Provincial Working Group, 1994; Trocme, Tam, & McPhee,
1995). At present child abuse rather than neglect is the framing concept for all
legislation in Canada, and neglect now appears as a subcategory of abuse.
Other subcategories are physical abuse, sexual abuse and exploitation (recently
gaining attention), and emotional abuse and neglect. In other words, abuse
now has a generic meaning as the main framing concept in child protection
and specific meanings, usually discussed as physical, sexual, or emotional
abuse and as neglect. The primary, secondary and tertiary levels of attention
to issues in child welfare over time could be depicted as in Figure 2-1.

Along with the identification of various forms of abuse, a debate has
developed about definitions of abuse in relation to intrusion by child welfare
authorities into the private family. This debate involves questions of whether
the rather broad and vague definitions of abuse found in legislation in the

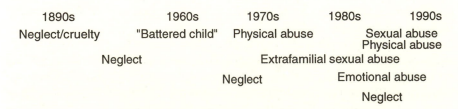

Fig. 2-1. Historical trends in protection issues.

1960s and 1970s allowed social workers too broad a mandate to interfere in family matters. At about the same time, Aboriginal groups began to speak publicly about the damaging effects of intrusive power in the hands of child welfare agencies and also about the ethnocentric views of white, middle-class social workers in defining abuse and neglect. In the early 1980s these debates became part of a public consultation conducted by the Ontario provincial government during the process of revamping its child protection laws. In general, on grounds that families would otherwise be denied needed services, social workers argued for continuing broad definitions of abuse. Social workers argued that they were capable of judging risk and trained to do so. Members of the legal profession, along with some client groups, argued that a criterion of mere risk as construed by a social worker left the door open for abuse of families by the authorities. They argued that definitions of abuse and neglect should be narrow, specific, and clear to prevent unwarranted intrusion into private family life. In the Ontario legislation that followed, the key criteria for defining abuse became "harm" and "substantial risk of harm," criteria favoring the narrow definitional approach. Also encoded in the new legislation was the "least intrusive" principle, directing authorities to take the least intrusive action consonant with protecting children from harm.

Another definitional debate of the 1980s concerned physical abuse. It was noted that the Criminal Code of Canada, as well as tradition, allowed "reasonable force" to be administered to children by parents and some others. For child welfare workers, this provision of the code brought into question the difference between discipline and abuse. By this time, many middle-class workers had come to feel that the administration of physical punishment was unacceptable, especially if the discipline resulted in bruising or other marks. Certainly, many parents disagreed and felt supported by the code. Particularly in areas receiving many new immigrants, the issue of differentiating between discipline and abuse arose in relation to culturally different parenting practices that allowed fairly substantial and frequent force in disciplining children.

Current Legislation

The 12 jurisdictions within Canada have each developed their own child protection legislation and definitions. There are of course many similarities among them. These include the idea that families are responsible for the care, supervision, and protection of their children; that children have rights that must be protected; that governments are responsible for protecting children from harm; that the "best interest of the child" is a guiding decision principle; and that the least intrusive form of intervention must be provided (Federal-Provincial Working Group, 1994, p. 7). All provinces also rely on some version of defining a child "in need of protection" or defining conditions signaling endangerment of the "safety and development of the child."

In addition to legislation, each jurisdiction has policy manuals, guides, and protocols providing working definitions of abuse and specifying criteria and procedures to be used in making determinations of abuse. In some cases, manuals help to clarify definitions that remain vague and broad in the actual legislation. They also tend to express the common practice understandings of social workers in the field. Saskatchewan's manual, for instance, suggests that a criterion for determining a child in need of protection is care that departs from that "reasonably expected of any parent." New Brunswick's guidelines suggest that the definition of a child in need of protection includes the caretaker's failure to anticipate injury or danger to a child. Although seldom mentioned in legislation, the problem of determining whether an event could have been anticipated is certainly one that preoccupies many protection workers.

Over the past two decades, most Canadian jurisdictions have in some way engaged in the debate concerning intervention into private family life by child welfare authorities. The two primary positions taken in legislation are generally thought of as the interventionist model, which provides broad powers to social workers to intervene without legal warrant and also to offer service, and the more legalized, noninterventionist approach, which narrows the grounds and procedures for intervention and service. According to Bala et al. (1991), only two provinces, Ontario and Alberta, have taken the noninterventionist approach favored in their book. Barnhorst's (1986) analysis suggests instead that Canadian jurisdictions can be viewed on a continuum between these two approaches. Using this method, Barnhorst found all but four jurisdictions (British Columbia, Newfoundland, Saskatchewan, and the Northwest Territories) had adopted the noninterventionist approach to some degree. In other words, both philosophy and practice have tended to move in the direction of nonintervention, a model in keeping with rights-based beliefs, due process, and limited service provision. Effects that flow from it include the framing of narrower definitions of abuse, accompanied by more attention to investigative processes; the least intrusive approach to service provision; increased attention to legal procedures in the processing of cases; and fewer children placed in care.

Among other jurisdictional differences in definitions of abuse is the definition of children by age. Table 2-1 shows the maximum age of coverage in child

Table 2-1. Age of Child as Defined in Canadian
Child Protection Legislation

Province	Age
Newfoundland	Under 16
Prince Edward Island	Under 18
Nova Scotia	Under 16
New Brunswick	Under 19
Quebec	Under 18
Ontario	Under 16
Manitoba	Under 18
Saskatchewan	Under 16
Alberta	Under 18
British Columbia	Under 19
Yukon	Under 18
Northwest Territories	Under 18

Source: Jurisdictional protection legislation.

protection legislation in Canada's 12 jurisdictions. The ages shown, of course, refer only to the definition of a child. For various purposes (e.g., extension of wardship), other ages are specified in different jurisdictions (Federal-Provincial Working Group, 1994, pp. 14–15). One province, New Brunswick, includes an unborn child in the definition of a child for protection purposes.

In general, definitions of abuse continue to rely heavily on understandings that the parent or guardian bears chief or exclusive responsibility for the protection and care of the child. All provincial protection legislation designates caretakers of the child, including parents, guardians, and "the person in whose charge a child is" as responsible parties. Clauses assume or state a wide variety of responsibilities this person must assume, including provision of basic needs, protection of children from all forms of abuse by others, the taking of "reasonable precautions" to safeguard children, and the provision of remedies for various problems.

Physical Abuse. Specific references to physical abuse are surprisingly few in most provincial legislation. Only Alberta provides a comprehensive list of "observable injuries" counting as abuse, while other provinces refer to injury or risk of injury. Although legislation in a number of jurisdictions remains vague or even silent in its specification of physical abuse, policy manuals and other guidelines used by workers spell out the meaning of abuse in more detail, often including lists of injuries that may signify abuse, from cuts and bruises to internal injuries.

In practice, the generally accepted definition of physical abuse has been "nonaccidental physical injury," a term used to include not only intentional acts but recklessness (Falconer & Swift, 1983). In legislation the concept of nonaccidental injury still defines physical abuse in many statutes. Canada's Criminal Code includes a clause providing that teachers, parents, and guardians are "justified in using force by way of correction toward a pupil or child . . . if the force does not exceed what is reasonable under the circumstances" (5.43). This legislation allowing use of force against a child continues to complicate the determination of what constitutes abuse for it sanctions an indeterminate amount of physical discipline, but does not address the issue of harm to the child. It also provides a strong defense for those who condone the use of force. The Northwest Territories statute, for instance, differentiates "reasonable disciplinary force" from physical abuse in language that could be seen to allow reasonable force even if some injury is sustained by the child. Other jurisdictions make this distinction in their policy guides and manuals.

Child Neglect. Definitions of traditional forms of child neglect continue to predominate in most legislation. Variations on themes concerning abandonment, children found in unfit and improper circumstances, failure of caretakers to provide necessities, lack of supervision and guidance, delinquent behavior by the child, denial of medical care, and failure to send a child to school are included in most provincial acts. A few provinces still include some of the original wording defining neglect, for instance, "a child found begging"

(Northwest Territories). A recent addition to the definition of neglect in some provincial statutes (e.g., Ontario) is failure to provide appropriate treatment or remedies for children's emotional, mental, or physical developmental needs. Prince Edward Island's policy specifies neglect as a phenomenon that goes on over a "substantial period of time," an understanding that is quite common in practice across the country (Swift, 1995a).

In practice, neglect has traditionally been defined in terms of care that is assumed should be given by the parent. With attention focused on abuse, little has been written about neglect, especially from a Canadian perspective, with the result that understandings developed by Americans such as Polansky, Bergman, and De Saix (1972), Polansky, Chalmers, Buttenweisser, and Williams (1981), and Kadushin (1988) dominate thinking about it. Because of both class and cultural differences between social workers and clients, the definition of neglect imposed in practice has been criticized as ethnocentric. In fact, Aboriginal people have considered that inappropriate application of the neglect definition has accounted for the apprehension and permanent loss of many of their families' children. The problem of distinguishing neglect from poverty has plagued workers for decades. To a small extent, the idea of "community neglect" has been employed to help workers identify deprivation children suffer because their parents are unable to provide for them. Recently the problems of parental (especially maternal) addiction, poor housing, and domestic violence have become more frequently discussed as features of neglect (Cohen-Schlanger, Fitzpatrick, Hulchanski, & Raphael, 1993; Swift, 1995a).

Emotional Abuse. Emotional and psychological abuses have been recognized for many years, but have been considered difficult to define and prove. As O'Hagan (1993) has written, understanding and defining this arena has been impeded by the use of "imprecise derivatives" used by professionals. These include "emotional neglect," "psychological abuse," and "emotional maltreatment." O'Hagan differentiates between emotional and psychological dimensions of abuse and argues that legislation should too. However, review of legislation shows that such a distinction has not yet been made explicit in a statute of any jurisdiction.

Issues related to emotional abuse are, however, increasingly incorporated in legislation. A common definition appears in Nova Scotia's act, which defines emotional harm or risk of harm as "demonstrated by anxiety, depression, withdrawal, or self-destructive behaviour." (Children and Family Services Act, 22(2)(f)). Alberta's statute includes a list of causes of such harm, including rejection, deprivation of affection, domestic violence, inappropriate criticism, and the mental state of the caregiver, including that affected by drug abuse. Another format (Prince Edward Island) is endangerment of the "emotional and mental health and development of the child" (Family and Child Services Act, Paragraph 1(2)(e)(g)). Only the Northwest Territories requires in its legislation that a psychiatric assessment be conducted to establish that a child's development is threatened. A relatively recent addition in several provinces is the inclusion of domestic violence and even "disharmony" as conditions possibly causing emotional harm.

Sexual Abuse. Sexual abuse according to Wells (1990) was not considered a serious problem until the late 1970s. Until then, victims were considered to be unreliable witnesses, an idea supported by Freud's theories (Masson, 1984) about sexual abuse as fantasy. In 1984, the Badgley Report was published (Government of Canada, 1984). This well-publicized report found that in Canada one of two females and one of three males were victims of unwanted sexual acts, ranging from witnessing exposure to sexual attack, and that four in five of these acts occurred in childhood. The report also stated that most assailants were known to the child and were often family members. These dramatic findings put child sexual abuse at the forefront of the child welfare agenda. Findings also challenged previous views of sexual abuse as primarily involving father-daughter incest with intercourse. The report included in its notion of "unwanted sexual acts" many behaviors that had previously not been conceptualized as abuse. Among the consequences of this report were concerns that ordinary acts of caring for children might come to be construed as abuse.

Law reform eventually followed the Badgley Report. Bill C-15, proclaimed in 1988, amended the Criminal Code of Canada and the Canada Evidence Act to make abusers easier to prosecute. Amendments to the Criminal Code dealt with topics that included 16 specific offenses that could apply to sexual abuse, ranging from touching and exposure to procuring and assault with a weapon.

This level of specificity has removed some of the definitional burden of sexual abuse from framers of child welfare legislation. However, Bill C-15 does not remove responsibility from child welfare authorities for intervening in cases of sexual abuse. The Criminal Code of Canada covers the issue of whether a crime has been committed; it does not include the question of whether a child is in need of protection, which remains the authority of protection agencies (Wells, 1990). Provinces (except British Columbia) therefore continue to include explicit reference to sexual abuse in their legislation, although, as in the case of physical abuse, mention is often rather cursory.

Issues and Trends in Defining Child Abuse

The issue of defining the line between discipline and abuse has not been resolved. Middle-class methods of discipline in Canada have moved considerably in the direction of foregoing physical discipline altogether. This direction is encouraged by the vast discourse on parenting (Swift, 1995a), which presents alternative methods of discipline as superior in style and effect. Canadians also take pride in living in a relatively peaceful country, an image in keeping with nonviolent disciplinary styles. However, many parents continue to favor physical punishment and are supported in this position by the Criminal Code of Canada.

Another confounding issue is cultural differences in disciplining children. Especially in Canada's main immigrant reception areas of Toronto, Montreal, and Vancouver where dozens of different cultural groups arrive and raise children, child protection authorities have struggled with definitional issues arising from culturally diverse child-rearing practices. Complex issues (i.e., whether female circumcision, required of young girls in some cultures, should be actively prevented or passively allowed) also confuse and frustrate both front-line protection workers and policy makers. The introduction of the concept of harm to the child as a criterion of abuse shifted the definitional focus from evaluation of parental morals and behavior to effects on children. However, this shift does not deal particularly well with cultural issues since what is considered harmful in one culture may be considered an important feature of childhood in another. Also, the question of whether gender should enter into the concept of harm has yet to be addressed. These are arenas in which practice may be leading policy; empirical research to determine how such ambiguous issues are being dealt with on a day-to-day basis is needed.

Research carried out by Trocme et al. (1995) in Ontario confirms that emotional abuse is a concern of social workers and the reporting public and that complaints of such abuse are increasingly being substantiated by authorities in that province. However, this category of abuse remains controversial and largely hidden. Recently, a film called "The Trouble with Evan" (Docherty, 1994) was aired nationally. Cameras placed in a family's home, with full consent, captured frequent, ongoing, and very disturbing scenes of parents' verbal abuse of one child. Such a graphic and widely displayed demonstration of nonphysical attacks may increase the profile of this issue in Canada.

Focus on sexual abuse continues, but with new and complex twists. The mass media have brought sexual abuse into the public domain in the past two years. Cases involving ritual abuse, large-scale sexual abuse on an intergenerational basis, abuse perpetrated by such trusted figures as priests and Christian brothers in children's institutions, child pornography and prostitution as lucrative and flourishing businesses, and charges of sexual abuse in the distant past, followed by the defense of false memory syndrome, keep sexual abuse in the forefront of public attention. This issue more than any other raises the question of whether traditional child welfare's almost exclusive focus on parents remains appropriate. Sexual abuse is also an issue that brings gender into the equation in an inescapable way since the majority of victims are girls, while nearly all perpetrators are males.

Neglect continues as the largest single category of cases. It also remains relatively noncontroversial. Neglect cases are generally less dramatic than those involving abuse, but they can involve just as much suffering for both parents and children as abuse (Swift, 1995a). These cases continue to present ambiguities to workers, with the most difficult problem remaining one of distinguishing between poverty and neglect. In a recent article, one author proposed that neglect issues be removed from child welfare legislation (Callahan, 1993b), to be replaced by family support for those in material need and prosecution for those parents engaged in acts of criminal negligence. The Criminal Code of Canada already contains a provision that encodes the withholding of the necessities of life as a criminal offense. Callahan's suggestion may become the basis of more serious discussion as federal funding for child welfare, along with that for other social services, decreases.

Underlying these various debates is the question of how the implementation of narrow abuse definitions and due process are affecting both practitioners and families. Many leading spokespersons hail the noninterventionist approach as representative of important progress, claiming protection of parental rights and family continuity as its benefits. However, this model has its critics. The focus on due process has led to the legalization of social work, in which assessment has been replaced by investigation (Thompson-Cooper, Fugere, & Cormier, 1993, October, p. 560). This central issue is revisited in the conclusion of the chapter.

The Reporting System

Just as definitions vary across jurisdictions, so too do reporting mandates. In general all jurisdictions have adopted some version of reporting requirements. As Thompson-Cooper et al. (1993) note, little history of the development of Canadian reporting laws has been written nor has much critique yet been developed.

Administration

The arrangements by which child welfare reporting structures are administered vary across the country. In the western and some eastern provinces, the mandated child protection organizations are departments of provincial governments, usually organized on a regional basis. Another model is that of Ontario, in which organizations are "semipublic" (Harris & Melichercik, 1986), operating as privately incorporated agencies with boards of directors, but dependent on government financing. The Quebec model is organized around regionally based social service centers that provide a broad range of health and social services to children and adults. Within each region is a Centre de protection de l'enfance at de la jeunesse (Child and Youth Protection Center) responsible for coordinating protection services. A recent change in this structure emphasizes more specialized and administratively separate child welfare services, including both protective services and institutional care facilities.

Mandated authorities, however organized, are accountable to the children's services department of their provincial ministry of welfare. Service costs have been funded under the Canada Assistance Plan (CAP) for the past several decades. CAP has provided 50% of health and social service costs from federal sources, subject to various restrictions, with the remainder paid by provinces and in some cases municipalities. In 1995 new legislation altered this arrangement. Now federal block funding, based on a predetermined formula, will be provided to provinces for health, postsecondary education, and social services, including child welfare. It is clear that federal contributions will be substantially reduced under the new plan. At the same time, provinces will have more power to determine how these funds should be allocated.

Effects of this major policy shift on child protection services remain to be seen, but cutbacks in program funding are a virtual certainty. Critics also fear effects on children of this apparent "unraveling" of Canada's social safety net, especially reduced accessibility to health services. In addition, other social programs benefiting child welfare clients are likely to be reduced or terminated, including child care and women's shelters.

The arrangements for child welfare on Indian reserves across Canada require special mention. Although family and child welfare are generally provincial matters in Canada, status (legally registered) Indians come under federal jurisdiction, which takes precedence. As a result, the federal government has traditionally had the primary responsibility for child welfare programs for this population (Armitage, 1993a). For this reason, Native people on reserves were not considered to be subject to or eligible for provincial child welfare services until the 1960s. Until that time, the federal government had jurisdiction but was unwilling to "duplicate" provincial programs by developing a child welfare service for on-reserve Indians. As well, large numbers of Native children, especially in western Canada, were required to attend residential schools off the reserve for most of the year, reducing the number of children likely to be in need of protection from their families. These residential schools were phased out during the 1960s, creating a new population of children potentially in need of child welfare services.

Many reserves were (and are) characterized by high levels of poverty, alcoholism, substandard housing, poor health and health services, and serious child welfare problems. Provincial authorities, especially in the western provinces, began to extend child welfare services to reserves in the 1960s and 1970s. Johnston's (1983) survey of the results of this intervention demonstrated that Native children were apprehended by provincial authorities in far greater numbers than the proportion of Native families in the population and in much greater proportions than non-Native children. Many of these children had been permanently separated from their families and communities. Many had been adopted outside the province and the country. Johnston termed this phenomenon the *Sixties Scoop,* the effects of which were that some communities had lost a whole generation. Reaction by Native people against this child welfare approach led to the development of new arrangements in the 1980s for administering child welfare on a reserve. The predominant model has been the "tripartite agreement" involving the federal government as the source of funds, the provincial government as the legislated authority, and one or more Bands (legally constituted groups of Aboriginal People) as the administrators of child welfare programs (Armitage, 1993a). As of 1991–1992 according to Armitage (1993a, p. 155), 38 Native-controlled agencies involving 214 Bands have these arrangements across Canada. Other Bands that do not have formal agreements in some cases follow procedures set out in these official agreements.

Who Makes Reports?

Since the 1960s, the trend in legislation has been toward mandatory reporting of child protection concerns. At present all Canadian jurisdictions except one include mandatory reporting clauses in their protection legislation. The exception is the Yukon, where only teachers and day care workers are required to report under the legislation governing their respective professions. Protection legislation contains various wordings concerning what is to be considered reportable. Most legislation uses the phrase "in need of protection" as a general designation of intent. Some legislation (that of Prince Edward Island) contains specific conditions such as abandonment, desertion, and physical ill-treatment that must be reported. The majority of acts indicate that reports are required to be made by "anyone" aware of a child in need of protection. In addition, professionals who work with children are especially mentioned in most legislation as those required to report, even if the information they report is otherwise considered confidential. Lawyers are generally exempt from reporting, although not in Prince Edward Island.

Reports in all jurisdictions are to be made to mandated child protection authorities even if the information has been given to others, for instance, to health or educational personnel. In many places, 24-hour services or telephone "hot lines" have been made available for reports outside regular working hours. Two basic models currently exist for determining whether reports should be made to child welfare authorities or to police. One (used in Quebec and Saskatchewan, for instance) is a division of responsibility based on familial versus "extrafamilial" abuse, with child welfare only responsible for the case if a family member is the alleged abuser. In these instances, child welfare personnel must still conduct the initial investigation and remain involved if a child is found to be in need of protection. The other model involves the extension of child welfare authority to include abuse by persons in positions of trust. Manitoba's legislation, for instance, includes babysitters, coaches, and teachers as persons in positions of trust.

In general the reporter is guaranteed confidentiality and protection from liability, provided the report is made in good faith. A few jurisdictions do provide penalties for false or malicious reports. In the Yukon, for instance, a fine of $5,000, or 6 months in prison, or both are possible penalties. Most jurisdictions, however, focus penalty provisions on those who fail to report. The most common penalty is a $2,000 fine, up to 6 months in prison, or both.

In practice, of course, many people are reluctant to make reports and remain unclear as to what is a reportable offense. Some are afraid of repercussions should they be identified by the parents, and professionals are often uncertain as to placement of loyalties. Also, the trend toward defining abuse as actual or clear risk of harm to a child stands in contradiction to the push toward reporting children who may be in need of protection, adding to public confusion. Nevertheless, reporting appears to have increased substantially over the decades since these laws have been introduced (Armitage, 1993b, pp. 51–52).

Investigations. All jurisdictions place responsibility for receiving reports on child welfare authorities. The investigation of reports, generally referred to as "complaints" or "signalments" in Quebec, is shaped and guided by several

layers of directives, including legislation, provincial and organizational protocols, legal precedent, and supervisory intervention. But it is the front-line
protection worker who is generally responsible for "intake," for screening
complaints, and for conducting a more complete investigation when deemed
appropriate. According to Callahan (1993a, p. 67) Canadian child welfare
workers are about 70% female with an average age of about 35. Approximately 60% have a bachelor of arts (BA) or a bachelor of social work (BSW),
and the average length of tenure is estimated to be from 18 months to 3 years.
In larger Canadian cities, the norm is to hire social workers at the BSW or
master of social work (MSW) level and to specialize the intake function.
However, British Columbia deregulated professional standards in child protection, making it more likely that non-social workers will be hired to do this
work. Canada's vast rural areas make the availability of social workers with
these credentials problematic in many locations. A study of rural child protection workers suggested that they nevertheless often adopt attitudes consonant
with the profession (Trute, Adkins, & MacDonald, 1994). More than half of
the Canadian jurisdictions offer mandatory training to workers, training that
varies considerably in both length and content. Others offer training that is
not mandatory. In other words, no generalizations about the preparedness of
investigators can be made.

Both tradition and provincial legislation require that mandated child welfare authorities respond to all referrals and requests for help (Harris & Melichercik, 1986), generally within a specified time period. Of course, it is not
considered that all reports must necessarily be pursued. The first decision to
be made is whether further action is required. Some jurisdictions allow a
24-hour response time for all complaints. Others have codes or risk levels that
specify allowed time periods for response based on presumed urgency. In
Nova Scotia, for instance, five risk levels and response times are designated:

Child in life-threatening circumstances:	1 hour
Child in immediate danger:	Same day
Child exposed to damaging circumstances:	2 days
Low risk for child:	10 days
No risk for child:	21 days

The screening of reports has assumed an investigatory nature that has
to some considerable extent replaced the idea of the social work assessment
(Thompson-Cooper et al., 1993). Bala and Vogl (1991) state that the "skills
required to investigate an allegation of abuse or neglect are similar to those
required in police work" (p. 38). The required procedures nevertheless differ
somewhat across jurisdictions. In some jurisdictions (i.e., the Northwest Territories), the worker's supervisor must agree to decisions concerning whether
action is necessary and determining the degree of risk involved. In others (i.e.,
Nova Scotia) a case conference provides a backup screening mechanism. Risk
assessment tools are used in some places. The report of the Federal-Provincial
Working Group (1994) identifies three in current use: the Washington State

Risk Factor Matrix (Nova Scotia), the Manitoba Risk Estimation System (Manitoba, some Ontario agencies), and the Child Welfare League of America's Child Well-Being Scale (some Ontario agencies). The three provinces with abuse registers direct workers to use these lists as part of the initial screening process for reports.

Most jurisdictions have moved within the last decade (Thompson-Cooper et al., 1993) toward mandatory notification of police by child welfare authorities when certain types of reports are involved. These generally include reports of sexual abuse, serious physical abuse, and sometimes serious neglect, as well as cases involving alleged perpetrators outside the family. This trend has certainly increased with changes to the Criminal Code of Canada that clarify types of sexual abuse. Most provinces have developed detailed protocols to separate areas of responsibility between child welfare authorities and police concerning investigation, communication, and monitoring. In general, police are to become involved and take the lead in criminal investigations, while child welfare authorities are to ensure that children are adequately protected. Apprehension of children, usually with a warrant if time and circumstances allow, is the province of child welfare in most cases. In a few jurisdictions, police may also apprehend, and it is becoming more common for police to accompany social workers when children are to be apprehended. All jurisdictions provide directives for obtaining medical examinations of children suspected of having been sexually abused or physically injured. Although it is preferred that guardians attend this examination with the child, provisions are made for the apprehension and examination of the child if the guardian refuses permission. In most central and western jurisdictions, provisions are made to consult the Bands and communities of Native children about whom reports are made.

Child Abuse Registers. Only three Canadian jurisdictions (Nova Scotia, Ontario, and Manitoba) have introduced child abuse registers. Several other provinces allow protection personnel access to computerized information concerning client families. Quebec's legislation stipulates that all cases of abuse be reported to the Youth Rights Protection Commission, a monitoring body concerned with children's rights. Certainly where registries exist the number of children registered has escalated over time. Information from Manitoba's Annual Reports (Table 2-2) exemplifies this trend. It is worth noting that Manitoba's child register shows the gender of reported children has changed from an even distribution in 1975 to almost twice as many females as males reported in 1992. This trend no doubt reflects increased attention to and reporting of sexual abuse during those years.

Nova Scotia's register, initiated in 1976, was revamped in 1991 to include perpetrators who are other than guardians of the child victim and to make the register more broadly accessible for screening purposes. Information is now available to specific parties employing individuals who work with children. Ontario's protection legislation requires that abuse be reported to the register, which is used to monitor and track cases, but not to screen employees. An

Table 2-2. Number of Children
Registered, Manitoba Child Abuse
Register, Selected Years, 1970–1992

1970	49
1975	83
1980	236
1983	578
1986	836
1989	1,870
1992	2,140

Source: Manitoba Annual Reports.

interministerial committee has been investigating the possibility of allowing additional access.

Trends and Issues in Reporting

Although substantiating data are not available, it is common knowledge among professionals in the field that the response directives present in legislation often cannot be implemented as written. Creative intake departments employ devices such as referrals, waiting lists, problem redefinition, and increasingly strict risk designations in an attempt to set priorities for the demand for investigation and service. Thompson-Cooper et al. (1993) argue, along with Solnit (1980) and others in the United States, that the inception of reporting laws has changed child welfare from a helping service to an investigative service. They claim the resources required to respond, even inadequately, to the increase in reports has redirected already scarce resources from the helping function.

The development of due process procedures in the investigation of abuse complaints has led to the institution of new training programs, new legislation, and procedures designed to bring increased specificity and "objectivity" to the evidence-gathering procedures of social workers investigating child welfare complaints. Workers have been advised to emulate the police system of "black book" recording their observations. As they investigate, they are encouraged to take notes that may be used as evidence in court and will lend credence to their recommendations. In some locations these procedures have replaced or reduced reliance on the traditional social work assessment as a form of recording. This trend can be seen as part of the legalization of social work, which emphasizes a proper investigation and the least intrusive approach. It is increasingly being argued (Callahan, 1993b; Swift, 1995a; Thompson-Cooper et al., 1993) that this approach runs counter to social work objectives, turning social workers into policing agents and support staff into a "network of informers" (Thomas, 1982).

A related issue is the newly developing relationship between social workers and the police. Only in the last 10 years or so have provinces developed policies requiring social workers to refer many cases to the police. As Thompson-Cooper et al. (1993) point out, this requirement means a report to child welfare is a report to the police in many instances, an eventuality that exposes the family to highly intrusive investigation. In addition, workers themselves may be exposed to legal risks. In a recent Ontario case, for instance, a worker was ordered to pay a large sum in damages to a father wrongly investigated for sexual abuse (*Yakabuski,* May 21, 1994). The father's complaint was, in part, that police were notified of the report of alleged abuse before he had a chance to explain his side of the story to the worker. The worker's defense was that she was following an agreed-upon protocol with police to allow them first chance to interview the accused. The court found for the father.

A nontraditional issue recently coming to the fore is that of child abuse registers. Originally the idea of registers was to assist social workers in keeping track of high-risk families who moved from one jurisdiction to another. In the past this kind of register has been seen as a provincial responsibility, although it has not really "caught on" across the country. The recent explosion of interest in extrafamilial sexual abuse, however, has given a new cast to this issue. Now a prominent concern is employment in child care jobs of individuals with past criminal records, especially of sexual abuse. The recent discovery of considerable ongoing sexual abuse of children in institutions by caregivers and administrators, including Catholic priests and lay brothers, has brought public attention to this issue in a way that has garnered broad public support for registers. Nicholas Bala, a well-known spokesperson and author on child welfare issues, has recently recommended the introduction of a nationwide information system, including access to employers, as a protective measure for children (Steed, 1993).

Reporting and Placement Trends

In this section, information about reports made and substantiated and children placed in various forms of care are discussed. Problems of data collection and comparison are necessarily discussed as well. Some common beliefs about reporting are supported by data, for instance, that fewer children are now being placed in care than in the 1970s. However some beliefs come into question as a result of the data, for instance, that the vast majority of complaints concern child abuse.

Information about trends in child welfare processes should be considered in relation to child and youth population trends in Canada, which show the proportion of children 0–14 years old increasing through the 1950s and 1960s, reaching a peak of 33% of the total population in 1966, followed by a decline and leveling off at about 20% of the population by the mid-1980s; the 15–24-year-old group has declined since 1986.

Reports and Investigations

Trends in reporting cannot be compared across Canada because of differences in the data available. Information was derived from provincial annual reports, from information assembled for this chapter by provincial staff, and from the report issued by the Federal-Provincial Working Group (1994). From this information base, some apparent trends can be identified, but some departures from those trends are also evident. Rather than reaching conclusions about "Canadian trends," this section points the way toward some unanswered questions and some directions jurisdictions might pursue in the future.

With respect to information about trends in reporting over the past two decades, data from Quebec are the most complete. In Quebec, mandatory reporting has been in effect since the 1975–1976 fiscal year. From 1982, detailed data have been kept on reports received, reports retained, investigations pursued, and cases substantiated. From these data, it is apparent that the introduction of reporting requirements resulted in a steep increase in reporting—a 100% increase from 1982 to 1989, with the sharpest rise occurring between 1986 and 1988. During this same time period, the number of reports retained for investigation decreased, from 68% to about 55%. Even with this decrease, the staff in 1989 had nearly 11,000 additional investigations to conduct over the number in 1982 (Quebec annual reports). Recent information (Federal-Provincial Working Group, 1994, p. 78) concerning substantiation rates shows that both the total number of reports received and the percentage of reports retained were lower in 1991–1992 than in 1989. Of those reports retained for investigation, 44.7% were substantiated in 1992. This means that only 19% of reports received eventually became substantiated cases. This does not necessarily mean that 81% of reports were false or inappropriate, since there are other explanations for reports not being retained or substantiated. Some reports for instance are duplications, while some concern children already served by child welfare authorities. Also, cases that may have been substantiated in the past may not be now given the trend toward least intrusive service.

The apparent trends revealed in the Quebec data suggest that considerably increased resources are now necessary for handling and investigation of reports. Data from British Columbia suggest similar, although less dramatic, trends. Investigations in that province show a steep increase from 26,000 to 33,000 reports between 1986 and 1990, followed by a considerable decline to 27,000 reports in 1994.

What this limited information suggests is that the introduction of reporting laws has dramatically increased the number of calls received and the number of investigations that must be carried out. As with most new procedures, the response may be expected to level. However the data also suggest that many reports do not result in substantiated cases. A recent study by Trocme et al. (1995) in Ontario shows the substantiation rate to be 28%, with an additional 31% of reports classified as suspected but unable to be substantiated. These figures are based on an annual incidence rate of 21 investigated reports per 1,000 children in Ontario in 1993 (Trocme, McPhee, Tam, & Hay, 1994).

Types of Complaints

Behind public support for mandatory reporting laws is the belief that the laws are effective in uncovering serious cases of child abuse. Given the substantial

Table 2-3. 1988 Quebec Reports by
Type of Allegation

Neglect	45.7%
Physical abuse	14.0%
Sexual abuse	13.5%
Child's behavior	22.4%
Abandonment	4.4%

Source: Quebec Ministere des Affaires Sociales
Rapport Annuel.

attention to sexual abuse over the past decade, it might be supposed that recent
reports would concern a high proportion of sexual abuse cases. It might also
be supposed that physical abuse would be well represented in reports. Available data do not fully support these beliefs. Information from Quebec's Annual Report of 1988 (Table 2-3) revealed neglect to be the greatest single
category of allegation reported. Annual reports in British Columbia (Table
2-4) also consistently show neglect as the highest single category of investigation, one that is increasing as sexual abuse diminishes slightly.

Available data concerning substantiated cases also show neglect as a significant category. In Saskatchewan, for instance, neglect consistently represents
nearly half of substantiated cases, while physical and sexual abuse each are
about a quarter of the cases. Emotional abuse stands at about 3% (Annual
Reports).

In Alberta, recent data show a somewhat similar trend, although with an
interesting twist. Of children declared to be "in need," 8.3% were in need due
to physical abuse, 11.6% due to sexual abuse, 20.4% due to neglect, and
59.7% were attributed to "other reasons." The large "other" category suggests
that traditional child welfare concepts may be inadequate to describe and
account for issues now faced in the field, a theme that recurs in other findings.
Available data from other jurisdictions (i.e., New Brunswick and Saskatchewan) show similar patterns by case type (Federal-Provincial Working Group,
1994).

Table 2-4. British Columbia Investigations by Type of
Allegation, 1986/7 and 1993/4

	1986–1987	1993–1994
Physical abuse	18.0%	22.7%
Sexual abuse	20.0%	18.4%
Neglect	27.7%	33.8%
Multiple	11.4%	12.6%
Other	19.6%	12.5%
Emotional	3.3%	—[a]

[a]Included in "Other" category.

Source: British Columbia Family and Children's Services Annual Reports.

Some provinces report data on abuse only. Nova Scotia's child abuse registry does not show neglect. The registry's reports of substantiated abuse show cases of sexual abuse rising from very few in 1982, to almost twice as many as cases of physical abuse in 1986, and continuing in this direction in 1992. Manitoba's annual reports show a less dramatic but similar pattern of sexual abuse reporting. In 1971 no cases of sexual abuse were reported. In 1991, 1,229 cases were recorded, representing about 22% more than reported cases of physical abuse. During those same two decades, reports of physical abuse increased from 40 cases to 956.

Implications of these figures are (i) that child neglect remains an important issue, seen as reportable; (ii) that reports of sexual abuse have indeed increased dramatically, although available data suggest they may comprise about one fifth to one quarter of all reports; (iii) at least in some locations, sexual abuse cases now outnumber cases of substantiated physical abuse; (iv) emotional abuse remains an unclear category, appearing to be an extremely low percentage of cases for which figures are available, but not always disaggregated as a separate category; and (v) various catchall and "other" categories, not comparable across provinces as now collected, represent a large proportion of reports and certainly deserve further examination given their size in some jurisdictions.

Children Placed

While the number of reports has escalated over two decades, the number of children taken into care has decreased. As Hepworth (1980), Armitage (1993b), and others have reported, the number of children in care reached frightening proportions in the 1970s in Canada. Although these data reflect in part the demographic bulge of the "baby boomers," the percentage of Canadian children in the care of child welfare authorities was certainly greater than in most industrialized countries.

Substantial information collected about this phenomenon demonstrated that high placement rates were attributable largely to the very high number of Native children apprehended and placed following the phasing out of residential schools in the 1960s. Hepworth (1980) demonstrated that as of 1977, 20% of all children in care were Native children. His very thorough study also showed that 3.5% of all Native children were in the care of child welfare authorities, compared to 1.35% for all Canadian children. The western provinces had particularly high rates of children in care, with Native children half of Saskatchewan's care population and 60% of Manitoba's in 1976–1977 (Hepworth, 1980, pp. 111–115). Hepworth also demonstrated that Native children were less likely than others to return home or to be placed for adoption.

The gathering and disseminating of information about high placement rates in the early 1980s no doubt contributed to the trends toward narrower definitions of abuse and the reduction in number of placements. The attention of scholars such as Bowlby (1969) to issues of attachment and loss also had a great impact on Canadian child welfare decision making. The debate concerning parents' rights and the tendency to due process also worked to support the trend to provide in-home services as often superior to apprehension and placement for children needing protection. Available data (Table 2-5) do show a significant decrease in placement as a percentage of child population, except in Manitoba, between the late 1970s and the early 1990s. These data must be viewed with caution since definitions of "in care" vary over time and among provinces.

Another way of looking at trends is in terms of actual numbers of children in care. For instance, Ontario's data show a significant decrease in numbers of placements over the past two decades, from 17,800 in 1971 to just over 10,000 in 1991. During this same time period, available data reveal that the number of children served in their own homes was high in proportion to children in care. Information from Ontario in 1988, for instance, shows 74,000 families being served, with only 9,712 children in care (Trocme, 1991). In Alberta for 1991–1992, 7,102 children were judged to be in need of protection as of March 31, 1992, with about half (3,535) of these served in their own homes (Federal-Provincial Working Group, 1994). These data suggest that a high proportion of children receive in-home care.

In the public mind, reporting laws and child welfare authorities operate in many or most cases to protect the very young and vulnerable child from perpetrators of abuse since these are the characteristics of cases most often receiving a high level of media attention. In Manitoba, indeed nearly half of all reports in 1991–1992 concerned children aged 10 years and under, while 30% of reports involved children aged 11 to 15 (Federal-Provincial Working Group, 1994, p. 107). However, the ages of children actually taken into care in some jurisdictions suggest a more complicated reality for child welfare services. Hepworth (1980) reported a high rate of older children in care through the 1960s and 1970s. Among the possible explanations Hepworth suggests for this phenomenon were a large number of older children in long-term care and a focus on trying to provide in-home care for younger children. This pattern of older children in care continues into the 1990s (Table 2-6). In British Columbia, 68% of children in care as of March 31, 1992, were 10 and older. In fact, 43% were 15 or older, while only 16% were 4 or younger (Federal-Provincial Working Group, 1994, p. 158) Alberta shows a similar trend. Nova Scotia's data show an even stronger trend toward adolescent care. In that province as of March 31, 1992, 82.1% of children in care were 10 or older, 12.5% were 19 or 20, while only 6.7% were 4 or younger. This trend is occurring in the context of a decreased proportion of population in the 15–24-year age range.

Few data are available concerning gender of children placed. British Columbia shows slightly more males than females in all age groups except older adolescents (Federal-Provincial Working Group, 1994, p. 158). Alberta also shows more males than females overall for 1992 (Federal-Provincial Working Group, 1994, p. 142). In the Northwest Territories, more girls are in placement than boys in all age groups. Alberta on the other hand shows more males (53.6%) than females (46.4%) in care. Information from New Brunswick shows about twice as many girls as boys in care for sexual abuse, but more

Table 2-5. Children in Care as a Percentage of Children Aged 0–14 Years by Province, 1976–1977 and 1991–1992

	Children in Care 1991–1992	Child Population 0–14 Years, 1991–1992	Children in Care as a Percentage of Child Population 0–14 Years		Percentage Change
			1976–1977	1991–1992	
Newfoundland	729	127,920	0.75	0.57	−24
Prince Edward Island	206	29,360	0.91	0.70	−23
Nova Scotia	1,561	184,360	1.42	0.85	−40
New Brunswick	1,187	151,220	1.44	0.78	−45
Quebec	a	1,378,175	2.06	a	a
Ontario	10,040	2,055,240	0.63	0.49	−22
Manitoba	5,412	239,730	1.54	2.26	+47
Saskatchewan	2,464	237,460	1.10	1.04	−5
Alberta	3,567	601,105	2.14	0.59	−72
British Columbia	6,084	662,250	1.62	0.92	−43

[a]Data not available.

Sources: Census of Canada (1991, 93–310–12), Federal-Provincial Working Group (1994), Hepworth (1980, p. 76).

Table 2-6. Older Children in Care, Selected Jurisdictions, March 31, 1992

	Age Group[a]	Percentage of Children
Newfoundland	12+	52.4%
Nova Scotia	10+	82.1
New Brunswick	13+	69.7[b]
Ontario	13+	53.4
Alberta	12+	51.1
British Columbia	10+	68.0
Yukon	12+	46.1
Northwest Territories	13+	29.5

[a]Comparable age groups not available.

[b]Permanent care only.

Source: Federal-Provincial Working Group (1994).

boys than girls for other reasons. These data are too scant to reach conclusions, but do suggest that vast numbers of girls have not been apprehended to protect them from sexual abuse as some may believe.

Native Children in Care

The main demographic story concerning Canadian children in care has for several decades been that of Native children. It may be generally believed that the shocking picture painted by Hepworth in 1980 has changed. Certainly efforts to turn this trend around have been made, including the use of tripartite agreements, increased involvement of Bands in child welfare procedures, the development of support agencies, and so on. However, it is far from certain that these efforts have seriously reduced placement of Native children. It can be said that the outright disappearance of Native children, especially through out-of-country adoption, has declined. A recent study in Saskatchewan (Rosenbluth, 1995), however, suggests that Native children are still at high risk of apprehension and placement. Fully half the sample in Rosenbluth's study was Native children. This study reveals not only continuing overrepresentation of Native children in care, but also that Native children are first placed at a much earlier age than other children (5.5 years on average as opposed to 8.5 years) and are more likely than others to become permanent wards of the state. Also, although duration of placement has been reduced on average for other children, this reduction is smaller for Native children.

Work concerning Metis (mixed Indian and European ancestry) children in Manitoba reveals that they also continue to be at high risk for apprehension. Barkwell, Longclaws, and Chartrand (1989) report that at the beginning of the 1980s in Manitoba, 40–60% of all children removed from their families in western Canada were Indian or Metis. They also show evidence to suggest that Metis children remain greatly overrepresented in the child welfare system. Both Rosenbluth and Barkwell et al. report that very high percentages of the Native children they studied were placed in non-Native homes.

Placement Types

In Canada, foster care is thought of as the mainstay of the alternate care system. In the 1970s, when so many children were in care, a vast number of foster homes were open and in regular use in Canada. A look at the current picture suggests some change in this arena. Most provinces do keep reasonably accurate information on placements, and it is possible to view this information not only over time, but across the country. This examination reveals that the number of children in foster homes across the country has diminished considerably, a trend to be expected in light of the diminution of children placed. The proportion of this form of care vis-á-vis other forms has distinct patterns in different jurisdictions, patterns that have changed markedly in some jurisdictions but not in others. Four patterns, using earliest and latest available data for each province, are shown in Table 2-7.

How can these disparate trends be explained? The data reveal only some surface clues to underlying social and historical patterns across the country. Saskatchewan, with an increase in the proportion of foster care, appears to have very few group homes or other specialized placements (Federal-Provincial Working Group, 1994, p. 126) and, as elsewhere, a decrease in adoptions (Annual Reports, Saskatchewan). Evidence of a decreased proportion of

Table 2-7. Trends in Numbers of Foster Placements and Foster Care as a Percentage of All Placements, Selected Jurisdictions, 1970s and 1990s

1. Decrease in numbers, increase in proportion:		
Saskatchewan:	1972	1992
	2,260 foster placements	1,990 foster placements
	(70% of placements)	(80% of placements)
2. Decrease in both numbers and proportion:		
British Columbia:	1975	1994
	5,965 foster placements	2,255 foster placements
	(60% of placements)	(36.3% of placements)
Ontario:	1970	1991
	11,207 foster placements	5,200 foster placements
	(63% of placements)	(51% of placements)
Nova Scotia:	1975	1992
	1,888 foster placements	448 foster placements
	(75% of placements	(50% of placements)
3. Decrease in number but approximately the same proportion:		
Alberta:	1975	1992
	3,826 foster placements	2,065 foster placements
	(61.4% of placements)	(57.8% of placements)
Quebec:	1978	1994 (Estimate)
	16,824 foster placements	6,800 foster placements
	(68.4% of placements)	(62% of placements)
4. Increase in number, same proportion:		
Manitoba:	1980	1992
	1,470 foster placements	2,143 foster placements
	(40.8% of placements)	(39.5% of placements)

Sources: Federal-Provincial Working Group (1994), Provincial Annual Reports.

foster care is harder to explain. In British Columbia, the figures show an increase during the last two decades in the use of other resource types, including group homes and "specialized resources." Between 1975 and 1994, specialized resource placements increased from 16% of the total placements to 34% (British Columbia Family and Children's Services Annual Reports; Federal-Provincial Working Group, 1994, p. 94). Ontario's placement picture suggests increasing variety in placement types as a possible explanation. Nova Scotia's placement picture shows a relatively large percentage of children in independent living situations (18.7%), with group homes and residential facilities accounting for quite small proportions of children placed (Federal-Provincial Working Group, 1994).

The third pattern in Table 2-7, showing a decrease in the number of foster homes but no change in foster care as a proportion of all placements, suggests a decrease in total placements over time. Quebec has traditionally relied on a greater proportion of institutional care than other provinces. Although efforts are being made to decrease institutional care as a proportion of the total, presumably with a concomitant increase in foster care, this trend has been slow to develop. During the 1980s institutional care remained at approximately a third or more of the total placements (Quebec Annual Reports). Finally, Manitoba's increase in the number of foster care placements can be explained by a 33% increase in the number of total placements between 1980 and 1992.

In none of these jurisdictions has kin care shown any great increase, nor have group home placements, except in British Columbia. There is some tendency toward a greater number of categories of placement, which confounds the picture but may also help to explain why proportions of traditional forms of care have diminished. Ontario, for instance, now includes agency-sponsored and "outside" foster care and group care in its list of categories (Ontario Association of Children's Aid Societies, 1990). About the only generalizations that can be made are that the number of placements has diminished in most jurisdictions and that existing placement categories are somewhat more numerous and complex than they were two decades ago.

Issues

Questions are now beginning to be raised about child welfare priorities given apparently low report substantiation rates. American reports suggest that only about 40% of reports become substantiated cases. Data cited in this section suggest that substantiation rates in Canada are as low or lower. It could be speculated that this low number, as well as the sizable "suspected" category found by Trocme et al. (1995), result from a contradiction between the least intrusive approach, which requires a high level of harm or risk for substantiation and case opening, and the trend toward mandatory reporting, which encourages public responsibility to prevent harm. Given the lack of a central database, it is not currently possible to evaluate the effects or effectiveness of mandatory reporting on a national basis. While mandatory reporting may seem at first blush to be based on acceptance of community responsibility for the health and safety of children, this notion needs more attention and thought. Seen from another perspective, reporting is a surveillance function, one that makes "informers" of the public but does not necessarily lead to safety or healthy development for children. The figures show that the vast majority of these reports, after all, do not lead to child welfare service provision. Of those that lead to protective care of children, neglect would appear to be the most prevalent problem identified, and neglect is an issue historically and presently associated with poverty (Swift, 1995a). As Thompson-Cooper et al. (1993) and others have argued, the resources now going to these investigations might instead be used for an increased level of services or a different kind of services.

Without doubt, least intrusive and in-home care are the watchwords of current Canadian child welfare practice. The lessons of the 1970s, demonstrating that removal of children from their families can easily escalate to unacceptable levels, are still fresh in the minds of most protection personnel. A few voices, however, are beginning to question the wisdom of an overpowering swing in the opposite direction. Kufeldt (1994), for instance, cites data to show that 89% of children and 75% of parents involved in alternate care situations thought that this solution had been in their best interests at the time it occurred. Kufeldt also cites research revealing that children are entering care at older ages and are more damaged due to failures of in-home services and prevention efforts. She suggests that we discontinue our efforts to employ the same strategies, whether they be alternate care or in-home service, for all. Rather she suggests a continuum of resources matched to the needs of specific children and families is what is needed. Some data presented here suggest that this is beginning to occur. At present very few evaluative data are available concerning the effectiveness of in-home care. In fact the current overwhelming belief in it as the best direction for most children in need of protection is largely based on faith in family and the importance of early attachments. In the final section of the chapter, some recent research on various approaches to both in-home and alternate care is discussed.

Data presented in this section show that large proportions of children in care continue to be older children. Very little attention to this phenomenon has so far been paid, although termination of care in late adolescence has become an issue for discussion (Raychaba, 1987, 1988). However current policies continue to provide very little ongoing support (emotional, social, or financial) for most youth leaving care.

Current Issues in Canadian Child Welfare

In addition to the issues raised in the three sections above, other issues are currently being debated in Canada.

Data Collection

Many laments concerning the lack of national child welfare data were noted during the preparation of this chapter. As Gorlick (1995) points out, identification of trends and evaluation of policy and programming are next to impossible without such a system. While no one argues against a centralized system, there are considerable difficulties in producing it. An important political barrier of course is the long-standing tradition of provincial jurisdiction over child welfare. To arrive at common definitions and data collection systems would indeed be a major and costly undertaking for all 12 jurisdictions. It might be argued also that this process would have a homogenizing effect not only on information, but on the functioning of systems that differ now for sound geographical, social, economic, and political reasons and that the richness of history and experience unique to Canada's different jurisdictions would be diluted. Gorlick (1995) nevertheless recommends that national data be collected on child protection issues. One recent development that might stimulate action in the direction of centralized data collection is the founding of the Child Welfare League of Canada, which has some data-collecting capacity and research support.

Culture/Race

The Canadian government is currently experiencing two important challenges to its authority. One is from Quebec, where separation and sovereignty will again be put to voters. The other is from the Native population, known politically as the First Nations. As Durst, McDonald, and Rich (1994) note, Native leaders view the survival of language and culture as depending on the achievement of self-governing structures. Because of the role child welfare has played in maintaining colonial relations between Native people and the dominant society (Hudson & McKenzie, 1981), a role referred to as "genocide" by prominent Canadian figures (Barkwell et al., 1989), child welfare remains a pivotal issue in this struggle. The tripartite agreements developed in various jurisdictions, most prominently in Manitoba, since the 1980s appeared at first to provide a solution by sharing authority among the involved parties. However, it is now apparent that power sharing is only part of the answer. Levels of abuse, addiction, domestic violence, and poverty continue unabated in many Native communities, and many Native children continue to be brought into care. The conditions of individual reserves may act as barriers to realizing the goals of self-government in the arena of child welfare even when authority has been passed in principle to Native people. In other words, it is not only a political but an economic struggle for Bands to assume control of their own child welfare issues. Durst et al. (1995) appropriately raise the question of how much control Native communities really have since economic development continues to depend almost exclusively on the federal government and its restrictive funding policies.

Another aspect of cultural issues in child protection involves differences in child-rearing practices. Over the past two decades, Canada has begun to accept many "nontraditional" (non-European) immigrants, a trend that has presented the social services generally with new service delivery issues. Concerns have been raised that children who are "different" are at higher risk of placement. In Montreal a recent study (Hutchinson, Nichols, Paré, & Pépin, 1991) in fact demonstrated the overrepresentation of Black children in care. Workers operate under a federal policy of "multiculturalism" that directs all Canadians to respect and celebrate the cultural diversity resulting from our immigration policies and our policies concerning Native people.

Certainly this diversity is having an enormous impact on child welfare in terms not only of issues, but also in terms of solutions, some of which have quite positive potential. For instance, as problems involving Native people unfold, it is clear that their experiences have much to offer child welfare service and philosophy. Among the most important of these are the emphasis on healing and spirituality and a focus on community forms of care (Longclaws, 1994; McKenzie, Seidl, & Bone, 1995).

New Service Approaches: In-Home and Alternate Care

Along with the least intrusive approach and concomitant reduction in the number of placements has been a focus on development of new programs, intensified programs, or both for serving children and families in their own homes. These include the "home-builders" approach, a brief, intensive, in-home service based on crisis theory. Another approach is the development of parent support networks to provide informal mutual aid and support for parents who are clients of child welfare agencies. Benefits of networks include social integration, emotional support, new education and coping skills, and concrete support. Evaluation of several such networks shows significant reduction in levels of out-of-home care for children whose parents were active in a network. Researchers determined this model could be used to increase client satisfaction, reduce risk of out-of-home care, and reduce agency costs (Cameron, 1995).

A somewhat different model is reported by Fuchs (1995), one based on strengthening informal social networks in the neighborhood setting. Demonstration projects carried out in high-risk communities showed that diversifying and enlarging networks resulted in increased information, as well as increased emotional and concrete support for resident parents, thus helping to reduce the risk of placement for children. Yet another model focuses on the extended family to facilitate a process of healing following abuse, as well as to help protect victims from further abuse (Burford & Pennell, 1995). In this model members of the family and sometimes the community group are brought together for a "conference" to discuss the abuse and recommend protective and healing strategies. Obviously this idea flies in the face of confidentiality since the details of the abuse become known to a much wider than usual circle of people. The total cost of a conference cited by the research team as an example was $158, spent mostly for travel costs and a meal for participants. Anecdotal evidence suggests client satisfaction, and more follow-up research is planned.

What these models share is a community approach to service provision. The traditional focus on the nuclear family, and especially on the parents, is broadened to include extended family, other client families, and communities. Such approaches, advocated by many in the past (e.g., Garbarino, 1978), show considerable promise. But because they move outside the traditional family unit, which is the current focus of child welfare legislation and service, they must struggle for credibility and official support.

During the 1980s publicity concerning the Richard Cardinal tragedy (Obomsawin, 1986) brought attention to the extent and damaging effects of "foster care drift." The diaries of the teenage Native child, which came to light after Richard hanged himself, gave evidence of at least 28 different placements in his short life and the desperate loneliness that resulted. A review of the Alberta child welfare system following this event led to new policies across Canada aimed to increase children's chances of permanent placements, either with their natural families or in a foster or adoption home. There is a wide-spread belief that these policies have wiped out at least the worst cases of drift. However, data collected recently suggest that this is not necessarily the case. Rosenbluth's (1995) recent study shows that such practices, while reduced, are far from over.

Concerning alternate care, an approach gaining credibility in Canada is specialized or "treatment" foster care. In this model, foster caregivers are viewed as professionals rather than as the child's new or substitute parents. The focus of this care according to Nutter, Hudson, Galaway, and Hill (1995) generally includes four elements:

1. It serves children who likely would otherwise be placed in relatively restrictive treatment settings.
2. It makes use of screened and trained foster care providers.
3. It involves individual treatment planning.
4. It promotes a program philosophy involving strong community links.

Review of these programs in Canada by Nutter et al. suggests that much more evaluation research is required in order to determine effectiveness of this program type for particular children.

Another study by Thomlison (1995) of specialized foster care shows that three quarters of the subjects in her study were discharged to family settings. Since all children included in the study were considered too difficult for family placement prior to the study, this finding suggests the programs were effective in meeting treatment goals and may be effective in facilitating eventual family reunion. Certainly the per diem costs of specialized care will be higher than for regular foster care, which has historically been kept at a very low level. Even so, as Hepworth (1993) notes, specialized care, which can be purchased at rates as low as $20 Canadian per day, is an inexpensive alternative to institutional care. Even at $50 Canadian per day, this alternative remains much less expensive than most other treatment resources.

An important approach to facilitating family reunion is increasing parent participation in foster care programming. The traditional view of foster care-givers as substitute parents has produced some role confusion for birth par-ents. There has been a concomitant tendency to exclude the original parents, who are seen as having "failed," from a service of which they are not a natural part. Richardson, Galaway, Hudson, Nutter, and Hill (1995) used a sample of treatment foster care programs to examine some effects of involving birth parents in foster care arrangements. They found that higher proportions of children whose parents participated in the placement were discharged because treatment goals were met. What these various studies suggest is that the traditional idea of simply moving a child to another family is not a sufficient approach to protective service in the 1990s.

Women and Child Welfare

Recently a feminist approach to understanding child welfare issues has begun to emerge in Canada. The focus on child sexual abuse, which involved mostly female victims of mostly male perpetrators, provided impetus for this direction, and the application of feminist theory to child welfare problems has now begun in earnest (Callahan, 1993b; Krane, 1990; Reitsma-Street, 1986; Swift, 1991). This analysis reveals a heavy focus on women as clients, often blamed for problems beyond their control; serious resource deprivation experienced by many female clients; the different relationship of women than men to both the labor market and the welfare system; and women's different life experiences as caregivers (Baines, Evans, & Neysmith, 1991). Also brought to the fore are "women's issues" such as wife abuse, which were previously seen by child welfare workers as different, separate, or irrelevant problems. Feminist analysis further reveals how the unpaid or very low paid caring labor of women has allowed the child welfare system to remain at such a low level of funding (Swift, 1995b). A feminist approach includes the social context within which problems occur. Sexual abuse for instance is not viewed as an inevitable problem, but as the product of larger social norms that are themselves in need of change.

Callahan's (1993b) important recent article suggests that a feminist analysis of child welfare leads to solutions involving the separation of child apprehension, with its quasi-judicial mandate, from voluntary services to families—the separation of crimes from needs. She cites examples of projects exemplifying this approach and delineates several models through which separate services could be developed. In any of these models the current emphasis on reporting, investigation, and identification of criminal and civil misbehavior would become matters of lower priority for child welfare authorities, while service provision would become the main priority. This approach, so different from the present due process approach, has considerable promise but will require much effort to establish itself as credible in the current social context of legalized child welfare.

The Purpose of Child Welfare: Residual Service
or the Well-Being of Children?

The conclusions of Callahan reflect the primary underlying issue in current Canadian child welfare debates today. Should child welfare remain a residual service, increasingly legalized to protect the individual rights of family members, or should child welfare reflect its name, focusing on the welfare of Canada's children? In recent years, with attention so riveted on the rights and intrusion debates, this question has been largely ignored. However, an increasing number of voices are taking the broader view. This is occurring in the context of a broad-based child advocacy movement intended to publicize the problems faced by Canadian children, as well as the inadequacy of current solutions. It has long been known that child welfare clients are "overwhelmingly drawn from the ranks of Canada's poor" (National Council of Welfare, 1979, pp. 2–3). Clearly poverty has long-term destructive effects for children, but as child welfare services are currently organized, such pervasive issues cannot be addressed.

Organizations like Coalition 2000 have begun to bring wide public attention to the fact of poverty for 1 in 5 Canadian children. First Nations groups have successfully advocated not only for changes in placement policies, but for holistic preventive services involving not just counseling but healing, recreation facilities, skill development, and other services for children whose families are poor. Wharf (1993, p. 217) recommends that a variety of broad policy strategies be considered, including universal payments for children and providing caregivers (including parents) an adequate wage. Wharf also recommends that provincial departments "get out of the business of delivering services" (1993, p. 224). He suggests instead partnerships between provinces and communities, with the former retaining authority for legislation and allocation of funds, the setting and monitoring of standards, and the operation of specialized services. Regular services in this model would be subject to "community governance," an approach allowing ordinary citizens to gain some understanding of child welfare complexities and also allowing the welfare of children to become a community concern and challenge.

Gorlick (1995) has made the point that the present national focus on public debt and unemployment, in tandem with reduced transfer payments from the federal government to provincial governments, will further erode child welfare services. Child protection as it now stands is quite isolated from other policy directions and is always at risk of being eliminated from the policy agenda. The recent child welfare policy conference sponsored by Health Canada represented an important opportunity for academics and policy makers to focus exclusively on child welfare issues. However such events are hardly sufficient to ensure improved service to children. Current policy changes and cutbacks are a serious matter given the long-standing underfunded nature of child protection and child welfare more generally. The funding crisis may provide some impetus for change for it begs the question of whether we can keep on doing what we are doing. The deeper question is, of course, should we?

References

Act to Amend the Criminal Code and the Canada Evidence Act (Bill C-15). 33rd Parliament of Canada (1986).

Act for the Prevention of Cruelty to and Protection of Children. Statutes of Ontario, (1893), c. 45.

Advisory Committee on Children's Services. (1990). *Children first*. Toronto: Ministry of Community and Social Services.

Alberta Department of Family and Social Services Annual Reports, 1975–1992.

Armitage, A. (1993a). Family and child welfare in First Nation communities. In B. Wharf (Ed.), *Rethinking child welfare* (pp. 131–171). Toronto: McClelland & Stewart.

Armitage, A. (1993b). The policy and legislative context. In B. Wharf (Ed.), *Rethinking child welfare* (pp. 37–63). Toronto: McClelland & Stewart.

Baines, C., Evans, P., & Neysmith, S. (1991). *Women's Caring: Feminist Perspectives on Social Welfare.* Toronto: McClelland & Stewart.

Bala, N., Hornick, J., & Vogl, R. (1991). *Canadian child welfare law.* Toronto: Thompson Educational Publishing.

Barkwell, L. J., Longclaws, L., & Chartrand, D. (1989). Status of Metis children within the child welfare system. *The Canadian Journal of Native Studies, 9*(1), 33–35.

Barnhorst, R. (1986). Child protection legislation: Recent Canadian reform. In B. Landau (Ed.), *Children's rights in the practice of family law* (pp. 255–298). Toronto: Carswell.

Bowlby, J. (1969). *Attachment and loss* (Vols. 1 & 2). New York: Basic Books.

British Columbia Family and Children's Services Reports and Statistics, 1972–1994.

Burford, G., & Pennell, J. (1995). Family group decision making: An innovation in child and family welfare. In J. Hudson & B. Galaway (Eds.), *Child welfare in Canada: Research and policy implications* (pp. 140–153). Toronto: Thompson Educational Publishing.

Callahan, M. (1993a). The administrative and practice context: Perspectives from the front line. In B. Wharf (Ed.), *Rethinking child welfare in Canada* (pp. 64–97). Toronto: McClelland & Stewart.

Callahan, M. (1993b). Feminist approaches: Women recreate child welfare. In B. Wharf (Ed.), *Rethinking child welfare* (pp. 172–209). Toronto: McClelland & Stewart.

Cameron, G. (1995). The nature and effectiveness of parent mutual aid organizations in child welfare. In J. Hudson & B. Galaway (Eds.), *Child welfare in Canada: Research and policy implications* (pp. 66–81). Toronto: Thompson Educational Publishing.

Canada Evidence Act. Revised Statutes of Canada (1985), c. C. 5.

Canadian Charter of Rights and Freedoms. Part I of the Constitution Act. (1982), c. 11.

Children and Family Services Act, Statutes of Nova Scotia (1990), c. 5.

Child Welfare Act. Statutes of Alberta (1984), c. C-8.1, as amended.

Cohen-Schlanger, M., Fitzpatrick, A., Hulchanski, J. D., & Raphael, D. (1993). Housing as a factor in child admission to temporary care. Toronto: University of Toronto, Joint Research Report of the Faculty of Social Work, and Children's Aid Society of Metropolitan Toronto.

Criminal Code of Canada. Revised Statutes of Canada (1985), c. C-46.

Docherty, N. (Producer & Director). (1994). *The trouble with Evan.* Canadian Broadcasting Company.

Durst, D., McDonald, J., & Rich, C. (1994). Aboriginal government of child welfare services: Hobson's choice? In J. Hudson & B. Galaway (Eds.), *Child welfare in Canada: Research and policy implications* (pp. 41–53). Toronto: Thompson Educational Publishing.

Falconer, N., & Swift, K. (1983). *Preparing for practice: The fundamentals of child protection.* Toronto: Children's Aid Society of Metropolitan Toronto.

Family and Child Services Act. Revised Statutes of Prince Edward Island (1988), F-2.01.

Federal-Provincial Working Group on Child and Family Services Information. (1994). *Child welfare in Canada.* Ottawa: National Clearinghouse on Family Violence, Health Canada.

Fuchs, D. (1995). Preserving and strengthening families and protecting children: Social network intervention, a balanced approach to the prevention of child maltreatment. In J. Hudson & B. Galaway (Eds.), *Child welfare in Canada: Research and policy implications* (pp. 113–122). Toronto: Thompson Educational Publishing.

Garbarino, J. (1978). Defining the community context for parent-child relations: The correlates of child maltreatment. *Child Development, 49,* 604.

Gorlick, C. (1995). *Listening to low income children and single mothers: Policy implications related to child welfare.* In J. Hudson & B. Galaway (Eds.), Child Welfare in Canada: Research and policy implications (pp. 286–297). Toronto: Thompson Educational Publishing.

Gouvernement du Quebec. Loi sur la protection de la jeunesse/Youth Protection Act (1977). Revised Statutes of Quebec, c. P-34.1.

Government of Canada. (1984). *Sexual offences against children: Report of the committee on sexual offences against children and youths* (Vols. 1 & 2) (Badgley Report). Ottawa: Ministry of Justice.

Harris, J., & Melichercik, J. (1986). Age and stage-related programs. In J. Turner & F. Turner (Eds.), *Canadian social welfare* (pp. 159–181). Don Mills, ON: Collier Macmillan Canada.

Hepworth, H. P. (1980). *Foster care and adoption in Canada.* Ottawa: Canadian Council on Social Development.

Hepworth, H. P. (January, 1993). *Overview of child welfare services in Canada.* Paper presented at the National Forum on the Future of Children and Families, Washington, DC.

Hudson, P., & McKenzie, B. (1981). Child welfare and Native people: The extension of colonialism. *The Social Worker, 49*(2), 63–66, 87–88.

Hutchison, L., Nichols, B., Paré, N., & Pépin, M. (1991). *Profile of clients in the Anglophone youth network: Examining the situation of the Black child.* Montreal: Ville Marie Social Service Center.

Johnston, P. (1983). *Native children and the child welfare system.* Toronto: Canadian Council on Social Development in association with James Lorimer & Co.

Kadushin, A., & Martin, J. (1988). *Child welfare services* (4th ed.). New York: Macmillan.

Kempe, C. H., Silverman, F. N., Brandt, I. S., Droegemueller, W., & Silver, H. K. (1962, July). The battered child syndrome. *Journal of the American Medical Association, 181,* 17–24.

Krane, J. (1990). Explanations of child abuse: A review and critique from a feminist perspective. *Canadian Review of Social Policy, 25,* 183–196.

Kufeldt, K. (May, 1994). *Child welfare interventions: Do we know what we are doing?* Paper presented at the National Research and Policy Symposium on Child Welfare, Kananaskis, Alberta.

Longclaws, L. (1994). Social work and the medicine wheel framework. In B. Compton & B. Galaway (Eds.), *Social work processes* (5th ed.) (pp. 24–33). Pacific Grove, CA: Brooks/Cole Publishing Co.

Manitoba Department of Family Services Annual Reports, 1970–1992.

Masson, J. (1984). *Freud: The Assault on Truth*. London: Faber and Faber.

McKenzie, B., Seidl, E., & Bone, N. (1995). Child welfare standards in First Nations: A community-based study. In J. Hudson & B. Galaway (Eds.), *Child welfare in Canada: Research and policy implications* (pp. 54–65). Toronto: Thompson Educational Publishing.

National Council of Welfare. (1979). *In the best interests of the child*. Ottawa: National Council of Welfare on the Child Welfare System in Canada.

New Brunswick. (1989). Guidelines for protecting child victims of abuse and neglect. Department of Health and Community Services.

Northwest Territories. Consolidation of Child Welfare Act, Revised Statutes of the Northwest Territories (1988), c. C-6, as amended.

Nova Scotia Department of Community Services Annual Reports, 1975–1992.

Nutter, R., Hudson, J., Galaway, B., & Hill, M. (1995). Specialist foster care program standards in relation to costs, client characteristics, and outcomes. In J. Hudson & B. Galaway (Eds.), *Child welfare in Canada: Research and policy implications* (pp. 201–218). Toronto: Thompson Educational Publishing.

Obomsawin, A. (Writer and Director). (1986). *Cry from a diary of a Metis child*. Montreal: National Film Board.

Ontario Association of Children's Aid Societies. (1990). *Fact sheets*. Toronto: Ontario Association of Children's Aid Societies.

Ontario Ministry of Community and Social Services, Children's Services Branch. Annual Reports and Statistics, 1970–1991.

O'Hagan, K. (1993). *Emotional and psychological abuse of children*. Toronto: University of Toronto Press.

Polansky, N., Bergman, R. D., & De Saix, C. (1972). *Roots of futility*. San Francisco: Jossey-Bass.

Polansky, N., Chalmers, M. A., Buttenweisser, E., & Williams, D. (1981). *An anatomy of child neglect*. Chicago: University of Chicago Press.

Quebec Ministere des Affaires Sociales. Gouvernement du Quebec Rapport Annuel, 1982–1992.

Raychaba, B. (1987). Leaving care—Where? *The Journal, 31*(9), 3–12.

Raychaba, B. (1988). *To be on your own with no direction from home: A report on the special needs of youth leaving the care of the child welfare system*. Ottowa: National Youth in Care Network.

Reitsma-Street, M. (1986). *A feminist analysis of Ontario laws for delinquency and neglect: More control than care*. Toronto: University Toronto, Faculty of Social Work, Working Papers on Social Welfare.

Richardson, G., Galaway, B., Hudson, J., Nutter, R., & Hill, M. (1995). Birth parent participation in treatment foster care programs in North America and the United Kingdom. In J. Hudson & B. Galaway (Eds.), *Child welfare in Canada: Research and policy implications* (pp. 219–232). Toronto: Thompson Educational Publishing.

Rosenbluth, D. (1995). Moving in and out of foster care. In J. Hudson & B. Galaway (Eds.), *Child welfare in Canada: Research and policy implications* (pp. 233–244). Toronto: Thompson Educational Publishing.

Saskatchewwan Social Services Annual Reports, 1972–1992.

Solnit, A. (1980). Too much reporting, too little service: Roots and prevention of child abuse. In G. Gerbner, C. J. Ross, & E. Zigler (Eds.), *Child abuse: An agenda for action* (pp. 135–146). New York: Oxford University Press.

Steed, J. (1993, Oct. 22). Forum examines how to prevent child abuse. *Toronto Star,* pp. D1, D2.

Swift, K. (1991). Contradictions in child welfare: Neglect and responsibility. In C. Baines, P. Evans, & S. Neysmith (Eds.). *Women's caring* (pp. 234–271). Toronto: McClelland & Stewart.

Swift, K. (1995a). *Manufacturing "bad mothers": A critical perspective on child neglect.* Toronto: University of Toronto Press.

Swift, K. (1995b). Missing persons: Women in child welfare. *Child Welfare, 74*(3), 486–502.

Thomas, B. R. (1982). Protecting abused children: Helping until it hurts. *Child and Youth Services, 4,* 139–154.

Thomlison, B. (1995). Treatment foster care and reunification with a family: Children likely to experience family placement after treatment foster care services. In J. Hudson & B. Galaway (Eds.), *Child welfare in Canada: Research and policy implications* (pp. 194–200). Toronto: Thompson Educational Publishing.

Thompson-Cooper, I., Fugere, R., & Cormier, B. (1993, October). The child abuse reporting laws: An ethical dilemma for professionals. *Canadian Journal of Psychiatry, 38,* 557–562.

Trocme, N. (1991). Child welfare services. In R. Barnhorst & L. Johnson (Eds.), *The state of the child in Ontario* (pp. 63–91). Toronto: Oxford.

Trocme, M., McPhee, D., Tam, K. K., & Hay, T. (1994). *Ontario incidence study of reported child abuse and neglect.* Toronto: Institute for the Prevention of Child Abuse.

Trocme, N., Tam, K. K., & McPhee, D. (1995). Correlates of substantiation of maltreatment in child welfare investigations. In J. Hudson & B. Galaway (Eds.), *Child welfare in Canada: Research and policy implications* (pp. 20–40). Toronto: Thompson Educational Publishing.

Trute, B., Adkins, E., & MacDonald, G. (1994). *Coordinating child sexual abuse services in rural communities.* Toronto: University of Toronto Press.

Wells, M. (1990). *Canada's law on child sexual abuse.* Ottawa: Ministry of Justice.

Whart, B. (Ed.). (1993). *Rethinking child welfare in Canada.* Toronto: McClelland & Stewart.

Yakabuski, K. (1994, May 21). When to come to a child's aid. *Toronto Star,* pp. B1, B4.

Young Offenders Act. Revised Statues of Canada (1985), c. 4-1.

3

England

Child Abuse Reports, Responses, and Reforms

DAVID BERRIDGE

The last decade in England has seen escalating concern about the abuse of children and its prevention. Following a lull in interest since the mid-1970s, widespread media and political attention was aroused by the deaths in London of Jasmine Beckford in 1984, Tyra Henry in 1984, and Kimberley Carlile in 1986. Public reaction was vehement and individual social workers were castigated, particularly as these children were ostensibly subject to official scrutiny at the time. With the benefit of hindsight, a number of common themes have been detected from these and other tragedies, including certain professional shortcomings and deficiencies in interagency communication and collaboration (Department of Health, 1991a; Reder, Duncan, & Gray, 1993).

A year later, a crisis of a rather different order occurred in Cleveland, a county in northeastern England. Here, over a 6-month period, some 125 children were diagnosed as having been sexually abused by their parents, with most children being removed from their homes. In this case it was pediatricians who received the most criticism as their diagnoses were perceived to have led to the children being peremptorily and insensitively removed. Hence, in the London cases professionals had done too little too late, while in Cleveland it was too much too soon—encapsulating the dilemmas of child protection. Doubts were raised about the state's right to intervene in family life, fueled interestingly by the public protests of the Cleveland parents and their allies, who constituted a rather broader social profile of families than is normally the case in child abuse investigations. The nature of evidence in sexual abuse cases compared with individual child deaths obviously also has important implications.

These and other developments influenced reforms throughout the 1980s in England affecting child care law, policy, and administration. Changes occurred in the concept of and approach to "child abuse." Negotiations also took place concerning the balance between children's and parents' rights and the boundaries between the family and the state. An understanding of child abuse reporting systems and placement trends in England (and Wales[1]) requires consideration of this wider child welfare and social policy context.

Detailed empirical research on how the English child protection system operates is only now coming to fruition. For the purpose of this chapter, important information is derived from these studies to attempt to ascertain how the reporting, and the overall child protection, system function. In contrast to this relative dearth of empirical information, social researchers have developed a range of theoretical perspectives in approaching the problem of child abuse. These challenge earlier, more individualized approaches, based on notions of psychopathology, by emphasizing the social context in which behavior occurs (see Parton, 1985). Thus, Frost and Stein (1989) highlight issues of power and inequality. A feminist analysis extends this to stress the nature of male sexuality and dominance (see Dominelli, 1989). Approaches have also been based on the work of Foucault (Parton, 1991). Furthermore, Fox Harding (1991) usefully outlines four alternative perspectives in child care policy, what she terms laissez-faire and patriarchy, state paternalism and child protection, a birth family and parents' rights approach, and children's rights and child liberation. This chapter reveals a sympathy with aspects of the last two perspectives (see also Berridge, 1994).

Legal and Administrative Context

Initially we need to consider the law and policy in England over the last decade before we can turn to the more specific issues of child abuse reports and responses. Measures to combat child abuse are contained within a framework to enhance the welfare of a wider group of "children in need," severely disadvantaged in other ways. There have been considerable developments recently in law and policy in this field that need to be understood.

The roots of reform can be traced to the mid-1970s when a wide range of commentators was expressing concern about the quality of public services for disadvantaged and delinquent children (see Parton, 1991, chap. 2). These doubts included the seemingly inexorable rise in the number of children being separated from their parents; unfocused work with children and families leading to long stays in public care; frequent insensitivity on the part of many social services departments to children's and parents' rights; increased use of compulsory powers; and, following several child deaths, disquiet about the extent to which children were being adequately protected (House of Commons Social Services Committee, 1984).

Grounds for concern were confirmed by the results from some 12 child care research studies. These had been strategically planned by the (then) Department of Health and Social Security (DHSS) and the Social Science Research Council in response to the issues discussed above (DHSS, 1985b). Prior to this there had been very little information about how child care services actually operated and what experiences children were likely to have. Using research in this way to inform policy was a positive process, appreciated by professionals in the field (Packman & Jordan, 1991). Results from the commissioned studies confirmed the concerns already expressed: social workers demonstrated a lack of planning in assisting children and families in need, the work was too often crisis oriented, parents tended to be excluded from the care process, and there was frequent instability in care placements and a general pessimism on the part of professionals about the care system (DHSS, 1985b).

The process of reform continued with the report of a government interdepartmental working party (DHSS, 1985a), which led in 1987 to a White Paper outlining proposed changes in the law. Following certain modifications, this eventually resulted in the Children Act 1989 (implemented in October 1991), which sets the current legal framework for the care, upbringing, and protection of children in England and Wales. It is obviously impracticable within a brief chapter to give comprehensive information about the focus of this legislation, but we need to convey its important elements before we can turn more specifically to the operation of the English child protection system. Some of the main themes of the Children Act 1989 therefore are as follows (Department of Health, 1989):

the child's welfare is the paramount consideration;

children are generally best looked after in the family and parents should be supported in this task;

the primary target for attention are "children in need", who are those who are unlikely to achieve or maintain a reasonable standard of health or development, or are disabled. Appropriate services should be provided for families with these children including: advice and counselling, social activities, assistance with travel, aid with arranging a holiday, home help, family centres and day care;

applications can be made to the courts for Care or Supervision Orders for children suffering, or likely to suffer, "significant harm", either in terms of ill treatment or impairment of health or development. These can last up to the age of 18 unless discharged earlier. "Parental responsibility" can be retained by the parents of children living away from home;

compulsory orders are to be avoided wherever possible, and the obtaining of emergency orders is made much more stringent;

a unified, more rational and flexible court structure is introduced, which is intended to reduce delays;

children's racial origin, cultural, linguistic and religious background must be considered; and, finally

children should be consulted on matters affecting them.

Child Protection in England

Having sketched the general child care framework, let us now narrow our discussion to the system organized to combat child abuse. This is presented in the official publication, *Working Together Under the Children Act 1989* (Home Office, 1991). The document clearly outlines the measures to be followed and the roles of different professionals and also raises issues of good practice. We begin by describing the legal and policy framework of the child protection system, including reporting arrangements, and then discuss some key issues, including recent influences and developments. Evidence is provided below to demonstrate how this system operates in practice.

Though local authorities as a whole have statutory obligations in this area, social services departments have the lead responsibility for child protection arrangements. Each area is required to set up an Area Child Protection Committee (ACPC), which acts as a forum to help ensure close working relationships and complementary policies among social services, the police, medical practitioners, community health workers, the education service, and relevant others.

Though aimed specifically at professionals, *Working Together* emphasizes that the community as a whole has a responsibility to ensure the well-being of children. Relatives, friends, and neighbors should be alert to circumstances in which children can be harmed and take appropriate action if this is suspected. Sensitive information from informants will be received confidentially. Social services departments should publicize ways by which such information can be conveyed, such as by calling a telephone number. Material can be displayed in venues such as public libraries, health clinics, community centers, and doctors' offices.

Social services departments are legally obliged to provide services to prevent ill treatment or neglect of children in their area. They must also investigate reports of children suffering, or likely to suffer, significant harm and take steps to promote their welfare. This charge covers all children, including those living in foster and residential care and boarding schools. "Significant harm" is elaborated as follows:

> Where the question of whether harm suffered by a child is significant turns on the child's health or development, his health or development shall be compared with that which could reasonably be expected of a similar child. (Home Office, 1991, S 31[10]).

This is clearly a very broad definition, and it will be interesting to see how it is interpreted by the courts. Useful work on developing this concept has been undertaken by Adcock, White, and Hollows (1991).

Social services are to set their child protection work in the wider context of provision for all children in need although, as we discuss below, there are doubts about whether this always occurs. The law requires other local agencies, particularly those dealing with education, housing, and health, to cooperate with social services in the planning and provision of services for children and families.

Working Together stipulates that if a child is perceived to be at risk of serious injury or death, immediate protective action must be taken. This may amount to a voluntary withdrawal of an adult (a relatively new development in England) or child or by seeking from the court an Emergency Protection Order, which allows initially for the removal of the child for a period of up to a maximum of 8 days (this is discussed further below).

For cases that proceed this far, an initial strategy discussion is supposed to be held between social services and the police to plan their joint roles and the investigation. The objectives of this are to establish the facts and the circumstances giving rise to the anxiety, decide if there are grounds for concern, identify sources and levels of risk, and decide if protective or other action is necessary. A Child Assessment Order may be sought from the court (for up to a maximum of 7 days) to help ascertain the basic facts about a child's condition (e.g., if there are no grounds to suspect an emergency, but parents are uncooperative).

When concern continues to exist, the next stage would be for cases to proceed to a Child Protection Conference. This is a forum attended by relevant professionals, and it is intended for the family, to share information, assess risks to the child, and make recommendations for future action. It is not within the powers of this conference to decide that abuse has occurred: This is a criminal offense and a matter for the courts. Child Protection Conferences are supposed to be held within 8 days of becoming aware of the seriousness of the situation and at most 15 days. The main decision to be made by a conference is whether or not to "register" the child. If so, a key worker will be allocated. It is emphasized that services may still be required if a decision not to register is made. When registration occurs, a written multiagency child protection plan is supposed to be produced. This plan includes arrangements for a comprehensive assessment, as well as what the responsibilities of each agency will be. We see below, from the findings of recent research studies, that a number of these initial requirements are not always followed, for example, conference attendance and timing and the provision of services. *Working Together* also deals with issues of implementation, review, and deregistration, discussion of which is beyond the scope of this chapter.

The document provides definitions of categories of abuse for registration and statistical purposes. More than one category may of course be relevant, and simultaneous registration can therefore occur. Definitions are reproduced in full below.

> *Neglect*: The persistent or severe neglect of a child, or the failure to protect a child from exposure to any kind of danger, including cold or starvation, or extreme failure to carry out important aspects of care, resulting in the significant impairment of the child's health or development, including non-organic failure to thrive.

Physical Injury: Actual or likely physical injury to a child, or failure to prevent physical injury (or suffering) to a child including deliberate poisoning, suffocation and Munchausen's syndrome by proxy.

Sexual Abuse: Actual or likely sexual exploitation of a child or adolescent. The child may be dependent and/or developmentally immature.

Emotional Abuse: Actual or likely severe adverse effect on the emotional and behavioural development of a child caused by persistent and severe emotional ill-treatment or rejection. All abuse involves some emotional ill-treatment. This category should be used where it is the main or sole form of abuse. (Home Office, 1991, pp. 48–49)

Measures may be taken in relation to unborn children. *Working Together* refers to other forms of abuse, such as that undertaken by other children, abuse of those already living in foster and residential care, and organized forms of abuse—a phenomenon about which very little is known in England as yet, although knowledge is increasing (e.g., see *Child Abuse Review, 2,* 1993). However, these categories are not specifically listed.

Clearly the definitions of the four main classifications quoted above are very broad and allow for substantial professional leeway. Some further elaboration of the four categories is provided in an earlier official publication for social workers undertaking a comprehensive assessment as part of longer term planning (Department of Health, 1988). This elaboration is reproduced in Table 3-1. However, as we see below, different policies and practices exist among local authorities. A variety of training initiatives has been encouraged and supported to raise social work standards, but there is no further attempt to standardize local practice on the part of central government. Categorization and registration are also essentially part of a social process, influenced by local interpretations and professional priorities, rather than simple reporting of objective facts. We return to this discussion below.

Policy Development

Let us now elaborate further on some of the issues raised so far, particularly regarding developments in child protection policy.

It is already clear from the previous section that, unlike the United States, England has no mandatory child abuse reporting laws. Furthermore, there seems to be no significant interest in moving in such a direction. This issue was considered by the interdepartmental working party referred to above (DHSS, 1985a), but was rejected for several reasons. Principally it was felt that the structure of health and social services care in England, which have been essentially public sector agencies, would render a mandatory system unnecessary because of the built-in channels of communication and the nature of professional accountability. What is more, relying on a mandatory approach, it was argued, might actually serve to diminish individual professional responsibility—say on the part of a doctor or health visitor—by being able automatically to refer suspected problems elsewhere. It was also felt that much work had

Table 3-1. Elaboration of Categories of Child Abuse

Injury or physical abuse	*Emotional abuse*
Minor	Rejection
Serious (e.g., results in fracture or head injuries)	Lack of praise and encouragement
	Lack of comfort and love
Premeditated/sadistic	Lack of attachment
Burns and scalds	Lack of proper stimulation (e.g., fun and play)
Bites	Lack of continuity of care (e.g., frequent moves)
Repeated abuse	
Resulting from lack of control	Lack of appropriate handling (e.g., age-inappropriate expectations)
Punishment with implements	
Genital/anal area injuries	Serious overprotectiveness
Shaking	Inappropriate nonphysical punishment (e.g., locking in bedrooms)
Poisoning	
Other	
	Sexual abuse
Neglect	Inappropriate fondling
Abandonment or desertion	Mutual masturbation
Leaving alone	Digital penetration
Malnourishment, lack of food, inappropriate food, or erratic feeding	Oral/genital contact
	Anal or vaginal intercourse
Lack of warmth	Exploitation for pornography
Lack of adequate clothing	Exposure to pornography
Unhygienic home conditions	
Lack of protection or exposure to dangers, including moral danger, or lack of supervision appropriate to child's age	
Persistent failure to attend school	
Nonorganic failure to thrive	

Source: Department of Health (1988).

been done recently to enhance interprofessional communication so that improved administrative procedures would make mandatory reporting nonessential.

These arguments have not been particularly challenged. However, it is interesting to note that, over the past decade, important social policy reforms have occurred in England so that large numbers of public sector workers are now employed in quite different and more autonomous structures such as health service "trusts" and schools that have "opted out" of local authority control. These more devolved structures, which are responsible for their own budgets, potentially pose greater coordination and communication problems. Moreover, they may not necessarily always give external issues such as involvement in preventive child welfare programs the highest priority. The impact of these new structures on the overall welfare and protection of children will have to be scrutinized closely.

A second point to make concerning the development of child protection services in England is the significant influence on policy that is exerted by specific crises. Murder, sexual abuse, and other extreme forms of child abuse are highly charged subjects to which governments are politically sensitive. Sometimes this can bring to the fore areas that have been previously neglected, for example, at long last residential child care in England is receiving greater attention following specific and widely publicized instances of malpractice.

The aftermath of the rapid diagnosis in 1987 of 125 cases of sexual abuse in Cleveland had a profound effect on public and political attitudes to both child abuse and social work more generally. Consequently, in very general terms, more sympathy is expressed toward parents' rights than hitherto, and fewer would align themselves automatically behind children and their protection. Specifically, the tone of the revised *Working Together* issued in 1991 signifies something of a shift, as can be detected from the preface to the work, which emphasizes especially the pitfalls of unwarranted intervention in families (Home Office, 1991).

These developments would be consistent with the wider ideological position: that of a government seeking to minimize the role of the state, restrain public spending, and encourage individual and family responsibility and solutions. There is also an espoused rhetoric about the sanctity of "the family." However, a full explanation of recent trends in child welfare goes beyond reactions to the Cleveland affair and government ideology as pointed out above; numerous research studies throughout the 1980s highlighted the frequent insensitivity of social workers toward parents and restrictions on children maintaining contact with their parents. This it is known is not in children's best interests (Millham, Bullock, Hosie, & Haak, 1986; see also Bullock, Little, & Millham, 1993). Hence, changes in policy in this direction were already foreshadowed and justified and not simply part of a wider ideology or the backlash to events in Cleveland. Interpretations of recent trends in child welfare and child protection as reflecting solely greater emphasis on the privacy of the family and the diminution of the role of the state are oversimplifications, as Parton (1991) acknowledges. Theories can sometimes be used to explain too much.

Another important development in child protection policy not unrelated to the above concerns the approach to emergency measures. Prior to the 1989 legislation, children felt to be in immediate danger could be removed from home for up to 28 days by magistrates granting a Place of Safety Order. The use of these orders had risen significantly in the 1980s. This reflected, no doubt, a changed professional culture influenced by the publicized instances of maltreatment and criticism of individual professionals and indicated a more defensive and controlling form of social work (Dartington Social Research Unit, 1985). Millham and colleagues' (1986) research revealed that as much as a fifth of their care sample had entered care on Place of Safety Orders. By no means were all of these individuals in care at risk of immediate danger as intended in the spirit of the law; indeed, a third were adolescents.

The widespread use of Place of Safety Orders, by routinely defining cases as "emergencies," could subsequently put families at immediate disadvantage before the court and in the eyes of other professionals. Applications by social workers were seldom challenged by magistrates, who could find themselves in an invidious position.

The Children Act 1989 brought about important reform in this area by replacing Place of Safety Orders with Emergency Protection Orders, which as discussed above (initially) could last up to only 8 rather than 28 days. Parents' rights of challenge were also strengthened. There was some resistance from professionals, who felt this was an insufficient period in which to undertake the necessary investigatory work. Nonetheless, in the first full year of operation of the new legislation, there was a reduction by more than half in the number of emergency measures brought (Department of Health, 1993a).

A final point to be considered in reviewing policy developments in child protection is variations in conceptualizing child abuse. The system of child abuse protection in England started in 1974 following the death of Maria Colwell (see Creighton, 1992, for an overview). Initially registers were for children felt to have been "nonaccidentally injured." This was expanded in 1981 to include other forms of abuse: physical neglect, nonorganic failure to thrive, and emotional abuse. Sexual abuse was added in 1988. In the same year, registers were renamed Child Protection Registers rather than Child Abuse Registers to reflect also future preventive concerns rather than simply a record of the past. In line with this, in 1988 a category was added, "grave concern." This was defined as follows:

> Children whose situations do not currently fit . . . (other) . . . categories, but where social and medical assessments indicate that they are at significant risk of abuse. These could include situations where another child in the household has been harmed or the household contains a known abuser. (See Creighton (1992) p. 7.)

However this category was subsequently withdrawn in 1991, by which time it was accounting for about half of all registrations. The use of this category was also felt to be one of the major inconsistencies in practice among local authorities (Department of Health, 1993c, p. 2). Further insight into local variations has been provided by Little and Gibbons (1993), who contrasted the numbers of children recorded on Child Protection Registers with a range of sociodemographic factors. Adjacent areas have been shown to demonstrate significant unexplained differences. Following statistical analysis, the authors revealed that approximately half the variation in the numbers on registers was attributable to operational rather than sociodemographic differences. Deregistration practices were found to be particularly important.

In the next section we turn to some of the more specific themes addressed in this book, referring particularly to child abuse reports, responses, and placements. This task is complex from an English perspective. As there is no mandatory element and as agencies have considerable professional leeway, albeit within a unified policy framework, national statistics on child abuse reports are not collected. Instead published statistics refer to children whose names are entered on Child Protection Registers as being in need of an interagency protection plan. It is only since 1988 that these statistics have been comprehensively gathered and published by the Department of Health. Before then figures were published by the voluntary agency, the National Society for the Prevention of Cruelty to Children (NSPCC) (Creighton, 1992). Although this provided useful indicators, the exercise covered only a minority of the child population. These statistics are analyzed further in the chapter.

It is therefore important to reiterate that the number of children recorded on these registers is not the same as the total who have been abused (Corby, 1990). Registers include children felt to be at risk of abuse who have not yet been maltreated in this way. On the other hand, some children are excluded who have been abused but are not felt to need further protection in the form of an interagency plan. Abuse can also remain undetected. Indeed, despite considerable definitional and methodological difficulties, self-report studies indicate that the extent of physical, sexual, emotional, and other forms of abuse far exceeds that which is officially notified and recorded (Parton, 1989).

A further complication is that a program of detailed empirical research in England on child abuse and its prevention has only recently been undertaken. Nonetheless researchers kindly made available to the author, prior to publication, copies of their reports, and these proved invaluable in writing this chapter. The four research studies that have been used are by Gibbons, Conroy, and Bell (1995), who investigated the operation of Child Protection Registers; Farmer and Owen (1995), concentrating on the process of intervention in child abuse; Sharland, Aldgate, Jones, Seal, and Croucher (1993), who explored similar issues relating specifically to child sexual abuse; and Cleaver and Freeman (1995), who focused on parents' perspectives when suspected of child abuse. The first three studies concern children and young people below the age of 16 years, while the upper limit for the last study is up to 18 years. As discussed below, they contain very important information that is highly pertinent to policy and practice (see also Department of Health, 1995).

Child Abuse Reports

In the Gibbons et al. (1995) study of eight local authorities in which a total of 2,758 reports of suspected abuse was received over a 16-week period, estimated monthly rates of reports to social services ranged from 0.84 to 1.81 reports per 1,000 children under 16 years of age. Overall this would average out to a monthly rate of approximately 1.13 reports per 1,000. (As the authors emphasize, the eight agencies were not selected as a representative sample, so caution should be used in any extrapolations. However as this is the best detailed English data available on child abuse reports, it is used here.)

The same study (Gibbons et al., 1995) revealed that sources of referrals varied considerably for different types of alleged abuse and also among the eight authorities. (This may account for the quite different pattern reported by Farmer and Owen, 1995, whose work was located in two shire counties). In total, in Gibbons et al.'s study, teachers, school nurses, and other educational professionals were responsible for nearly a quarter (23%) of all reports.

Health staff and lay people—including household members, other relatives, friends, and the child involved—each contributed about 17% of reports. Other social services colleagues made 13% of referrals, followed by police or probation personnel (12%). Only 6% of reports were anonymous. Farmer and Owen discovered more family reports and fewer by professionals, while the largest number of referrals in Sharland et al's (1993) sexual abuse sample (based in one English county) came from the nonabusing parent, followed by those referrals from teachers. (Cleaver and Freeman's 1995 survey of records did not cover all professional groups, although the role of the school clearly emerges as significant.)

There were also wide differences among Gibbons et al.'s (1995) eight authorities in the types of abusive behavior reported. Average figures were physical abuse, 40%; neglect, 26%; sexual abuse, 23%; and "safety" (including children being left alone), 21% (some reports concerned more than one category). Nearly twice as many girls as boys were the reported recipients of sexual abuse, but fewer girls were reported for physical abuse or neglect. Girls were reported at older ages than boys in each category: for neglect, the average ages were 5.1 years (boys) and 5.4 years (girls); physical injury, 5.6 years (boys) compared to 7.1 years (girls); and sexual abuse, 7.4 years (boys) as opposed to 8.0 years (girls). In the other three studies, children for whom sexual abuse reports were made tended to be older.

Despite a recent official exhortation (Department of Health, 1991d), issues of ethnicity have been insufficiently addressed in English child care research. Regrettably, with the exception of Gibbons et al. (1995), the studies under consideration here do not include this as a significant element. Gibbons et al. show that Black and Asian families were overrepresented (58%) among reports for physical injury compared with their White counterparts (42%), but there were relatively fewer sexual abuse referrals (20% for Blacks and Asians and 31% for Whites). Culturally appropriate sanctions posed dilemmas for social workers.

The characteristics of families implicated in reports of abuse are consistent with what is known from other studies of the child welfare system (e.g., Packman, Randall, & Jacques, 1986). The most typical family structure in Gibbons et al.'s (1995) research is that headed by a lone parent (36%), with reconstituted families constituting a further 22%. There was widespread experience of poverty, including unemployment, dependence on income support, and temporary accommodation. However, families reported because of suspected sexual or emotional abuse were less likely to be materially disadvantaged than those reported in the neglect or physical injury categories. The profile of Farmer and Owen's (1995) (and Cleaver and Freeman's 1995) sample is similar to the above. They pose the interesting question: What happens when sexual abuse occurs or is suspected in middle-class families for which social services seems not to have a significant role?

Parents implicated in child abuse reports had an unenviable range of personal and social problems. Gibbons et al. (1995) reveal, from an analysis of social work records (which no doubt underestimate difficulties), that over a quarter (27%) of women were stated to have been subjected to violence by their partners, a fifth (20%) of parents misused drugs or alcohol; 13% had criminal records, while the same percentage had been treated for mental illness and had been abused themselves when young. Also two thirds (65%) had been in prior contact with social services, including 45% who had previously been investigated for child abuse. If anything, Farmer and Owen's (1995) group appears even more disadvantaged, with violence—again overwhelmingly from men to their female partners—affecting three families in every five.

Cleaver and Freeman's (1995) results generally point in a similar direction, although they usefully distinguish among five different types of families suspected of abuse: multiproblem families (43%), specific problem families (21%), acutely distressed families (13%), outside perpetrator families (13%), and infiltrating perpetrator families (9%).

Responses

The four recent studies referred to above also provide valuable information on the actual operation of the child protection system in England, including the way in which cases are filtered out at various stages. It is important to know the consequences of such decisions. This dimension is dealt with most comprehensively in Gibbons et al.'s (1995) research. Just over a quarter (26%) of all reports were filtered out of the system very early without further investigation by duty staff, usually after making telephone checks with other agencies. This varied considerably from 15% in one of the eight participating authorities to more than double this figure, 32%, in another. (Sharland et al.'s 1993 study specifically of sexual abuse cases produced figures at the top of this range, with a third of referrals eventually being closed within a month.)

The second stage occurs when investigations are held but it is decided not to proceed to an inter-agency case conference. The researchers found this to apply to more than two in every three of the cases that were investigated, or to put it another way, half of all the reports filed were pursued but did not lead to a formal, interprofessional meeting. The researchers went a stage further in this and explored whether or not "appropriate" cases were being included or omitted. They argued that few cases were unnecessarily proceeding to conferences, but that conversely a significant minority when there were grounds for concern was being "missed." Again there were substantial differences among authorities. Gibbons et al. (1995) conclude that, given the large number of cases for which further intervention was felt to be unwarranted, too many families were unnecessarily being incorporated in the child protection system.

The next stage of the procedure concerned cases reaching an interagency child protection conference (24% of all reports). At these, Gibbons et al. (1995) discovered that about half of cases discussed were placed on the Child Protection Register. (The Farmer and Owen 1995 finding was virtually identical, although for the sexual abuse cases in Sharland et al.'s 1993 study, about one in five of all initial reports were estimated eventually to have been registered. Cleaver and Freeman's 1995 survey of child abuse suspicions in one local authority came up with a slightly higher figure.) Although children referred with allegations of neglect or emotional abuse were significantly less likely to reach an initial case conference, those who did had an equal chance of being placed on the register. Following investigation, a significant minority of cases were registered under a different category than initially presented.

Gibbons et al. (1995) usefully summarize the operation of these filtering mechanisms in Table 3-2. They demonstrate that more than six in every seven children who initially entered the child protection system were filtered out without their name being placed on a register. With about 29,500 new registrations each year in England at the time, this would suggest in total something like another 175,000 reports over the same period that were investigated but excluded. The research concludes that there is a greater problem of children with significant problems being missed rather than cases being unnecessarily selected for conference. Considerable differences existed among local authorities.

Placements

Significantly, Gibbons et al. (1995) revealed that almost 90% of children in their study remained at home during the period of child protection investigation, and in only 4% of all reported cases were children removed on emergency orders. Sharland et al.'s (1995) and Cleaver and Freeman's (1995) research contained similar evidence. Gibbons et al. also showed that, during the investigation, action was taken to remove the alleged perpetrator from the household—by compulsion or persuasion—in 4.5% of physical abuse cases and 13% of sexual abuse. The adult concerned was charged or cautioned by the police in 4 and 16% of cases, respectively.

In a 6-month follow-up period after conferences, it was similarly discovered that more than five in every six "registered" children had lived continuously with their families. The equivalent figure for children whose names had not been entered on registers was over 95%. Of those living away, 84% were in foster family care or living with relatives and only 16% were in residential settings. Sharland et al.'s (1993) results point in a similar direction.

Gibbons et al. (1995) also monitored children's and families' experiences and "outcomes" over the 6 months. The percentage continuously allocated a key worker ranged across authorities from 25% to 90%. (There was also one

Table 3-2. Operation of Filters in Child Protection System

Entry point: New incident	1,888 ⟶	42 lost cases
1st filter: Checks	1,846 (100%) ⟶	478 (26%)
2nd filter: Further investigation	1,368 (74%) ⟶	925 (50%)
3rd filter: Child Protection Conference	443 (24%) ⟶	128 (7%)
Retained in system after conference	315 (16%)	
Of whom: On register	272 (15%)	

Source: Gibbons et al. (1995).

area, experiencing a prolonged social work strike, in which no cases were continuously allocated a key worker.) Disconcertingly, apart from general social work contact and support, most families and children did not receive specific help to overcome problems and bring about improved and more appropriate parenting. This has also been discovered in other research (Gough, Boddy, Dunning, & Stone, 1987) and is a point to which we return below. (The conclusions of Cleaver and Freeman's 1995 intensive study of 30 families tend to be more optimistic.) Few offers of services were not taken.

Legal action of some form was taken over the 6 months in one in five cases that reached the conference stage. On the other hand, about 13% of those whose names were entered on registers were discharged. There were pronounced differences among the eight local authorities in this, extending from 0% to 35%. The use of registers was clearly more purposeful in some areas than in others. Those agencies with the highest deregistration rates were found to adhere most closely to child protection procedures, to be better managed and organized, to hold reviews on time, and to examine situations critically. Consequently, children remained on registers for shorter periods.

Over the 6-month follow-up period there was repeated concern of suspected abuse or neglect in almost a third of cases placed originally on registers and one in five that were not. It is of course difficult to know to what extent this reflects differences in possible maltreatment or levels of surveillance. (Farmer and Owen's 1995 follow-up after 20 months found that about a quarter of their sample had been reabused or neglected; Cleaver and Freeman's 1995 results were similar.) By the end of the follow-up, 63% of those placed on registers had remained at home throughout, 18% had left home but returned, and the remainder (19%) were separated from parents before the initial conference and remained so 6 months later. Figures for those not on registers were 71%, 15%, and 14%, respectively.

Farmer and Owen's (1995) follow-up over 20 months found that a lower percentage had remained at home throughout. At this stage, 47% of the sample were in this situation, plus another 21% had been removed and later returned. At 20 months, a third of the children had been removed and were still away (compared with Gibbons et al.'s 1995 figure of 19% after 6 months).

Trends in Child Protection Registrations

As stated above, writing this chapter poses particular problems from an English perspective: there is no mandatory child abuse reporting system nor comprehensive statistics on referrals. For this reason this discussion relies on recent empirical research and one study especially. This also makes it difficult to attempt an authoritative account of trends in reports of, and responses to, child abuse.

Nonetheless some national statistics exist that help form part of the picture. These refer to child protection registrations only. Since 1988 they have been published by the Department of Health and, prior to that, for some local authorities by the NSPCC. It is necessary, however, to be cautious about their use and interpretation. For example, as we have already seen, the way in which child abuse is conceptualized varies over time (as with the category of "grave concern"). NSPCC statistics included different local authorities over the years. In addition, ages of children covered has also altered: under 15 years in the 1970s, rising to under 17 years in the 1980s. Department of Health statistics now go to 18 years.

The total number of children on Child Protection Registers between 1984 and 1992 is estimated in Table 3-3[2]. It is apparent from the figures that registrations in England rose markedly throughout the 1980s. Indeed, between 1984 and the end of the decade it more than tripled. This growing official intervention was no doubt influenced by the heightened public concern about child abuse and the widely publicized deaths in particular. There were important consequences for both the volume and nature of social work activity.

However, the final statistic for 1992 is an intriguing one, revealing a reduction of some 15% over the previous year (Department of Health, 1993c). Over this period registrations decreased by about 13% and deregistrations increased by 17%. (The respective figures for the previous year had been increases of 5 and 10%. The 1993 statistics show a further drop of 16% to 32,500; Department of Health/Welsh Office, 1994.)

It is difficult to know exactly why this reversal of the trend occurred, although some possible explanations can be suggested. First, as we discussed above, grave concern was discontinued as a category for registration with the introduction of the Children Act 1989 in October 1991. The numbers represented under this heading fell significantly. A second explanation may be that, although still in its very early days, the new legislation with its greater emphasis on partnership and prevention may already have been having some influ-

Table 3-3. Total Number of
Children on Child Protection
Registers in England, 1984–1992

Year	Number
1984	12,388
1985	17,622
1986	23,755
1987	29,766
1988	39,200
1989	41,200
1990	43,600
1991	45,300
1992	38,600

Note: 1984–1987 statistics are from Corby (1990). Later statistics are derived from annual Department of Health Series (for example 1993b). 1984–1986 statistics include Wales.

ence on the style of social work interventions. There was a corresponding drop in the number of statutory orders more generally, as well as in the total number of children being "looked after" by local authorities. Some may also feel finally that the increased financial constraints affecting local authorities and the introduction of other reforms may have influenced the capacity for child care work. As historical research has demonstrated, the numbers of children in public care in the 20th century may have been more influenced by supply-related rather than demand factors, notably the state of the economy (Parker & Loughran, n.d.). To put it crudely, children and families probably get what it is decided can be afforded, rather than what they need.

More detailed analysis of registration trends is complex because of the deficiencies in the data highlighted above. Nonetheless, let us tentatively summarize what the figures seem to suggest.

- Child protection registration rates per 1,000 children fell between 1975 (0.97) and 1980 (0.72) before rising in the mid-1980s (1986, 2.18). Since then they have stabilized (1992, 2.3).
- This overall pattern applied generally to different types of abuse. However the rate of sexual abuse registrations increased sevenfold between 1983 and 1986 before declining slightly thereafter. The 1992 statistics for different categories of registrations were physical abuse, 0.6 children (per 1,000 children); sexual abuse, 0.4; neglect, 0.3; emotional abuse, 0.2.
- The average age of children registered increased from 3.7 years in 1975 to 7.1 years in 1986 before dropping to 6.2 years (1992). The earlier rise was no doubt influenced by growing awareness of the problem of sexual abuse.
- Presumably for similar reasons, the percentage of girls involved rose from 43% in 1975 to 56% in 1986, but has since consolidated at just over 50%.
- Registrations of children from minority ethnic groups have remained at between 6 and 10% over the past decade. Given the relatively younger age structure of the minority population, this would seem an underrepresentation.
- In line with increasing child and family poverty in the United Kingdom over the past 15 years (Bradshaw, 1990; Kumar, 1993), the proportion of families with registered children receiving income support grew from 41% in 1975 to 59% at the end of the decade. It is difficult to see how rising poverty could be expected to do anything other than increase tensions and therefore child abuse within families.
- The proportion of cases for which the "index of suspicion" was "certain" or "very suspicious" fell from 77% in 1975 to 67% in 1986. It dropped further to 45% in 1989, but this would have been influenced by the change from Child Abuse to Child Protection Registers (see Creighton, 1992, p. 54).
- For children named on Child Protection Registers, the out-of-home

placement rate almost quadrupled in the decade from 1975, but still stood at just over 1 child in 1,000 children of all children in England.

- Estimates can be made of the numbers of children on Child Protection Registers living in different types of placement on any one day, not over the period of a year. In 1992 the largest number, 2.7 children per 1,000 of all children, were living with relatives, usually parents. The equivalent figure for foster family care was 0.4 children and for residential care of all types it was 0.1 children.

Placement Issues

Let us now widen this discussion to look more generally at some current issues and concerns relating to placements for abused and other children in the welfare system. The bulk of this chapter so far, by concentrating on reporting and registration arrangements, gives an incomplete view of the problem of child abuse. In particular, it tends to focus attention on the circumstances of younger children coming to the attention of agencies. Some, albeit a minority, of these children will grow up in the care system, and their experiences of abuse will require attention over prolonged periods from social workers and foster and residential caregivers. For example, significant neglect or injury was felt to be a factor in the backgrounds of over half of all residents living in a sample of 20 children's homes studied (Berridge, 1985). Furthermore some older children, including adolescents who have experienced abuse in the past, will come to the attention of agencies. This will be part of a broader range of problems that need addressing, and the young people involved therefore may not experience the child protection system in quite the same way as described above.

The main three placement options for children and young people in England are at home with parent(s), with foster families, or in residential care. We deal briefly with each in turn.

Living at Home

We saw above that most children coming to the attention of the child protection system in fact remain living at home with one or both parents. There has also been a significant number of children in England legally in public care but allowed to live with a parent or guardian; this constituted some 12% prior to the legal categories being changed under the new legislation. It had actually reached 19% a decade earlier (Department of Health, 1993b). Bullock et al. (1993) have shown that the vast majority of children eventually return home, and this is in their best interests. This gives added weight to their earlier work, which demonstrated the considerable barriers preventing parents and separated children from maintaining contact; often it seems this was not what social workers intended (Millham et al., 1986). Clear evidence was presented to show that continuing contact with parents was strongly associated with positive emotional development, stability in care placements, and an enhanced likelihood of eventual return.

Despite these advantages of family contact, actually living at home is not without its problems. For example, Rowe, Hundleby, and Garnett (1989) revealed that this was in fact often one of the most unstable arrangements, with a third of placements ending prematurely. Moreover, using their outcome criteria, barely a third of placements at home were considered "successful."

Farmer and Parker (1991) provide additional evidence of children legally in care but placed in what was called "home on trial." In placements lasting on average about three years, a quarter of those returned home were reabused or neglected. However, few had to be removed. Interestingly, the researchers also comment that, though deemed adequate to look after their children, few of the parents would meet the criteria to be approved as a local authority foster caregiver. Older adolescents returning home after leaving care have also had mixed fortunes, but it should not be underestimated how difficult most find it (Garnett, 1992; Stein & Carey, 1986).

Returning more specifically to the child abuse population, the empirical studies discussed earlier highlight an issue of major concern. This applies generally to placements but, as discussed above, most children remain at home so it is introduced here. The point to be made is that once abuse has been investigated, children and parents receive insufficient help to deal with the effects of the mistreatment and to enhance the quality of adult care. We see below that this has wider implications, but we deal first with the specifics.

Gibbons and colleagues (1995) revealed that families received a range of general social work support services, but there was very little specialist help forthcoming. Farmer and Owen (1995) provided confirmatory evidence and demonstrated the inadequacy and perhaps also injustice of what was offered to the nonabusing parent. Following the investigation of abuse, in two-parent families attention often moved away from the abusing father figure onto the mother. A range of wider child care concerns was raised, and the issue was often redefined as the ability of the mother to care. Thus, a moral judgment could be introduced. This seems particularly harsh given the fact that in three in every five families fathers were violent to mothers as well as the child.

Even more surprisingly, a lack of specialist help has also been identified in cases of child sexual abuse. Sharland and colleagues (1993) found that fewer than a quarter of their sample received any therapeutic services, which had been promised to some additional families, but resources were scarce. Almost half the children known to have been abused received no direct professional input after the investigation. The investigation, it seems, is paramount, and any follow through is of secondary importance. We return to this below.

Foster Family Care

For children and young people in public care who have to live away from home, including those who have been abused, foster care is now generally the preferred option, especially for preadolescents. Thus at any one time almost 60% of all those looked after will be with foster caregivers compared with 16% in residential settings (Department of Health, 1993b). The nature of young people accommodated in foster homes has changed significantly in the past 20 years, and children with special needs, acute behavioral problems, and sibling groups are now frequently to be found in family settings.

A range of issues can be identified in England relating to foster family care (Berridge, 1996). Here just two are discussed that are felt to be among the most pertinent, supply factors and the quality of care.

Being a foster caregiver is probably one of the most difficult undertakings one can envisage. Residential child care staff may end up with the most difficult young people, but their work is structured differently, not usually requiring 24-hour-a-day dedication. There are no doubt satisfactions arising from providing security, continuity, and affection to disadvantaged children, but many aspects of foster care are unattractive. Remuneration is often poor, and local authorities responsible for overseeing placements are not always as sensitive, thoughtful, and supportive as they could be (Berridge & Cleaver, 1987). Children are also frequently defiant and appear ungrateful. As the number of residential homes decreases, the problems posed by young people are likely to worsen, so it is difficult to see these problems being alleviated.

It is not surprising then that many agencies experience difficulties in recruiting and retaining an adequate supply of foster caregivers. National statistics provide some support for this view. Although the proportion of all children looked after who are placed in foster homes has continued to rise, this has largely been because of a reduction in the overall care population rather than an absolute increase in the numbers fostered. Indeed, the total number of children living at any one time in family placements has actually fallen over the past decade by 3%, from 35,749 to 34,766 (Department of Health, 1993b). An English study of a county that closed all of its own residential facilities and instead placed most children in foster families reported that it faced acute problems of supply. There was frequently a tendency for children to go where a vacancy existed rather than somewhere that was carefully assessed as being an optimal placement to meet young people's needs. In addition, most Black children were placed in White families (Cliffe, 1991).

Some might deduce from this that there is a finite supply of families in society wishing to offer care placements. Bebbington and Miles (1990) have contrasted the known characteristics of foster caregivers with the socioeconomic profile of different local authorities and concluded that the supply is likely to be much more plentiful in some areas than in others. This has been confirmed by a recent study undertaken in an area that would emerge as one of the lowest in terms of likely supply. It was discovered that the authority had no foster caregivers of its own living within its boundaries (Sinclair, Garnett, & Berridge, 1995).

Parker (1978) has also argued that wider social change is likely to have an adverse effect on the supply of foster caregivers. Greater proportions of women, including those with (young) children, are working outside the home; cohabitation is becoming more popular and marriage less so; and families are having fewer children, with the birth of the first child being postponed. These factors are likely to lead to fewer women being available to act as foster caregivers. The 1980s and early 1990s in England have also been a period of profound economic and social change. As government has pursued more of a "free market" approach to economic (as well as social) policy, values that have been emphasized have related to individualism, materialism, and self-reliance. It may be speculative at this stage, but there would seem to be a tension between this approach and wider civic responsibilities: In particular, if society is becoming less altruistic, this might be expected to have an adverse effect on the propensity to offer foster placements.

All this of course assumes a rather traditional model of foster care compared with a more "professionalized" approach. There is evidence that agencies paying more competitive rates for foster caregivers, as well as providing training opportunities and proper support, can both recruit and retain families to work even with the most difficult children. However the professionalization of foster family care in England is a contentious issue. It would not be supported by a significant number of foster caregivers, who claim a contradiction between demonstrating genuine affection and concern and being paid. Not all would be convinced that the increased professionalization of residential care, bringing with it, for example, shorter working hours and unionization, has necessarily led to improvements. The economics of increased foster care professionalization would also pose complications: It would have significant resource implications, which would be especially unattractive in the current climate. Nonetheless, despite these problems, a recent study has concluded that an increased move toward professionalization must be the way ahead for mainstream foster family care in England (Berridge & Cleaver, 1987).

This leads into a related issue, that of ensuring adequate quality of care in placements. Problems do not apply exclusively to foster family care (DHSS, 1985a), although there are some specific concerns in this area. For example, not all foster caregivers have been prepared to work in an "inclusive" manner and welcome continuing contact with parents (Rowe et al., 1984). As we discussed above, maintaining links in this way tends to work to children's advantage in both the short and longer terms. The Children Act 1989 emphasizes issues of partnership with parents; these issues were reinforced in the specific guidance and regulations on family placements (Department of Health, 1991b). It would be useful for research to be undertaken to see what impact the new legislation, guidance, and associated training have had on the practice of foster family care (Berridge, 1994, 1996).

Particular concerns have been expressed regarding the quality of care provided to children from minority ethnic groups (House of Commons Social Services Committee, 1984), although again this applies to placements generally and not just to foster family care. Many authorities find difficulties in recruiting caregivers from all sections of the community (Cliffe, 1991), but where a strategic approach has been adopted and agencies have been prepared to invest resources, a more representative and appropriate service has resulted (e.g., Caesar, Parchment, & Berridge, 1994).

Furthermore, problems for family placement in England have arisen regarding continuity of care. Overall most children benefit from their stays in family (and residential) settings (Colton, 1988). However, placement breakdown affects a significant minority of children, and it is known that this can inflict further damage (Rowe et al., 1989). Comfort should be drawn from the fact that disruption rates seem not to have deteriorated over the years as the diversity and difficulty of children being fostered has increased. Nonetheless, studies have shown that something like half of all planned long-term placements break down within a period of three to five years. Encouragingly, levels of disruption for other types of family placement seem significantly smaller (Berridge & Cleaver, 1987). The likelihood of placement failure has been positively associated, as one might expect, with the age of the child and extent of behavioral problems posed (Triseliotis, 1989). Other related factors have been revealed as the inclusiveness of placements, maintenance of children's social networks, and foster caregiver's experience, training, and support (Berridge & Cleaver, 1987).

Residential Care

As discussed above, though catering at any one time for a minority of children in public care, residential care in England is currently receiving more attention than the other categories of placement reviewed. This situation has arisen following several scandals of sexual and other forms of abuse of residents by staff. In addition to the previous mistreatment by their own parents that many of these children have experienced, this situation obviously requires urgent attention. Though government and professional concern are to be welcomed, it is regrettable that such a position was reached before positive action was taken.

Of the many current issues associated with residential child care in England, we try to identify some of the most significant. In doing this, it will be seen that there are a number of common concerns between residential and foster family care. For example, recruitment and retention of residential staff is also a problem for many employers. Exacerbated by recent crises, residential care generally is not held in high esteem, and this has influenced morale. This is despite the fact that outcomes for children placed in residential facilities are not demonstrably inferior to those for children in foster families (Berridge, 1994; Cliffe, 1991). Though some improvements have occurred in pay and working conditions, residential care is clearly not an easy way to earn a living. Consequently the most able candidates have not always been attracted to residential child care or wanted to make it a long-term career option; this no doubt influences the quality of care offered.

A major impediment to the quality of residential care, and an issue of much debate, has been that of training. Whereas virtually all field work staff are now professionally qualified, a survey discovered that this applied to less than one in three residential child care staff: 80 per cent of heads of residential homes held a relevant professional qualification, but the same applied to only half of assistant heads and barely a quarter of other staff (Department of Health, 1991c). Given that residential establishments generally deal with the most problematic young people, this is clearly inadequate. A current initiative is seeking to ensure that all heads of residential homes will be professionally qualified within a short period. In addition, there are efforts to integrate more effectively group care issues and experiences in generic social work training (Central Council for Education and Training in Social Work, 1992). There is also a government-sponsored project to develop more common standards in residential settings run by different agencies such as health and education authorities and in independent schools (Kahan, 1994).

The quality of care therefore could be enhanced in many group care environments. Practitioners can become too preoccupied with the daily problems of residential life and lose sight of the wider factors that necessitate children living away from home. Colton (1988) has shown how much residential care is insufficiently child oriented and more directed at maintaining order, almost as an ultimate objective in itself. Unhelpful restrictions can be imposed on visits and contact with families inappropriately controlled as a sanction. Educational progress is insufficiently prioritized (Berridge, 1985; Jackson, 1987). Moreover, preparation for departure could be improved in all care environments, not just residential care, especially for young people who will subsequently be living "independently."

These problems are not eased when individual residential facilities have to cope with a wide assortment of young people with contradictory needs, for example, when emergency placements arrive to disrupt the whole proceedings or an inappropriate combination of abused and abusers occurs. There is an unfortunate tendency sometimes to use residential homes as "dumping grounds" for young people for which no other solution is forthcoming. If homes are used in this way it should be no surprise if positive results do not emerge. Inadequate management must take much of the responsibility for these and other deficiencies, as several official inquiries have demonstrated (e.g., Levy & Kahan, 1991).

Another issue of considerable concern to service providers has been the cost of residential services, especially specialist facilities. Official statistics have reported the cost of residential placement being six times that for foster care, but it has been shown that presenting figures in this way is misleading. The two services tend to provide for different age groups, and so one is not comparing like with like. The foster care figure also conceals a wide range of hidden costs, especially social work support. Once these factors are taken into account, the cost differential persists but is much narrower (Knapp & Fenyo, 1989). Furthermore, it is relevant to point out that the recent evaluation of services in the English county that discontinued its use of residential care discovered that the county saved no money as a result and felt that it would have been unwise to have set out to do so. The policy only had a chance of working if additional family and young people's support services were provided from the corresponding savings (Cliffe, 1991).

As a result of the above factors, there are clearly problems in residential services in several regions of England. Difficulties also arise in managing unruly behavior, which often attracts widespread local publicity. Some of these problems are being addressed, albeit rather late in the day. However a reminder should be made that residential child care can, and usually does, make a positive contribution (Department of Health, 1991c; Department of Health, Social Services Inspectorate, 1993; Rowe et al., 1989), and that there are political and professional choices about how the service is perceived, organized, and provided with resources.

Conclusions

This chapter on child abuse in England finishes with some general conclusions. However, as a range of subjects was covered, it may be helpful first to summarize briefly some of the main points that have emerged so far.

Child abuse is currently an issue of major concern and is having a significant impact on wider child care policy. Political and public attitudes have been inconsistent over the past decade, varying from encouraging a more interventionist approach to one of not interfering unnecessarily in family life. The balance has now tilted back against intrusion. Though the two positions are not mutually exclusive, the social worker in the middle is in an unenviable situation.

The policy framework in England incorporates child abuse as part of a broader range of services for children in need. Considerable legal reform has occurred over the past decade in response to deficiencies in services. Consequently, the Children Act 1989 has been welcomed as a positive measure, and its implementation was carefully planned. It is felt that this legislation strikes a good balance among emphasizing themes of partnership with parents, avoiding coercive measures whenever possible, and giving children a stronger voice.

National child abuse procedures are outlined in detail and generally adherence is good. There is particular emphasis on the roles of different professionals and interagency collaboration. Social services departments are legally obliged to prevent children in their areas from suffering ill treatment or neglect. Categories of abuse are identified, but these are very broad and allow for much local variation.

England has no mandatory child abuse reporting laws, and there seems no particular urge to move in this direction. Perhaps for this reason there are no comprehensive statistics on referrals. Thus discussion in this chapter relies on recent empirical studies, especially Jane Gibbons and colleagues' (1995) useful study. This research demonstrates the key role of teachers and other education staff in alerting social services departments to suspected abuse. The families concerned experience multiple economic and social deprivation. Social services are successful in maintaining the overwhelming majority of children at home throughout the investigation process as well as subsequently. Some six in every seven reports are filtered out without children's names being added to Child Protection Registers. Questions are raised about whether they should all have fallen within this system in the first place.

The number of child abuse registrations rose considerably throughout the 1980s, especially in the category of sexual abuse. However this has leveled off more recently. A major problem that has been identified is the lack of specialist help for families after investigation, including cases in which sexual violations have occurred.

Most children who have to live away from their families have been found to benefit. However, problems were highlighted in both foster family and residential care concerning maintaining an adequate supply of caregivers, ensuring quality of care, and issues of professionalization. Specific concerns exist about aspects of residential care, including shortcomings in management.

Having now sketched this scene, what concluding messages should the international reader have about the child protection system in England? As this book is primarily concerned with policy issues, the focus here is on three current major concerns: the relationship between the child abuse and wider child welfare systems, organizational issues and the danger of fragmentation of services, and the climate of opinion toward children and the new legislation specifically. Each of these has been touched on already, and to some extent they are interrelated. They are also relatively new phenomena. Discussion here, therefore, is inevitably tentative, and the concerns expressed may or may not materialize. It is hoped that they do not.

The official system to protect children in England has been tightened considerably over the past 20 years. If possible parental mistreatment is suspected by, say, a teacher or health visitor, then this concern is more likely to be expressed through formal channels and inquiries result. This will not in itself of course guarantee that children will always be safe, but it is an important prerequisite.

However what has emerged is a tendency for child welfare cases increasingly to become defined in terms of child protection. Keeping a child alive must obviously be the overriding consideration, but there are major drawbacks in lowering the threshold too far. Cleaver and Freeman's research (1995), discussed above, reveals that too many minor cases are unnecessarily dealt with by child abuse procedures. Bringing too narrow a focus to the work has also meant that broader considerations of social and emotional development are often ignored. Cases not defined in this way may automatically and inappropriately be perceived as lower priority. This may be happening to adolescent services, for which one study has found inexperienced social workers routinely being allocated (Sinclair et al., 1995).

Another consequence of preoccupation with protection rather than welfare, discussed in the review of the empirical research, is that attention concentrates specifically on investigation of the neglect of services that can help alleviate problems. The investigation, it seems, is becoming an end in itself. Children and especially mothers will frequently benefit from specialist services even when the danger of significant harm is felt not to be present. At the moment, studies show that by no means is this always happening.

Government has taken steps to discourage local authorities from unduly setting priorities and approaching cases in this way, including reminding them that it is illegal. Nonetheless, a survey by Aldgate, Tunstill, and McBeath (1993) revealed that, although there were imaginative policies and good practice to be found, too many agencies were neglecting wider child welfare concerns in the way suggested here. This is likely to become a major issue for the remainder of the 1990s, and the welfare of thousands of children hinges on it.

The second subject to be raised is that of the organization of services. Here there has been a timely and perceptive reminder from the U.S. visitor Schorr (1992). Questions about resources are especially contentious in England. Governments over the past 15 years have been elected on mandates to constrain public spending, yet often take exception when it is pointed out that this has been achieved. Bewildering statistics are produced from all sides to support favored positions. However, Schorr, in using terms such as "the declining slope," argues that the personal social services in England are seriously overburdened and lack resources.

Moreover, the structure of services is also questioned. One has the impression that English social services departments are in a state of constant reorganization: New directors it seems join, reorganize, and promptly leave, to be followed by someone else who does exactly the same. No doubt some structural arrangements are better than others, but it is by no means apparent that this effort is always rewarded. Some senior managers have explicitly and successfully set out to create staff anxiety, believing this to be an established private sector strategy to enhance performance. How this befits a caring organization is unclear.

Two reforms in particular are influencing the structure of organizations in the area of social policy. Already mentioned is the movement toward smaller, autonomous units in health and education as hospitals and schools, for example, opt out of public sector management. It is too soon to know what implications this will have. However, it was shown earlier that much of the effort in the field of child protection over the past 20 years has concerned improving professional collaboration. The present reforms could pose some threat to this as lines of accountability and communication are multiplied. Furthermore, individual managers responsible for budgets may not always look positively at wider preventive programs that do not bring associated funding. Fragmentation of services therefore may undermine some of the progress that has been made in combatting child abuse.

Another organizational reform that is generating much debate concerns the introduction of a system of internal markets, particularly the division of English departments along "purchaser/provider" lines. This has been introduced by law to health services and to social services under "community care" reforms for those who are elderly, mentally ill, or with disabilities. Government intentions have been to increase efficiency and, ideologically, to encourage the take-up of private and voluntary sector services.

Whatever its relative merits for these other client groups, it appears that many departments are also introducing a purchaser/provider structure to children's services without thinking through the specific implications. Concerns include the fact that community care legislation and the Children Act 1989 stem from quite different value bases and may not therefore be compatible. Moving to a more explicit model of rationing services for children in need would also raise ethical concerns. Furthermore, it is not apparent how parental responsibility can be split between purchasers and providers. In addition, children's situations may be much more volatile than those of other client groups, making a formalized and separate approach toward assessments inappropriate (Sinclair et al., 1995). For these reasons, concerns exist about the welfare and protection of children that have not as yet been fully addressed.

Finally, this chapter ends on a note of further speculation. Throughout this brief view of the English scene it has been possible on the whole to maintain a positive perspective. Despite funding disputes and a tendency toward "moral panics" in child welfare (Parton, 1985), the law, policy, and practice have nevertheless made steady progress. The Children Act 1989 is envied by professionals in many other countries as an example of forward-looking, well-grounded, child-centered legislation (Pires, 1993). It is emulated by Scotland and Northern Ireland. Within England, it shines like a beacon compared to most other social policy legislation in the past 15 years.

Yet there is a feeling that these painstaking reforms do not always command the political support they deserve. Sections of the legislation seem threatened under the guise of deregulation, as if this were a good thing in itself. Some politicians' disapproval of social workers also has become tinged with increasing bitterness.

As a society we may also be becoming less compassionate toward children. Halsey (1992) describes this period of history as one of "low fertility and low morality"; men in particular, by embracing individualized values may be increasingly putting their own needs before those of the young. In any case England is not renowned as the most child centered of nations. The NSPCC estimates that between three and four children in Britain are killed each week because of abuse or neglect (some feel this is an overestimate). Although this figure may seem enviably low to some countries, and it has been argued that the numbers have decreased (Pritchard 1992, 1993), it confirms Schorr's cogent observation that "civility is a thin veneer, especially as it addresses children" (Schorr, 1992, p. 32).

It also sometimes seems from the press and media broadcasts that children are increasingly being blamed for society's ills. Moreover, some commentators imply that the Children Act of 1989 can be held responsible for virtually all challenges from the young. Politicians speak over the heads of children to adults, who would appear to command increasing sympathy at their expense: They are of course able to vote. Whatever other radical economic and social ventures pursued, it is hoped that there is no departure from the consensus achieved on policies for child welfare and protection, otherwise the lives, bodies, and minds of children may be put at risk.

Notes

I am grateful to Jane Aldgate, Isabelle Brodie, Susan Creighton, Elaine Farmer, Jane Gibbons, Anne Hollows, Rupert Hughes, Michael Little, and Helen Wenman for comments on an earlier draft of this chapter. I would also like to thank Susan Creighton of the NSPCC for her help in compiling statistics on registration.

1. Issues discussed in this chapter apply to both England and Wales, although official statistics are published separately for the two countries. Law and policy are different for Scotland and Northern Ireland. For the sake of brevity, the term *children* refers throughout to children and young people to the age of 18 unless stated otherwise.

2. Figures for 1993 and 1994 were issued late in the production of this book. They are 32,500 and 34,900, respectively.

References

Adcock, M., White, R., & Hollows, A. (Eds.) (1991). *Significant harm: Its management and outcome.* Croydon: Significant Books.

Aldgate, J., Tunstill, J., & McBeath, G. (1993). *Highlights from a national study on the implementation of Section 17 of the Children Act 1989 in England.* Leicester, England: University of Leicester, School of Social Work.

Bebbington, A., & Miles, J. (1990). The supply of foster families for children in care. *British Journal of Social Work, 20*(4), 283-307.

Berridge, D. (1985). *Children's homes.* Oxford, England: Basil Blackwell.

Berridge, D. (1994). Foster and residential care reassessed: A research perspective. *Children & Society, 8*(2), 132-150.

Berridge, D. (1996). *Foster care: A research review.* London: Her Majesty's Stationery Office.

Berridge, D., & Cleaver, H. (1987). *Foster home breakdown.* Oxford, England: Basil Blackwell.

Bradshaw, J. (1990). *Child poverty and deprivation in the UK.* London: National Children's Bureau.

Bullock, R., Little, M., & Millham, S. (1993). *Going home: The return of children separated from their families.* Aldershot: Dartmouth.

Caesar, G., Parchment, M., & Berridge, D. (1994). *Black perspectives on services for children in need.* Barkingside, England: Barnardo's/National Children's Bureau.

Central Council for Education and Training in Social Work. (1992). *Setting quality standards for residential child care: A practical way forward.* London: CCETSW (Central Council for Education and Training in Social Work).

Child Abuse Review. (1993). 2, 4.

Cleaver, H., & Freeman, P. (1995). *Parental perspectives in cases of suspected child abuse.* London: Her Majesty's Stationery Office.

Cliffe, D. (with Berridge, D.). (1991). *Closing children's homes: An end to residential childcare?* London: National Children's Bureau.

Colton, M. (1988). *Dimensions of substitute care.* London: Avebury.

Corby, B. (1990). Making use of child protection statistics. *Children & Society, 4*(3), 304-314.

Creighton, S. (1992). *Child abuse trends in England and Wales 1988-1990.* London: National Society for the Prevention of Cruelty to Children.

Dartington Social Research Unit. (1985). *Place of safety orders: A study for the DHSS review of child care law.* Bristol, England: University of Bristol.

Department of Health. (1988). *Protecting children: A guide for social workers in undertaking a comprehensive assessment.* London: Her Majesty's Stationery Office.

Department of Health. (1989). *An introduction to the Children Act 1989.* London: Her Majesty's Stationery Office.

Department of Health. (1991a). *Child abuse. A study of inquiry reports 1980–1989.* London: Her Majesty's Stationery Office.

Department of Health. (1991b). *The Children Act 1989 guidance and regulations: Volume 3 – Family placements.* London: Her Majesty's Stationery Office.

Department of Health. (1991c). *Children in the public care.* London: Her Majesty's Stationery Office.

Department of Health. (1991d). *Patterns and outcomes in child placement: Messages from current research and their implications.* London: Her Majesty's Stationery Office.

Department of Health. (1993a). *Children Act report 1992.* London: Her Majesty's Stationery Office.

Department of Health. (1993b). *Children in care in England and Wales March 1991.* London: Department of Health.

Department of Health. (1993c). *Children and young people on child protection registers. Year ending 31 March 1992, England.* London: Her Majesty's Stationery Office.

Department of Health. (1995). *Child protection: Messages from research.* London: Her Majesty's Stationery Office.

Department of Health and Social Security. (1985a). *Review of child care law: Report to ministers of an interdepartmental working party.* London: Her Majesty's Stationery Office.

Department of Health and Social Security. (1985b). *Social work decisions in child care: Recent research findings and their implications.* London: Her Majesty's Stationery Office.

Department of Health, Social Services Inspectorate. (1993). *Corporate parents: Inspection of residential child care in 11 local authorities.* London: Department of Health.

Department of Health/Welsh Office. (1994). *Children Act report 1993.* London: Her Majesty's Stationery Office.

Dominelli, L. (1989). Betrayal of trust: A feminist analysis of power relationships in incest abuse and its relevance for social work practice. *British Journal of Social Work, 19*(4), 291–307.

Farmer, E., & Owen, M. (1995). *Child protection practice: Private risks and public remedies – Decision making, intervention and outcome in child protection work.* London: Her Majesty's Stationery Office.

Farmer, E., & Parker, R. (1991). *Trials and tribulations.* London: Her Majesty's Stationery Office.

Fox Harding, L. (1991). *Perspectives in child care policy.* London: Longman.

Frost, N., & Stein, M. (1989). *The politics of child welfare: Inequality, power and change.* London: Harvester Wheatsheaf.

Garnett, L. (1992). *Leaving care and after.* London: National Children's Bureau.

Gibbons, J., Conroy, S., & Bell, C. (1995). *Operating the child protection system: A study of child protection practices in English local authorities.* London: Her Majesty's Stationery Office.

Gough, D., Boddy, F., Dunning, N., & Stone, F. (1987). *A longitudinal study of child abuse in Glasgow.* Glasgow: University of Glasgow and Greater Glasgow Health Board, Social Pediatric and Obstetric Research Unit.

Halsey, A. (1992). Changes in the family. *Children & Society, 7*(2), 125–136.

Home Office, Department of Health, Department of Education and Science, and Welsh Office. (1991). *Working together under the Children Act 1989.* London: Her Majesty's Stationery Office.

House of Commons Social Services Committee. (1984). *Second report from the Social Services Committee, Session 1983–84: Children in care.* London: Her Majesty's Stationery Office.

Jackson, S. (1987). *The education of children in care.* Bristol, England: University of Bristol, School of Applied Social Studies.

Kahan, B. (Ed.) (1994). *Growing up in groups.* London: Her Majesty's Stationery Office.

Knapp, M., & Fenyo, A. (1989). Economic perspectives on foster care. In Carter, P., Jeffs, T., & Smith, M. (Eds.), *Social work and social welfare yearbook 1.* Milton Keynes, England: Open University Press.[edq31]

Kumar, V. (1993). *Poverty and inequality in the UK: The effects on children.* London: National Children's Bureau.

Levy, A., & Kahan, B. (1991). *The Pindown experience and the protection of children: The report of the Staffordshire child care enquiry 1990.* Stafford, England: Staffordshire County Council.

Little, M., & Gibbons, J. (1993). Predicting the rate of children on the child protection register. *Research, Policy and Planning, 10*(2), 15–18.

Millham, S., Bullock, R., Hosie, K., & Haak, M. (1986). *Lost in care: The problems of maintaining links between children in care and their families.* Aldershot, England: Gower.

Packman, J., & Jordan, B. (1991). The Children Act: Looking forward, looking back. *British Journal of Social Work, 21*(4), 315–327.

Packman, J., Randall, J., & Jacques, N. (1986). *Who needs care? Social work decisions about children.* Oxford: Basil Blackwell.

Parker, R. (1978). Foster care in context. *Adoption and Fostering, 93,* 3.

Parker, R., & Loughran, F. (n.d). *Long-term child care trends. Report to the Economic and Social Research Council.* Bristol, England: University of Bristol, Department of Social Policy and Planning.

Parton, N. (1985). *The politics of child abuse.* London: Macmillan.

Parton, N. (1989). Child abuse. In B. Kahan (Ed.), *Child care research, policy and practice* (pp. 55–79). London: Hodder and Stoughton.

Parton, N. (1991). *Governing the family: Child care, child protection and the state.* London: Macmillan.

Pires, S. (Ed.). (1993). *International child welfare systems: Report of a workshop.* Washington, DC: National Academy Press.

Pritchard, C. (1992). Children's homicide as an indicator of effective child protection: A comparative study of Western European statistics. *British Journal of Social Work, 22,* 663–684.

Pritchard, C. (1993). Re-analysing children's homicide and undetermined death rates as an indicator of improved child protection. *British Journal of Social Work, 23,* 645–652.

Reder, P., Duncan, S., & Gray, M. (1993). A new look at child abuse tragedies. *Child Abuse Review, 2,* 89–100.

Rowe, J., Caine, M., Hundley, M., & Keane, F. (1984). *Long term foster care.* London: Batsford.

Rowe, J., Hundleby, M., & Garnett, L. (1989). *Child care now.* London: British Agencies for Adoption and Fostering.

Schorr, A. (1992). *The personal social services: An outside view*. York, England: Joseph Rowntree Foundation.

Sharland, E., Aldgate, A., Jones, D., Seal, H., & Croucher, M. (1993). *Professional intervention in child sexual abuse*. London: Her Majesty's Stationery Office.

Sinclair, R., Garnett, L., & Berridge, D. (1995). *Social work and assessment with adolescents*. London: National Children's Bureau.

Stein, M., & Carey, K. (1986). *Leaving care*. Oxford: Basil Blackwell.

Triseliotis, J. (1989). Foster care outcomes: A review of key research findings. *Adoption & Fostering, 13*(3), 5–16.

II

Family Service Orientation — Mandatory Reporting

4

Sweden

Toward a Deresidualization of Swedish Child Welfare Policy and Practice?

SVEN E. OLSSON HORT

A State that Snatches Children?

If one were to single out a country that in practice resembles the model welfare state, postwar Sweden would definitely be a contender. It has been said that this country of the Far North is the closest one comes to Richard Titmuss's (1974) institutional model of social policy. Everybody is included under the universal social safety net.[1] Public spending on social protection, including child welfare, is thus substantial and usually is looked on as investment in human capital. The general disadvantages of this system are of course the problem of overconsumption and the necessity of high taxes to fund such fancy programs. The international competitiveness of Swedish trade products is supposed to have become weakened, although this belief is contradicted by many experts in the field. Furthermore, in the early 1990s high unemployment levels and increasing interest payments on a burgeoning public deficit have created macroeconomic distortions of a magnitude hitherto unknown. This aspect of Swedish welfare policy is not further discussed here.

However, there are other types of supposed deficiencies as well. The opposite of the institutional model is the residual model, a social policy model by which the state only cares for the poor. Such a system involves a high degree of social control as it is important to draw the line between the worthy and the unworthy poor and destitute. A residual social policy in highly developed countries can be seen as a descendant of the old relief system for the poor.

Despite what is generally regarded as the success of universal welfare policies — material poverty has virtually been eliminated in Sweden — there are still social policy areas for which the achievements are much more in doubt. These involve the screening of individuals, in particular children, for compulsory care. In the early 1980s Sweden was widely accused in the international press of being "a state that snatches children." Measures taken by the state against families and children were considered too harsh and humiliating. Sweden held the world record for "the numbers, more precisely the percentage of children taken into custody" according to reports in the international media (cited in Gould, 1988, p. 55).

As Gould (1988) explains, the international press was deliberately used as an instrument in domestic lobbying by a coalition of rather diverse local interest groups that for very different reasons advocated less public intrusion in family matters. Nonetheless, the children's gulag scenario haunted Swedish policy makers and policy implementers for years to come. Intervention — including the prevention of child abuse and other kinds of maltreatment of children — in the private lives of families became a delicate matter for social workers. When the child of a German immigrant and his wife was murdered by the stepfather in the late 1980s in a remote rural area in northern Sweden, an outcry against social authorities for being too lenient and unwilling to immediately intervene followed suit (Olsson & Spånt, 1991, p. 50). Since that time, issues related to the care of children have occasionally topped the public agenda in Sweden.

In this chapter the problem of making residual policies more institutional is illustrated through an analysis of child abuse reporting systems and placement trends in Sweden. The overall purposes of this specific book, as pointed out by the editor at the start of this volume, to specify different definitions of child abuse, to illuminate various approaches to the design of child abuse reporting systems, to analyze trends in reporting and dispension of cases, to explore contemporary issues that different countries face in dealing with the problems of child abuse, and to identify policy options that are currently under review. This is also done in this chapter, and through an analysis of the peculiarities of the Swedish case I also hope to shed some light over my overarching research topic (Olsson, 1993; Olsson Hort, 1996).

I will not further dwell on the subject of social policy models, although I briefly return to this subject at the end of this chapter. However, I would like to point out that of those dealing with the practice of residual policies in Sweden, several (e.g., Gunnar and Maj-Britt Inghe and Gustav Jonsson) have been the foremost critics of the inadequacies of the universal welfare system (Olsson, 1993). In their footsteps an impressive range of research has followed in recent years that this chapter builds on apart from digging into official statistics concerning child welfare and child abuse. Overall, official statistics are very good in Sweden. Nevertheless, from a comparative perspective there are, as shown below, clear deficiencies in the administrative collection of statistics on child abuse and maltreatment.

Defining Abuse

Child abuse — in both emotional and physical terms — is a widely used notion in Sweden. Acts of physical abuse of human beings are of course forbidden by the general penal code, and successively more specifically corporal punishment of children by first teachers and then parents was prohibited. From child welfare legislation and practice it is still difficult to give the concept of child abuse an absolute meaning and strict definition. Actually specific conditions, signs, levels of severity, and empirical indicators are not part of the written law and thus are not specifically applied in social work practice. But, following international classifications of symptoms for physical examinations, medical doctors apply the diagnosis of child abuse. Physicians are under an obligation to report suspected cases of child abuse. However, according to available health records and reports received at social welfare agencies, no studies have been conducted of the occurrence of such reports to social authorities. Thus, no national statistics based on health registers are currently available as regards child abuse.

During the last three decades, the child abuse topic has been highlighted by volunteers as well. The National Association for the Protection of Children's Rights in Society (Swedish abbreviation, BRIS) is an organization of adults that acts as a representative for the child vis-à-vis public authorities as well as those in parental authority. Since 1980 BRIS has operated a round-the-clock call-in service called the Children's Help Telephone that on average receives 4,000–5,000 calls a year, most of them from teenage girls and from children in families, often a single-parent household, experiencing conflict. Roughly 20% of all phone calls are related to mental and physical abuse, another 5% have been classified as cases of sexual abuse (this figure has increased in recent years), and 4% percent concern children taken into care or those having trouble with foster homes (BRIS, 1991). For many years BRIS has also promoted the establishment of an Office of the Child Ombudsman; legislation finally passed and the office was established in 1993. The task of the Ombudsman is to insure that Sweden fulfills the U.N. Convention on the Rights of the Child and in particular to scrutinize the situation of vulnerable and disadvantaged children.

Compared to many other countries such as the United States, in Sweden access to public child welfare services is not primarily gained via a child abuse report. Child abuse or neglect is not a necessary or even typical precondition for beginning child welfare services. It is part of the normal course of life that children receive public child health and welfare services. Child abuse is of course regarded as abnormal, and the abuser—if convicted and sentenced—is considered a criminal. In many cases however, as a father or mother the abuser still has the "right" to the abused child. Thus, the victim, and the abuse as such, is not particularly well defined in Swedish legislation although national victim statistics on this type of crime against children have been collected from the early 1980s. Actually, apart from the penal code and the general Social Service Act and its supplemental Care of Young Persons Act, there is no law specifically regulating reports of child abuse that are not considered for investigation by social welfare authorities. The focus on child abuse is relatively recent, although medical personnel brought it to general attention in the late 1950s (Boethius & Kjellander-Ahlberg, 1982). Physical abuse of children became part of a wider concern spurred by professionals as well as feminists in the 1970s about family violence and wife battering. Somewhat later the issue of child sexual abuse rose to the top of the public agenda (Hallberg & Rigné, 1994).

However there is a prehistory that dates far back in time. Prior to child welfare legislation introduced in the early 1900s, children were taken to correctional prison, and punishments were generally harsh and authoritarian for grown-ups and children alike. However, more than two and a half centuries ago in 1741, taking children below age 7 to prison was forbidden by law; at that time institutions for the care of young boys and girls were established, most often through philanthropic initiatives (Sandin, 1986). Some of them were known as protection homes and were based on the concept of saving and disciplining children who were abandoned, neglected, and socially rejected.

Child maltreatment and the rights of the child have been the object of Swedish public debate at least since early in this century (Key, 1900/1909; Therborn, 1993). In 1902 the first Child Welfare Act was passed by Parliament. However it was not until the replacement of the first act by a second in 1924 that child neglect was truly recognized. The tone and spirit of the first act were in many senses couched in the language of 19th century moral evils. The Child Welfare Act was born out of both child labor and criminal penalty legislations and introduced the ultimate instrument for protecting society-at-large against the dangers that children of the laboring classes were considered to represent. Initially it was a law directed toward children themselves, which made it possible to take them forcibly into care, and was thus strongly influenced by the notion of social control (Lundström, 1992).

One, if not the main, reason why the 1902 legislation was amended in two decades was that it did not offer the possibility of taking children who were suffering from abuse and neglect by adults into care. This was partly changed by the 1924 Child Welfare Act, which came to include an additional paragraph specifically about taking children into compulsory care due to child neglect and abuse. Still social control was central to this piece of legislation, which remained mainly concerned with the deprivation and misbehavior of youth. At this time, however, the concept of the best interest of the child became the main criterion for all practical regulations of child-adult relationships in general family law.

The 1924 Child Welfare Act remained in force until 1960 when Parliament passed new legislation that placed greater emphasis on preventive measures and the need for correct legal procedures. Under the 1960 legislation the rules governing case documentation were made more specific. The theories of child welfare changed in important respects in the 1960 legislation, from explanatory models based on moral precepts to models based more on psychological insights. Thus there was a shift away from the individual-oriented and moralistic practice toward medical-psychological explanations for socially deviant behaviors. Still the legislation was influenced by concerns for social control. As a part of the general growth of the welfare state, the number of public institutions such as youth schools and children's homes grew.

Another aspect of the definition of abuse involves corporal punishment, which was used in both homes and schools as a way of disciplining children in Sweden. The attitude toward the use of physical punishment to discipline children changed gradually during the first half of this century and radically since the 1950s. In 1958, the teacher's right to beat children physically in schools was abolished, and by 1966 parents also lost their right to use corporal punishment. In 1979, as a final measure in this area, Parliament enacted the new Code of Parenthood, which contains prohibitions against physical and other humiliating treatment of children. The fact that this law was unanimously supported by all political parties indicates that the majority of the Swedish people were, and still are, against corporal punishment of children. Recent opinion polls support this statement. In effect the law has provided a protective shield for children, as well as an instrument for child lobby groups.

Today children and adolescents who are abused, neglected, or suffer other forms of maltreatment are first subject to the 1980 Social Service Act. This is a highly ambitious piece of legislation that reflects the general spirit of the Swedish approach to social citizenship. Ideas related to social control were explicitly abandoned in favor of an emphasis on individual citizen's social rights. With the introduction of the general Social Service Act, specific child welfare legislation was officially abolished.

Concerning children, the 1980 Social Services Act is fairly general and makes no mention of child abuse as such. The closest it comes is in the initial paragraph on children and young persons, which states that the municipal

> social welfare committee shall (1) endeavour to ensure that children and young people grow up in good and secure conditions, (2) act in close co-operation with families to promote the comprehensive personal development and the favourable physical and social development of children and young persons, and (3) ensure that children and young persons in danger of developing in an undesirable direction receive the protection and support they need and, if their best interests so demand, are cared for and brought up away from their own homes.

A central feature of the Social Service Act was the emphasis on the right of birth parents to provide continuing care and, at least, to have ongoing contact with their children if out-of-home care was required. The major intention of this reform was to reduce sharply the nonvoluntary (i.e., forced) removal of children from their homes. Although involuntary out-of-home placement can still be accomplished when deemed necessary, the legislation requires a hearing before the Social Service Advisory Board before any child can be removed from home on a long-term basis. Furthermore this reform indirectly promoted the development of residential family care in which parents and children were placed together in residential or foster family care to preserve the family (Barth, 1992, pp. 36–37).

The right to public assistance is not defined with great precision in the Social Service Act, which simply indicates that assistance must guarantee the individual a "decent standard of living." The current interpretation of this statement is that the level of public assistance should correspond to the general level of living standards in society; in other words there should be a fairly narrow range in the distribution of material resources among various population groups.

The lawmakers' ambition was to replace the old poor law with a law designed to promote the universal approach to welfare policy. It was thus an attempt to break with a past that had relied far too much on control and compulsion. The Social Service Act focuses attention on the totality of an individual's situation as various attempts are made to solve his or her problems. The implicit normative focus is on adults and families.

Apart from financial support to families and individuals, the law nevertheless contains special regulations to protect minors. For instance, help according to the Social Service Act is also to be provided in the form of care in a foster home or in institutions such as children's home, youth welfare schools, and similar establishments. As mentioned, the focus is on preserving families and maintaining contacts between biological parents and their children. There is a strong emphasis on voluntary measures and the rights of parents.

In addition to voluntary placement in foster care or an out-of-home institution, another form of assistance provided by social welfare authorities involves a contact person or contact family (Andersson, 1993; Barth, 1991). If a family, usually a single-head-of-household family, is in need of help, the social authorities try to find an individual volunteer or a volunteering family to assist them and carry out various services, for example, taking care of a child over the weekend. This way mainly single female mothers get some relief, and their children have an opportunity to become acquainted with another family or person. However all services provided by the Social Service Act are optional or preventive, and the contact family or individual is not supposed to, and in general does not, act as an agent of social control (Andersson, 1991, 1992; Gould, 1989). In cases of child neglect or abuse this form of assistance generally applies to an earlier stage in the process of prevention and a rather late stage in the process of rehabilitation.

The Social Service Act is supplemented by a special coercive law, the 1990 Care of Young Persons Act (Swedish abbreviation, and commonly referred to as, LVU), which regulates compulsory committal for care of children and adolescents who are neglected or display what is regarded as deviant behavior. This act tightens the regulations governing placement of a young person into compulsory care. The law covers compulsory care related to both the behavior of a child or adolescent and the inadequacy of the home environment. These are the two specific reasons for taking children and young persons into custody.

It is the second category, inadequacy of the home environment, that is most relevant in the case of child abuse; here the requirement for intervention on behalf of the state is that "due to physical abuse, exploitation, deficiencies of care or some other circumstances in the home, there is a palpable risk of the young person's health or development being impaired." Thus compulsory care may be involved in cases of physical maltreatment and other kinds of physical abuse, like sexual abuse, as well as cases in which the mental or social development of the minor is endangered as a result of, for example, the misuse of alcohol or drugs by the parents or the parents' character or behavior in general. While compulsory care due to the behavior of the child or adolescent tends to involve persons above age 12, compulsory care because of an inadequate home environment usually involves younger children.

As mentioned, no signs, conditions, levels of severity, or other empirical indicators of maltreatment are specified in the text of the prevailing law. The concept of maltreated children, which is widely used but not part of the legislation, includes children exposed to various forms of violence, cruelty, or neglect in the family. Under the law children are covered up to 18 years of age. Finally there are no trends discernible toward extending or narrowing the definition, an increased specification of conditions, or new types of indicators.

Filing of Reports

Long before the introduction of child welfare legislation in Sweden, children had been taken into custody or placed out of home by local authorities. The practice of child welfare has always been the task of local government, though the actual provision was, as already mentioned, carried out by philanthropic organizations. But with the 1902 legislation, the municipalities assumed the explicit task of preventing criminality and other wrongdoing among children and in general overseeing their social development (Svård, 1992).

Swedish municipalities were run by local people long before the full democratic breakthrough of the early 20th century. A kind of popular or semipopular predemocracy has existed throughout the centuries, thus rendering a sharp distinction between state and society superfluous. Through the Lutheran State church, the central state had representatives in the form of priests all over the country, but since medieval times independent landholders, farmers never subjugated to feudal lords, had a strong voice in local affairs in rural communities, while merchants and artisans held similar powers in the towns. Thus Sweden has a long tradition of lay involvement in public affairs.

When the first child welfare legislation was enacted in 1902, it was literate but not necessarily educated laypeople who had to implement the act. Professionals were basically absent from this field, with the partial exception of the clergy and school teachers. Rather soon however a national voluntary association, the Swedish Poor Relief and Child Welfare Society, started to organize and educate local child welfare committee members. The central actors within this organization were persons with some expertise in pediatrics, child rearing, and law (Ohrlander, 1992).

The medical corps, especially the pediatricians and the psychiatrists, were the ones who theoretically spearheaded the development of the treatment of what were considered disturbed children (or less often, children in disturbed families). In their efforts to understand deviant behavior they introduced scientific theories, especially those of psychopathology. Medical interest however was limited to those children who had already developed some form of deviant behavior. Very young children who were abused or, according to the thinking of the time, ran the risk of negative development because of parental moral deficiency were not the focus of concern (Sundell et al., 1992).

However, parallel to the theories of deviant behavior, other more instrumental techniques for classification and diagnosis were being developed through the standardization of forms, guidelines for how the minutes of the child welfare committee were to be written, and standards for giving legal advice and information. This took place to a large extent within the framework of the Swedish Poor Relief and Child Welfare Society, which was a voluntary, reformist organization with strong ties to the government and national welfare administration. Thus laypeople all over the country became accustomed to the habit of writing protocols and filling in forms.

In the big cities, professional child welfare bureaucracies began to develop in the 1930s following the establishment of professional social work education in the 1920s. Nationwide, however, it was not until the late 1960s and early 1970s that laypeople handed over the paperwork in this area to professional employees, mainly social workers. Although professionals prepared the reports, the ultimate decisions were still made by elected laypeople in the child welfare committees after reviewing written and oral recommendations by the social workers (Lundström, 1992). Thus Sweden is still a lay society in which the role of professionals in the social welfare sector is not yet firmly grounded.

Never in history has there been any formal requirement to register nonactivated child abuse reports. It is still the case that reports that do not lead to action by a caseworker will not be filed and archived. As long as social workers do not evaluate a report about suspected child abuse as having strong enough evidence to set in motion an investigation of a family, such a report does not figure in Swedish national statistics and most likely not in local social welfare archives either. Social workers may keep these reports in their desks for a while, but if no further indications spur an investigation the reports will eventually be discarded. Such reports may sometimes appear in the minutes of local social boards, but to this author's knowledge no inquiry of the incidence of such reports has been conducted in Sweden.

In Sweden there is nevertheless far-reaching legislation designed to protect children from ill-treatment in their own families. As mentioned, the ban on corporal punishment in the family code applies to all forms of physical and mental punishment. Under the Social Service Act, municipalities are to ensure that children and young people at risk of developing in an unfavorable manner receive the support and protection they need. If parental care is inadequate and there is a risk that the child's health and development will be endangered, the local social welfare committee is responsible for intervening to protect the child. For instance, the Social Service Act explicitly states that children who, for physical, mental, or other reasons, need special support for the sake of their development are to be allotted preschool places earlier than is normally the case (i.e., before age 1½ years), and it is the obligation of the social welfare committee to oversee that these places are utilized as intended and further to inform parents about the purpose and activities of preschools. In this manner preschool teachers — most of them public employees and part of the local social welfare service department — are called on to play an important role in preventing child abuse (Sundell, Lundström, Sjöberg, & Wettergren, 1992).

In principle the measures taken when children are at risk should be of a voluntary nature; they ought to take place in agreement with the parents (custodians) and with the consent of the child if he or she has reached the age of 15 years. As mentioned, an important principle involves supporting parents as far as possible to discharge their parental responsibilities by providing various forms of public assistance. In the local social welfare department a professional social worker is the key person who, on behalf of the local social welfare committee, thoroughly investigates each case and coordinates various activities. It is mandatory that persons who have custody of the child — as well as the child himself, if over age 15 — participate in the decision-making process and truly understand why and how decisions are achieved. Not surprisingly, research shows that these investigations and decisions involve a painful process that creates a lot of anxiety among social workers (Claezon, 1987).

Placements outside the home environment normally take place with the consent of the parents. Furthermore, the Social Service Act states: "If a minor is being cared for, by authority of this Act, in a home which is not his own, the social welfare committee is to consider, at least once every six months, whether this care is still necessary." By this the guiding philosophy of family reunification is strongly underlined. The alternative of adopting a child is rarely considered as a viable option. When a child is placed out of the home it is expected that the parents shall make a reasonable contribution, as defined by the government, toward the costs incurred by the municipality. It is however rarely the case that parents contribute to these costs.

The social welfare committee is responsible for ensuring that the child's access to his or her parents is facilitated. Moreover, the idea is that in normal circumstances it should be possible for the child to return to its biological parents, and the social welfare committee shall prepare a plan of treatment and follow up the child's circumstances after the child has been placed in care.

As already noted, when there is reason to suspect that a child is being maltreated, the social welfare committee is required to investigate the circumstances without delay. Any person who discovers that a child is being maltreated at home is obliged to report this to the social welfare committee. The casual reporter however is provided anonymity only as long as the case is not taken to court, which obviously creates the possibility of the threat of retaliation. The authorities in health care and social welfare services are also under an obligation to report child maltreatment. Mandatory reporters include teachers, doctors, nurses, midwives, and those in certain other professional categories in the private sector. According to a recent study, preschool teachers often tend to avoid reporting cases of child abuse to other social authorities; instead they do preventive work themselves with the families (Sundell et al., 1992).

Although work in the area of child abuse lays a heavy emphasis on voluntary agreements with the concerned parties, if a voluntary agreement cannot be reached, the social welfare authorities may nonetheless intervene in certain cases and take a child into public care. The exceptions to the voluntary principle are regulated by special legislation, the Care of Young Persons Act (LVU).

A decision to take a child into care according to the 1990 Care of Young Persons Act is issued by the county administrative court following an application by the municipal social welfare board. A certificate by a physician must always be included in the application. An appeal can be lodged against this decision, and the petition can be taken to the administrative appeal court and the Supreme Administrative Court. The decision of the administrative court involves only an order that someone is to be taken into care, and it will then be a matter for the social welfare board to put the order into effect. In so doing the board, according to the circumstances of the case, may choose to place the young person in a family other than his or her own or send the young person to a suitable institution. Furthermore the social welfare committee prepares a treatment and placement plan to prepare for the return of the child to his or her parents. As mentioned, this plan is reviewed every 6 months as part of a reconsideration of the necessity of nonvoluntary care. Care ceases automatically however when the adolescent reaches the age of 18 or, if the taking into care has been occasioned by the adolescent's behavior, when the adolescent reaches the age of 21.

Reporting and Placement Trends

In Sweden, it is difficult, based on records from social authorities, to obtain indications of reporting trends concerning child abuse. Reports that are not considered cases for investigation and intervention by social workers and the municipal social welfare committee are not systematically filed, archived, and passed on to national authorities. Furthermore, as long as care is classified as voluntary, no specific reason is noted in the official statistics based on local agency practice. As a research topic, child abuse has remained marginal (Sundelin, 1993). However when care is of a compulsory nature, it is possible to make a distinction between cases related to the behavior of the child and those that involve inadequate parental attention, which often reflects some form of child abuse but, of course, not exclusively so.

In addition to data kept by the social welfare authorities, certain child abuse offenses are registered under the penal code. Of roughly 1 million offenses registered by the police in 1993, some 3,400 offenses concerned allegations of child abuse (see Table 4-1). Criminal statistics focus on the crime and persons suspected of this offense, and a distinction can only be made between abuse directed toward two different age groups (children 0–6 and 7–14 years). Thus it is not possible to draw firm conclusions about the number of victims and annual substantiation rates from the victims' perspective. The figure given above includes more registered offenses than actual victims as multiple cases of abuse are often reported as independent offenses. Just above half of these offenses are further scrutinized by the police, with roughly half of them taken to court by a prosecutor. In some cases during 1 year the number of registered

Table 4-1. Abuse of Children 0–14 Years of Age per 1,000 Persons in the Population Ages 0–14 Years

	1982	1986	1989	1992	1993
Offenses reported to police[a]	0.7	0.9	1.2	1.9	2.1
Offenses cleared[b]	0.4	0.5	0.6	1.0	1.2
Percentage in which suspicion remains	48	50	53	49	43
Crime participations[c]	0.2	0.2	0.5	0.5	0.5
Percentage of court cases	18	23	28	27	22
Persons suspected of offenses	0.2	0.2	0.3	0.4	0.5
Percentage of which were females	12	15	13	18	18

[a]Offenses reported to the police during 1 year.

[b]Offenses cleared during 1 year by the police (the offenses could have occurred during the previous year or earlier).

[c]Crime participations: Crime for which suspicion remains and a suspect exists according to a prosecutor.

Source: Statistics Sweden (1994, p. 5) (and earlier editions).

suspected offenses is larger than the number of reported offenses because a single suspected offender/abuser at one point in time is reported to have committed several offenses against one or more children.

These police statistics date to the early 1980s. Over the years the number of registered offenses, the number of court cases, the total number of suspected abusers, and the number of female abusers have all increased roughly fourfold as regards victims ages 0 to 6 years. A fairly stable two thirds of these cases can be characterized as acts of family violence. However, between 1982 and 1993 the percentage of convicted child abuse cases for this victims' age group has oscillated between 15 and 31% with no clear trend. Concerning abuse of children ages 7–14 years, which according to criminal statistics is four times as common as against younger children, the number of registered offenses and the number of female abusers have trebled while the number of court cases and the total number of suspected abusers have roughly doubled. For this age group only one third can be characterized as clear acts of family violence. Furthermore, between 1982 and 1993 the percentage of convictions for child abuse cases for this victims' age group has oscillated between 24 and 43% with a tendency toward the lower relative figure at the end of the period. A summary for both age groups is presented in Table 4-1.

Taken together, criminal statistics show a sharp increase in allegations of child abuse, as well as in the number of court cases and convicted child abusers. In 1982 the number of registered offenses for both age groups was just above 1,000, a figure that 10 years later had more than trebled. Likewise, the number of cases taken to court increased from 427 in 1983 to almost 700 cases 10 years later, and the number of suspected offenders/abusers increased from almost 300 (of which 33 were women) in 1982 to about 750 offenders/abusers 11 years later, of which 133 were females. The increase in reported offenses of child abuse is more likely due to a growth in the awareness of this offense than an actual increase in the number of crimes committed.

Swedish social statistics are basically concerned with state intervention in family life and out-of-home placements. Once again it is pertinent to stress that not all of these cases can be classified as child abuse or neglect. To take a closer look at intervention and placement trends it is appropriate to start with the latest figures available.

The total number of children and young persons for whom care outside the home was in effect at some point during the last year for which statistics is available (1993, regardless of when the placement began) was 16,439 or 8.5 per 1,000 of the population ages 0 to 17 years. These figures include those in both voluntary and compulsory care, and placements were due to a variety of reasons, including child abuse and neglect. For 5,274 of these children and young persons or 2.7 per 1,000 of the population ages 0 to 17 years, the care was initiated in 1993, of which 1,311 children (0.6 per 1,000) were taken into immediate compulsory custody. Of this last category, 824 were placed in compulsory care that year (0.4 per 1000 of the population ages 0 to 17 years).

The rate of compulsory care outside the home initiated in 1993 increased somewhat compared to the previous year and so did the number of voluntary care placements based on an agreement between the parents and social authorities. However voluntary care is often of shorter duration, and roughly a fourth of all initiated voluntary care terminated within 1 month. Only 6% of all initiated compulsory care is terminated within the same length of time (Statistics Sweden, 1994).

A look at the numbers at a given date each year—in the Swedish case, December 31—of children in out-of-home placements makes it possible to discern certain trends. Over a longer time span voluntary care dropped from the 1930s to the late 1970s, from nearly 20 per 1,000 of the population under age 21 years to less than 5 per 1,000 (Gould, 1989, p. 57). This reflects developments under the old, more repressive child welfare legislation, although the figures refer to voluntary measures. This downward trend has been attributed to the reduction in material poverty and the decline of serious illnesses such as tuberculosis, which caused many parents to be unable to look after their children (Johansson, 1980). During the same period the rate of compulsory or forced out-of-home care hovered between 4 and 5 per 1,000 below the age of 18. With the change in legislation in 1982, compulsory care soon dropped considerably (from less than 4 to roughly 2 per 1,000 children below age 18 years), while voluntary care outside the home increased somewhat to about 6 per thousand below age 18 years and hovered around that figure throughout the 1980s. The last figure does not include such preventive measures as the contact family service (which has increased since its inception in 1982). Thus the two trends partly offset each other.

Figures 4-1 and 4-2 show developments between 1982 and 1993 for voluntary and compulsory care, respectively, per 10,000 of the population in the age group below 18 years. Figure 4-1 gives the trend for voluntary care starting with total (ongoing, initiated, and terminated) measures during 1 year (60 per

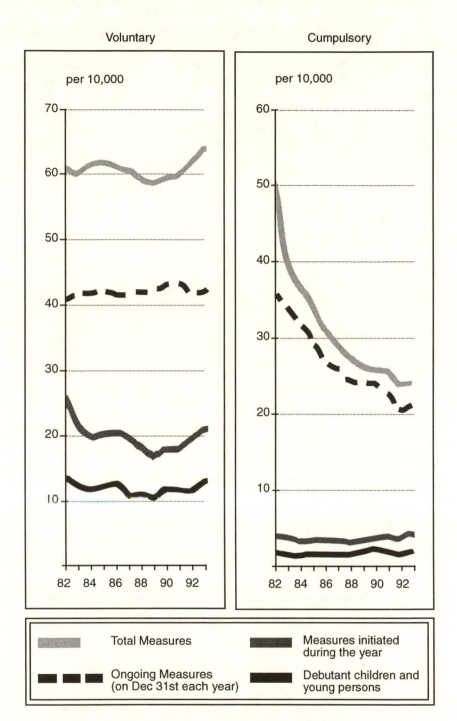

Voluntary

per 10,000

Cumpulsory

per 10,000

Total Measures

Measures initiated during the year

Ongoing Measures (on Dec 31st each year)

Debutant children and young persons

Fig. 4-1. The trend for voluntary care between 1982 and 1993 per 10,000 population below age 18 years.

Fig. 4-2. The trend for compulsory (nonvoluntary) care between 1982 and 1993 per 10,000 population below age 18 years.

117

10,000), followed by ongoing measures on December 31 the previous year (40 per 10,000), measures initiated during the year (20 per 10,000 in 1993), and finally at the bottom debutant children and young persons (just above 10 per 10,000). Figure 4-2 gives similar trends for nonvoluntary care. The latter figures include children taken into custody both due to their own behavior and due to deficiencies in the home environment.

Despite the increase in compulsory care during the most recent years, there is overall a downward trend since the 1980s, reflecting the fact that more cases were terminated than initiated. Thus the total number of children per 1,000 in the population below age 18 years in compulsory care has been decreasing (from 5 to less than 3), but the number of children taken into care each year was fairly constant, or roughly 0.5 per 1,000 in the population below age 18 years. This indicates a decrease in average time of ongoing care. Whether the recent increases will continue and create a true break in the downward trend remains to be seen. The dramatic rise in unemployment in Sweden in the early 1990s has, according to many social observers, created a meaner society and more stress in families, placing children at risk of negative developments.

Figure 4-3 illustrates the trend in total numbers of those in initiated care during the years 1982–1993 for voluntary care, contact families, and compulsory care, while Figure 4-4 gives placement of children by type of care (family or foster care, "own home," and institutional care of various types) (see Table 4-2 for specifications) on December 31, 1993, for voluntary and compulsory care.

Table 4-2 gives absolute figures for voluntary and compulsory care outside the home for the period 1983–1992. No specific reason is given for placement in voluntary care, and the proportion of child abuse cases cannot be exactly specified from this figure although a substantial proportion may be classified

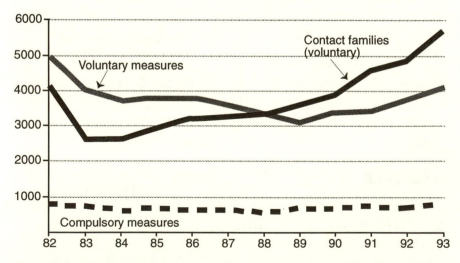

Fig. 4-3. Initiated voluntary and compulsory measures for children from 1982 to 1993 under the Social Service Act. *Source*: Statistics Sweden.

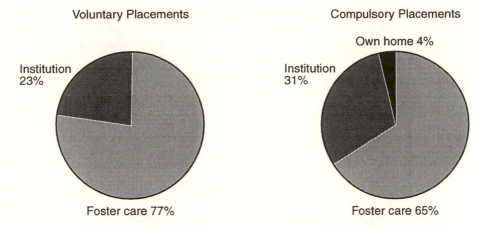

Fig. 4-4. Placements of children December 31, 1993.

as child abuse. Regarding compulsory care, if only those taken into care due to deficiencies in the home environment—the closest one comes to the definition of child abuse—are taken into consideration, the numbers are roughly half the total shown in Figure 4-2.

Not all those taken into immediate compulsory custody due to a deficient home environment are going into out-of-home placements: 391 of 526 cases in 1983 compared to 501 of 681 cases in 1992. The increase in the last couple of years has caused some alarm, which is discussed below. It is not possible to separate Swedish statistics by, for instance, minority status (i.e., immigrant children, ethnic origins, etc.) (Hessle, 1984). However, Table 4-2 reveals that while girls are overrepresented among those taken into immediate compulsory custody, the numbers are equal for boys and girls with regard to those placed in compulsory out-of-home care. Perhaps this reflects a general problem in making cases of sexual abuse, especially of girls, fully convincing (Martens, 1990, 1991).

Table 4-2. Number of Children in Voluntary and Compulsory Care

	1983	1986	1989	1992
Care outside the home (voluntary)	4,038	3,818	3,131	3,735
Immediate compulsory custody due to deficient home environment (total)	526	452	451	681
Boys	248	197	212	334
Girls	278	255	239	347
Compulsory care due to deficient home environment (total)	391	346	402	501
Boys	194	168	208	251
Girls	197	178	194	250

Source: Statistics Sweden.

Since the new social welfare law went into effect in 1982, the average stay in out-of-home placements has varied among different types of placement. The most common type of arrangement is family care, which covers both traditional foster care and what in other countries is known as kinship care or the care by close relatives. In Sweden, however, the notion of kinship care is sometimes applied to care in "own home," which in many cases is a euphemism for the absence of any care. (These cases are almost all teenagers who have been taken into compulsory care due to their own behavior but whose admittance is refused by institutions and family care as well.) Although placements in family care can involve one or several foster children, the use of "big foster homes" has been widely criticized. Finally there is also the fairly rare possibility of residential family care, which is a rather ambitious form of institutional treatment of both parents and children together.

Table 4-3 indicates that the average number of months for those staying in kinship care has been generally constant since the mid-1980s, while the average length of time in foster care, as well as various types of public and private institutional care, has increased somewhat in the early 1990s. Institutional care of various types is of shorter duration than foster care and also is much more expensive.

Does the Specter of a Children's Gulag Still Haunt Sweden?

There are definitely groups of children in Sweden who have not been sufficiently included in the general pattern of economic welfare and material progress despite considerable public efforts in this direction. Over the years the social services have been criticized for paying too little attention to the needs of socially disadvantaged children. Recently children who are maltreated have become an official priority group under a government initiative to improve the situation of vulnerable and disadvantaged children. According to government policy such children and their families need to be supported by a network consisting of both relatives and outside assistance. The welfare state should not strip parents of their responsibility, but should offer individual families a

Table 4-3. Average Stay in Out-of-Home Placement by Type of Placement (in Months)

	1983	1986	1989	1992	1993
Kinship care	5	7	7	8	7
Foster care	24	25	23	27	29
Publicly run children's home	5	5	6	7	8
Privately run children's home	3	9	10	11	10
Children's psychiatric clinic	5	5	4	4	10
Other	10	7	8	9	10
Average	18	18	17	18	20
Special supervisory homes (only "own behavior")	7	10	7	6	10

Source: Statistics Sweden, 1994 Report No. S32 SM9401 and earlier reports.

spectrum of supportive measures and should intervene to protect the children in question. An action program has been drawn up to develop competence within the social services regarding the needs of children in this category. The government has also allocated funds for this purpose. A Public Health Institute as well as a special national evaluation research unit have been set up and the endeavors of nongovernmental organizations are regarded as highly important.

Overall, these initiatives are designed to increase awareness of child abuse on the part of social workers and others who work with children. Special attention has been directed to children in families in which there is an alcohol problem. Stiffer sentences for sexual abuse of children are also being considered. Maltreatment of children is often closely connected to battering or other use of force against women. The government has declared the urgent need to extend efforts to prevent the use of violence against women by means of special initiatives (Socialdepartementet, 1994).

Furthermore a review of the present social welfare legislation proposed to strengthen the rights of children significantly along the lines of the U.N. Convention on the Rights of the Child (SOU, 1994). This also reflects a concern that the existing laws have emphasized the right to parental access to parents' biological children, while abandoned and abused children have become "swinging door children," moving back and forth between their parent's home and a multitude of out-of-home placements. Recently a child's right to grow up under stable and secure conditions with adults who show affection has been more thoroughly stressed. Still, adoption is not an issue and actually not an option in the Swedish child welfare discourse, which reflects the strength of the earlier emphasis on parental bonding and access to children placed out of home.

In the current review of the present social welfare legislation, some specific proposals have been put forward that most likely will become part of a new law. For instance, concerning out-of-home placement, the age of consent of the child will probably be lowered from 15 to 12 years. In addition, the mandatory reporters of child abuse category will be expanded to include such employees of public welfare authorities as janitors and secretarial office workers, as well as those employed in private but government-subsidized welfare services. By this the law comes closer to the ambition that any person who discovers that a child is being maltreated at home or outside the home should report this to the municipal social welfare committee.

Toward a Deresidualization of Swedish Social Welfare Policy?

Children who suffer abuse or neglect require protection. Notwithstanding legislation that heavily emphasizes the obligation of society-at-large to intervene when it is feared that a child is suffering in some way, children may be exposed to carefully guarded secret acts of cruelty. In recent years some steps have been taken to encourage a more profound understanding of these problems among professionals working in the field and laypeople responsible for decisions in these cases. The upcoming revision of the present social welfare legislation will most likely promote this approach and at least partially diminish the earlier emphasis on parental access to children taken into custody.

The increase in recent years in the number of children taken into voluntary custody has caused some alarm. So has a 60% increase in the number of calls to the Children's Help Telephone. These disturbing signs of social pathology have been attributed mainly to the major social problems that hit Sweden in the early 1990s: unemployment on a scale unknown since the Great Depression and an increase in the number of families living under stressful financial conditions. As long as no major changes are in sight, these overarching social problems will continue to plague all those involved in managing child welfare services. Both individuals and institutions will have to come to terms with decreasing resources at the same time that problems such as child abuse will most likely grow. Whatever the changes in legislation and administrative practice, there are no obvious, simple solutions to these challenges.

Overall the voluntary approach to social problems will definitely survive and remain at the center stage. Although the universal welfare policy has been much debated, most trends point toward a continuation of the traditional Swedish approach — in spite of continuing financial difficulties for the national state as well as for local authorities. Thus the deresidualization of Swedish social policy will continue (Olsson Hort, 1996). Coercive actions against families will continue to be a marginal phenomenon in social work practice. Nevertheless, such measures — in particular when children are involved — will remain highly visible and open to much criticism. A strengthening of the rights of children — to be protected by the state, courts, law enforcement and social welfare agencies, hospitals, child day care centers and schools, as well as by laypeople and their organizations in civil society — may lead to a renewal of the state-snatches-children accusation.

Notes

Apart from the members of the working group, and in particular the editor of this volume, the author thanks Christina Andersson, Gunilla Hedengren, Tord Jacobson, Karin Rosell, and Ulla Wittrock for comments and most helpful assistance in the preparation of this chapter. I bear responsibility for any remaining errors.

1. This is not to say that poverty — or at least economically weak and vulnerable social categories — have completely disappeared in Sweden. Despite the existence of a broad and fairly generous social security system, a considerable number of (particularly young) persons are periodically relying on a means-tested social assistance system as a last resort of support (see Salonen, 1993).

References

Andersson, G. (1991). *Socialt arbete med små barn*. Lund: Studentlitteratur.
Andersson, G. (1992). Social Workers and Child Welfare. *British Journal of Social Work, 22*(3), 253–269.

Andersson, G. (1993). Support and relief: The Swedish contact person and contact family program. *Scandinavian Journal of Social Welfare, 2,* 54–62.

Barth, R. (1991). Sweden's contact family program. *Public Welfare, 49*(3), 36–46.

Barth, R. (1992). Child welfare services in the United States and Sweden: Different assumptions, laws and outcomes. *Scandinavian Journal of Social Welfare, 1*(1), 36–42.

Boethius, M., & Kjellander-Ahlberg, B. (1982). *Barnkunskap.* Stockholm: Sparfrämjandet.

BRIS. (1991). *BRIS—Children's rights in society* [Mimeo]. Stockholm: Barnens Rätt i Samhället (BRIS).

Claezon, I. (1987). *Bättre beslut—en studie av socialsekreterarenas handläggning av omhändertaganden av barn.* Unpublished doctoral dissertation, Institutionen för socialt arbete Umeå, Sweden.

Gould, A. (1988). *Control and conflict in welfare policy—The Swedish experience.* London: Longman.

Hallberg, M., & Rigné, E. M. (1994). Child sexual abuse—A study of controversy and construction. *Acta Sociologica, 37*(2), 141–163.

Hessle, S. (1984). "Omhändertag ande av invandrarbarn." In H. Soyan (Ed.), *Socialtarbete och invandrare.* Malmö: Liber.

Johansson, S. (1980). *Barnens välfärd—Hur ser den ut och hur mäter vi den?* [Mimeo]. Stockholm: Swedish Institute for Social Research.

Key, E. (1900). *Barnens århundrade.* Stockholm: Bonniers. (English edition 1909)

Lundström, T. (1992). *Tvångsomhändertagande av barn* (Rep. No. 61, dissertation). Stockholm: Stockholm University, School of Social Work.

Martens, P. (1990). *Sexualbrott mot barn—de misstänkta barnen.* Stockholm: BRÅ.

Martens, P. (1991). *Sexualbrott mot barn—de misstänkta förövarna.* Stockholm: BRÅ.

Ohrlander, K. (1992). *I barnens och nationens intresse—socialliberal reforpolitik 1903–1930.* Stockholm: Almqvist & Wiksell International.

Olsson, S. E. (1993). *Social policy and welfare state in Sweden* (2nd ed.). Lund, Sweden: Arkiv.

Olsson, S. E., & Spånt, R. (1991). *Children in the welfare state: Current problems and policies in Sweden* (Innocenti Occasional Papers, EPR No. 22). Florence: UNICEF/ICDC.

Olsson Hort, S. E. (1996). Children in the welfare state: Policy and practice in Sweden. In A. G. Cornia & S. Danziger (Eds.), *Child poverty and depravation in industrialized countries.* Oxford, England: Oxford University Press.

Olsson Hort, S. E., & McMurphy, S. (1995). Social work in the institutional welfare state. In D. Elliott, M. Nayades, & T. Watts (Eds.), *International handbook of social work theory and practice.* Westport, CT: Greenwood Press.

Salonen, T. (1993). *Margins of welfare—A study of modern functions of social assistance.* Torna Hällestad, Sweden: Hällestad Press.

Sandin, B. (1986). *Hemmet, gatan, fabriken eller skolan* [The family, the street, the factory or the school] (Doctoral dissertation). Lund, Sweden: Arkiv.

Socialdepartementet. 1994. *National programme of action for the survival, protection and development of the child.* Stockholm: Ministry of Social Affairs.

SOU. (1994). *Förslag till ny socialtjänstlag.* Stockholm: Socialdepartementet.

Statistics Sweden. (1994). *Insatser för barn och unga 1993.* Stockholm: Statistiska centralbyrån (and earlier editions).

Sundelin, W. M. (1991). *Utveckling och överlevnad—en studie av barn i psykosociala riskmiljöer*. Unpublished doctoral dissertation, Stockholms unviersitet, Pedagogiska institutionen.

Sundelin, W. M. (1993). Development and survival: A study of children at risk living in adverse psychosocial milieu. *Child Abuse and Neglect, 18*(9), 715–723.

Sundell, K., Lundström, U., Sjöberg, E., & Wettergren, L. (1992). *Se till mig som liten är — en undersökning av socialtjänstens samverkan kring utsatta förskolebarn*. Stockholm: Socialförvaltningen (FoU-Byrån).

Svärd, H. (1992). *Mångenstädes svårt vanartade . . . — Om problem med det uppväxande släktet*. Dala Floda: Zenon.

Therborn, G. (1993). The politics of childhood: The rights of children in modern times. In F. Castles et al. (Eds.), *Families of nations — Patterns of public policy in western democracies*. Aldershot, England: Dartmouth.

Titmuss, R. (1974). *Social policy*. (B. Abel-Smith & K. Titmuss, Eds.). London: Allen and Unwin.

5

Denmark

Voluntary Placements as a Family Support

VITA L. BERING PRUZAN

Child Abuse

Legal Context

In Denmark a well-known children's doctor, Svend Heinild, deserves to be mentioned as the person most responsible for bringing the concept of "child abuse" to public attention in the 1960s. Dr. Heinild's efforts were inspired by the influential work of the American children's doctor Henry Kempe.

In the decades that followed, the term *child abuse* has been discussed and received many nuances. Evident examples of child abuse such as violence against children and sexual abuse are identified as criminal acts in the penal code. In addition to these criminal offenses, a topic that has aroused much debate from time to time has been the parental right to inflict corporal punishment (*revselsesret*), reflecting a tradition that is deeply integrated in the Danish child-rearing culture. "Child abuse/neglect has always existed and will always exist as long as the tradition for punishment of children is part of our culture" (Merrick, 1984).

The legal basis for a parental right to inflict corporal punishment on children dates to the Danish Law codex of 1683 (section 6-5-5). This right is still in existence, and the courts of justice define the borderline between legal punishment and illegal violence at a given time. The right of corporal punishment existed in schools and in institutions until 1967.

Through decisions over the last decades the courts have restricted the range of parental rights. The question of doing away with the right of parents to punish their children has been a matter of debate on several occasions during the last decades. Abolition of this right in the other Scandinavian countries (Sweden in 1979, Finland in 1983, and Norway in 1987) of course caused debate in Denmark.

The results of several opinion polls indicate that the majority of people are against abolition of the right of parents to inflict corporal punishment on their children. This is an indication of the traditional culture, under which punishment is still considered a normal part of bringing up children. The opposition is also based on an expressed fear that abolition of this right will mean that society can interfere too much in the private life of the family.

The Children's Commission was established by the government in 1975 to examine and illuminate the conditions of children growing up in Denmark. The commission's report (Børnekommissionens betænkning, 1981) expressed reluctance to recommend the abolition of corporal punishment, although it considered corporal punishment an inappropriate form of discipline for children. There is a general reluctance to criminalize parental acts as they are not covered by the penal code, especially parental acts of temper.

Discussion of the parental right to inflict corporal punishment on children is again on the agenda in Denmark. As an advocate of abolishing this right explains, the likelihood that parents will not use corporal punishment on their children is greater if this is not allowed compared to a situation where they are unsure about how far they can go when punishing their children (Vestergaard, 1993, p. 46). The result of a recent (1995) opinion poll, however, suggests that corporal punishment is not likely to be done away with in the immediate future since about half of the population still finds it an acceptable method of disciplining children.

Violent abuse of children is of course illegal. As judicial practice is restricting the area of legal "parental violence," the area of violence considered a crime under the penal code is widening. Since criminal statistics do not distinguish categories of victims or whether the crime is committed in the family or not, statistical data on parental violence are not registered.

An area of abuse included in the penal code is child sexual abuse. Within the last 20–25 years this problem has been a focal point of concern. The problem was first called to public attention by psychologists and psychiatrists who were in search of methods to handle treatment of sexual abuse victims. The extent of the problem has been estimated in a survey by Leth and Stenvig (1988), which included a demographically representative sample of individuals ranging in age from 18 to 50 years. (The participation rate was 66%.) The survey data were analyzed with the explicit goal of finding how many of the participants interviewed had been victims of sexual abuse as defined in the penal code. The findings revealed that 8% of the population had been exposed as children to criminal (penal code) sexual abuse from adults and 2.5% had been exposed to incest as defined by the penal code.

Social Policy Context

Social policy in Denmark is designed to facilitate a voluntary, family-oriented approach to the problem of child abuse. One of the basic principles of the Social Welfare Act of 1976 recognizes that family problems should be regarded — and worked on — as a whole. According to this approach problems of children and adolescents should not be considered apart from the family unit.

When these problems arise and call for public intervention, efforts should be made in cooperation with parents and others and should be considered as an offer of help to child and parents.

Seen from technical-legal and systematic viewpoints the Social Welfare Act was a continuation of legislation that had been evolving since 1958. The main line of legislative reform was directed at replacing the distinction between preventive child care and placement outside the home with the concepts of voluntary and involuntary (or forced) placement as the focal points for legal protection. The special legal safeguards for placement outside the home set forth in previous legislation were replaced under the 1976 act by legal safeguards for forcible placements.

However the conditions for forcible placements were defined somewhat loosely. The 1976 law states that a decision to place a child outside the child's home without consent from the person who has custody could only be taken when placement was undoubtedly necessary taking into account the "well-being" of the child or the adolescent because

1. The child or the adolescent had demonstrated grave difficulties in adjusting to everyday life, to school, or to society in general, and the parents could not cope with the child rearing.
2. The child or the adolescent was living under circumstances that caused mental or physical health or development to suffer seriously, or there was a danger of such suffering.
3. The parents did not ensure that the child or adolescent received the necessary mental care or other necessary treatment for mental or physical ailments.

But what constitutes the state of well-being? Critics of this concept said it was not only unclear, but from the point of view of language, indefinable. This was more than a matter of quibbling over language; the essential concern was that conditions for so radical a step as forcible placement outside the home should clearly be stated in the law and not hidden in a "magical formula" such as "undoubtedly necessary taking into account the well-being of the child or the adolescent."

In response to this concern, among other reasons, the government established an Expert Committee to clarify the conditions for involuntary placement of children and legal protections for families. Based on the Report of the Expert Committee (*On the Legal Framework for Efforts to Support Children and Adolescents*; Betænkning No. 1212, 1990) extensive amendments to the Social Welfare Act (Law No. 501 of June 24, 1992) were implemented in 1993. These amendments stipulate that the following conditions must be met before steps may be taken to remove a child or an adolescent from their home — even if the parents, the adolescent, or both objects: There has to be an obvious risk of serious harm to the health or development of the child or the adolescent. By using the terms *obvious risk* and *health or development* it is indicated that consideration must be taken of both the present condition of the child or adolescent and future conditions while growing up. This means that intervention can take place before serious harm has occurred.

Thus in 1993 the criterion of well-being was replaced by that of obvious risk of serious harm to the health or development of the child or adolescent. This new criterion is supplemented by an exhaustive numeration of the circumstances relating to the parents, the child, or both that have to be met before a forced placement can be imposed. These circumstances can involve either neglect on the part of the parents or harmful behavior by the child or adolescent.

Parents' neglect is reflected in the law as:

1. Insufficient care or treatment of the child or the adolescent
2. Violence or other serious assaults

Children's or adolescents' problems are defined as:

1. Abuse, criminal behavior, or other serious social problems
2. Other behavioral or adjustment difficulties

The term *neglect* is not used in the law. It is a normative term that can be defined broadly as not living up to one's obligation to care for children, an obligation that varies by time and place (Gelles, 1987). In recent years, several attempts have been made to define neglect operationally (Merrick, 1984; Michelsen, Christensen, Ovelund, Merrick, & Weicher, 1985). Jørgensen and Nissen (1990) suggest that the term is useful when describing circumstances under which the child or adolescent is threatened because unlike maltreatment and violence, for example, neglect involves a range of behaviors that cover unintentional actions and negligence. However the authors conclude that the term needs to be defined more precisely, a task that Christensen (1992) has undertaken in her study analyzing types and rates of neglect/abuse among children 0–3 years old in Denmark. One aim of this study was to get a valid picture of how many Danish children are victims of child abuse/neglect. The study, which achieved an 83% participation rate, involves a survey of all the families being served by child care nurses in Denmark; the survey made neglect operational according to four categories of active and passive behavior:

1. active physical neglect/abuse when a child is hurt by willful actions by an adult,
2. passive physical neglect/abuse when a child is exposed to serious negligence by an adult,
3. active emotional neglect/abuse when a child constantly is exposed to verbal offences, confinement, constant threats and rejection, and
4. passive emotional neglect/abuse when a child is exposed to neglect/abuse or understimulation because of parents' lack of ability to offer security, care and affection, e.g. due to mental illness, drug abuse (alcohol, medicine, narcotics), social problems, etc. (Christensen, 1992, p. 17).

The four categories of neglect/abuse are further specified so that they constitute a number of observable indications or symptoms that child care nurses are able to note in their regular contact with the families. The child care nurses were not asked to make global judgments about how many children they think are exposed to neglect/abuse, but to consider the circumstances of each child in light of a number of specific indicators that could be possible signs of neglect/abuse. The concrete representation of these indicators draws on the definitions of abuse/neglect formulated in *The Encyclopedia of Child Abuse* (Clark & Clark, 1989). The indicators used in each of the four categories are active physical neglect/abuse, passive physical neglect/abuse, active emotional neglect/abuse, and passive emotional neglect/abuse.

Active physical neglect/abuse is characterized as a parent's nonaccidental actions in which injury is actively inflicted on a child. Most often injuries result in marks or other such signs as, for example, broken bones, injuries of soft body tissues, burns, bruises, or hemorrhages under the hard membrane of the brain. Child care nurses were asked to note any of eight specific indicators (Christensen, 1992):

1. Broken arms, legs, ribs, and so on
2. Bruises on body, limbs, face
3. Burns (heat source, cigarettes, scalding)
4. Marks from physical punishment (seat, cheeks, limbs)
5. Marks from human bites
6. Scratches or abrasions near mouth, lips, gums, eyes
7. Scratches or abrasions on outer genitals
8. Strong reddening and irritation around mouth or outer genitalia. (p. 37)

Passive physical neglect/abuse is characterized as the lack of satisfaction of physical needs, which may endanger the child's health. The specific observable indicators were as follows:

1. The child is left to himself without any adult supervision for certain periods of time (1–2 hours or more).
2. The child is repeatedly not picked up at the kindergarten or day care.
3. The child has been left alone by parents for periods of up to several days.
4. The child suffers from malnutrition due to poorly balanced diet, not enough food, or too irregular meals.
5. The child suffers from malnutrition because of too much of the wrong food.
6. The child fails to receive necessary visits to doctors when sick or when preventive health examinations should take place.
7. The child is unusually limp or tired.
8. The child looks uncared for, untidy, neglected, or dirty.
9. The child is not dressed suitably considering the time of the year or the weather. (p. 38)

Active emotional neglect/abuse is characterized by a child being exposed to harmful nonphysical actions by a parent, which were operationally defined as follows:

1. The child is periodically confined.
2. The child is threatened with violence/beating.
3. The child is threatened with loss of affection or important relations.

4. The child is spoken to or spoken about in an offensive manner (i.e., called wicked, stupid, ugly, impossible, a child nobody likes).
5. Periodically parents act openly hostile toward the needs of the child (regard the child as an enemy, as someone who opposes the parents).
6. The child is periodically actively ignored by the parents. They are not willing to listen or talk to the child.
7. The child is prevented from being together with other children, adults, or both.
8. The child is taken care of by a large number of different adults.
9. The child is mostly taken care of by nonadult big brothers or sisters. (p. 38)

Passive emotional neglect/abuse is characterized by the child being exposed to serious emotional harm as a result of the parents' inability to offer security, care, and affection. This form of negligence involves risk of developmental damages. The specific indicators were

1. The child has observed physical maltreatment of its mother or other forms of violence at home.
2. The child has often been taken care of by adults who are under the influence of alcohol and drugs.
3. The everyday life of the child is unpredictable.
4. The child's parents have only a limited capability of reacting to the child's emotions. Primarily, they react to their own emotions.
5. The child's parents have only a limited capability of understanding the child's physical signals concerning pleasures/displeasures and limits.
6. The child is often rejected emotionally by the parents. (p. 39)

(The last three indicators were not as concrete as most of the others and required somewhat more professional judgment by the child care nurse.)

This specification of active and passive behaviors that are indicative of neglect/abuse offers a set of objective criteria to determine whether there is an obvious risk of serious harm to young children. They also help to clarify the conditions for involuntary out-of-home placement of children set forth in the 1993 amendments to the Social Welfare Act. According to these criteria set forth by Christensen (1992), the survey of families served by child care nurses found that at least 4% of Danish children from 0–1 years old are exposed to some form of neglect/abuse.

How Reports and Investigations Are Made

According to the Social Welfare Act of 1992 the local authorities are responsible for the situation of children and adolescents in their community. Section 28 of the law states:

> The local authority may offer single persons and families free day-to-day guidance and is *obliged* through field-work to direct such efforts *to all persons who can be considered to be in need hereof.*

Specifically in regard to children and adolescents, section 32 of the law notes:

The local authority supervises the living conditions of children and adolescents under the age of 18 years, and it is an obligation for the authority to offer parents guidance when a child or adolescent has problems with its surroundings or in other ways is living under unsatisfactory conditions.

According to section 20 of the Social Welfare Act it is a duty of every citizen to notify the local authorities if a child or young person under the age of 18 years is "subject to neglect or humiliating treatment or lives under conditions that will endanger its health or development." Besides this, there exists a special duty for public employees to report if in the course of professional duties they notice any conditions that could indicate need for public action.

If a child is suspected of being in special need of support, the municipal council is obliged to investigate the child's circumstances and determine whether intervention is required and, if so, what kind of intervention. This includes notification of the police. In daily practice, however, investigations of cases are conducted by caseworkers from the administrative departments of social affairs. The course of an investigation usually begins with the receipt of a report of critical signals concerning a child. This report will often come from a child care nurse, a doctor, day care personnel, or a psychologist — seldom from the general public. Also parents or the children themselves could approach the administrative department.

The caseworker is the central person in the local administration who serves cases concerning children and families. The caseworker is responsible — on behalf of the local authority — for looking thoroughly into the case and coordinating activities. If a decision about an investigation is reached, it is mandatory that the person who has custody over the child (as well as the child if he or she is an adolescent at least 15 years old) participate in the decision-making process and fully understand how and why the decison was reached.

The result of the investigation must be a reasoned position on whether there are sufficient grounds to initiate further actions and, if so, which steps to take. There is a range of alternatives involving family services, supports, and out-of-home placements. These measures from Section 33 of the Social Welfare Act include

1. Providing consultative assistance with regard to the situation of the child or adolescent, including that the child or adolescent attend a day care institution, youth club, place of education, or the like
2. Providing practical, pedagogical, or other assistance in the home
3. Providing family treatment or similar support
4. Establishing residential institutional care for the holder of parental custody, the child or the adolescent, and other family members
5. Establishing a relief scheme
6. Designating a personal adviser for the child or adolescent
7. Providing financial support for costs related to measures listed in items 1–5 should the holder of parental custody not have the necessary means
8. Providing financial support for the cost of avoiding placement out of home, the bringing forward of a return to the home, or for support to make a sub-

stantial contribution to stable contact between parents and children while one or more children are placed out of home

9. Providing financial support for a boarding or continuation school should the holder of parental custody not have sufficient means

10. Placing the child or adolescent outside the home at a residential institution, with a foster family, or at another approved location considered suitable to meet the special needs of the child

These measures can be offered individually or in combination. Although the list does not represent any order of priority, the act stipulates that helping the child or adolescent to remain in the home is an important objective of public intervention. This does not imply that every alternative within the home must be tried before placement even though the placement will always entail greater dislocation for the child or the adolescent than the other measures. It is important from the outset to choose the measure that is likely to be most effective in solving the problems. When out-of-home placement is deemed most appropriate, the family must be offered this alternative.

Furthermore the act prescribes that the measures must be terminated when their objective has been fulfilled or when the measures are no longer considered to serve any purpose, but at the latest when the adolescent reaches the age of 18 years. With the consent of the adolescent, supports such as a personal adviser or placement in a residential institution may continue until the adolescent reaches the age of 20 years.

When an investigation results in the recommendation for an out-of-home placement, the Social Welfare Act (as amended in 1992) requires that a detailed plan be developed prior to any placement. The four central components of the plan involve

1. A description of what the placement is expected to achieve
2. The expected duration of the stay
3. A description of the child's education, care, and other circumstances
4. Measures to support the family during the placement

This planning requirement emerged in response to criticism of earlier practice when placements were often considered as an end of the case and no more efforts were put into supporting the family after a child was placed out of home. The placement plan not only provides parents an understanding of what is to be achieved and the anticipated time frame, it also affirms the social administration's continuous responsibility for the case in question.

Even though a parent, an adolescent who is 15 years old or more, or both may oppose placement decisions, it is possible to initiate these measures on an involuntary basis. Decisions on forcible measures are made by the Child and Adolescent Committee, which consists of five members, of which three are chosen from the local authority council, a group of elected officials who represent the lay element, the fourth member is a judge, and the fifth a pedagogical-psychological professional.

The question of what type of public body should have the authority to make decisions on forcible placements was thoroughly discussed during the

1992 amendments to the Social Welfare Act. The critical issue was whether authority for involuntary placements should remain in a communal body such as the elected children's board or should be placed in a body that more resembled a law court. The decision for this authority to remain in the local elected body was based inter alia on the premise that a placement should not be considered as a goal in itself but as part of a process that includes past, present, and future initiatives for the family. The policy makers thought that this process would be better managed and continuity more assured by a Children and Adolescent Committee than a legal court. Furthermore it was considered potentially harmful to have a procedural form in which parents and children could be looked at — and could look at each other — as opposing parties, particularly since the larger objective of public intervention is to assist the family as an entity. A pedagogical-psychological consultant and a judge were included in the committee, the latter to ensure a high degree of legal security in connection with forcible placements. The strong influence of the majority of lay members on these local committees suggests that practices will differ throughout the country. The seriousness of a forcible placement is emphasized by the fact that normally every decision requiring forcible placement has to be reconsidered by the committee every year.

Placement Trends

To make sound comparisons between Denmark and other countries with respect to the actual number of children and adolescents that are placed outside their homes, it is necessary to describe the Danish statistics on placements. In a Nordic context, on first sight Denmark appears to have a much higher rate of out-of-home placements than other Scandinavian countries (except Iceland). It is necessary to take a closer look at the figures, however, to determine the extent to which out-of-home placement rates really differ and what these figures represent in each country.

There is different legislation concerning reporting and out-of-home placement arrangements among the Nordic countries, which most people otherwise consider to have similar cultures. From one country to another, for example, legislative variations create alternative definitions of what constitute out-of-home placements (Grinde, 1989, 1993). In Denmark these placements take the following forms:

- Residential institutions (group homes, treatment homes, institutions for the mentally and physically handicapped, youth homes, etc.)
- Private family
- Sociopedagogical community and the like
- Boarding school and the like
- Own room
- Hospital or on a ship

The costs of placements in residential institutions vary considerably depending on the groups and purposes being served, as well as the region of the country.

For a municipality in the Copenhagen area, the estimated monthly costs range from D.Kr. 66,000 ($11,000) in treatment homes, D.Kr. 53,000 ($8,800) in institutions for the handicapped, D.Kr. 52,000 ($8,600) in youth homes, D.Kr. 38,000 ($6,300) in school homes, and D.Kr. 35,000 ($5,800) in group homes. The costs in other placement categories tend to be lower, for example, D.Kr. 17,000 ($2,800) in private family settings, D.Kr. 34,000 ($5,700) in a sociopedagogical community, D.Kr. 9,000 ($1,500) in boarding school, D.Kr. 6,000 ($1,000) for a room for an adolescent, and D.Kr. 32,000 ($5,300) for placement on a ship.

As noted above, the Danish system of out-of-home placements includes the financing of stays in boarding, youth, or continuation schools and lodging for adolescents to live independently away from their parents. These habitations constitute about 20% of all living arrangements that are registered in Denmark as out-of-home placements. In the other Nordic countries such living arrangements are financed under other types of legislation and are not included in the statistics on placements out of home (Andersen, 1989).

In addition to alternative types of living arrangements, another difference in the way countries operationally define their placement statistics concerns the children who are included in the category of "children and adolescents placed out of home." Since 1980 Danish statistics on out-of-home placements include all placements of physically and mentally handicapped children in specialized institutions. In 1993 the number of placements in institutions for handicapped children amounted to one quarter of all the out-of-home placements in residential institutions.

Regarding the category of placement with a "private family," the Danish statistics include placements both with relatives such as grandparents, if the foster family is paid by the public authorities, and with a family to which the child or adolescent is not related. The data on placements do not distinguish between kinship care and care by nonrelated families. Children and adolescents who are placed with a family that does not receive a grant from the public authorities are not included in the statistics on out-of-home placements. According to Christoffersen's (1988) analysis, almost 20% of all children in publicly subsidized out-of-home care with private families in Denmark live with a family to whom they are related — an arrangement referred to as kinship foster care, which is becoming the predominant form of out-of-home placements in the United States.

As noted above, various living arrangements are included in the statistics on out-of-home placements in the Danish system. These arrangements have not remained static. Indeed, since the 1960s, several features of this system have undergone significant change. Christoffersen (1993) describes three important trends in out-of-home placements that have evolved over the last few decades.

First, the rate of forcible placements — that is placement without parents' consent — declined from more than a third of all placements in 1965 to about 6% in 1992 (see Fig. 5-1). (Over this period neither out-of-home placements nor family reunifications that occurred against the wishes of adolescents were

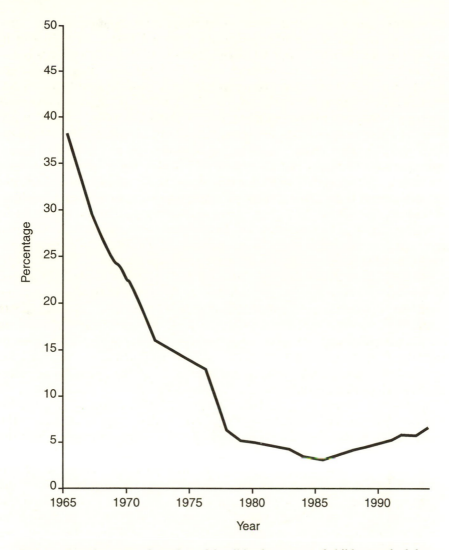

Fig. 5-1. Development of number of forcible placements of children and adolescents as percentages of all out-of-home placements calculated on a specific day of the year, 1965–1994. Preliminary calculations of The Danish National Institution of Statistics are used for the year 1994. *Source:* Danmarks Statistik in Christoffersen, 1993, p. 14.

considered to be forcible placements in a legal sense.) This significant reduction in involuntary placements came as a result of the Child Care Acts of 1958, 1961, and 1964 on which the Social Welfare Act is based. This stream of legislation advanced the basic principle that assistance to children and adolescents should be carried out — as an offer of help rather than an imposition of public authority — in collaboration with their parents (Grønhøj & Pruzan, 1974).

Another noticeable development is that the proportion of placements with private families has grown dramatically since the mid-1970s. As illustrated in Figure 5-2, between 1950 and 1992 the number of children and adolescents placed in family care increased from about 16% to more than 40% of all out-of-home placements. Legislation in 1958 and 1964 as well as the Social Welfare Act (1976) and its amendments up to 1984 contained more or less explicit requirements to favor family care over placement in residential institutions. The data in Figure 5-2 suggest that administrative practice first changed in response to these requirements in the beginning of the 1970s. As noted above the costs of family care are considerably lower than those of residential placements. Between 1980 and 1992 the percentage of placements in private families increased by about 7% as placements in residential institutions de-

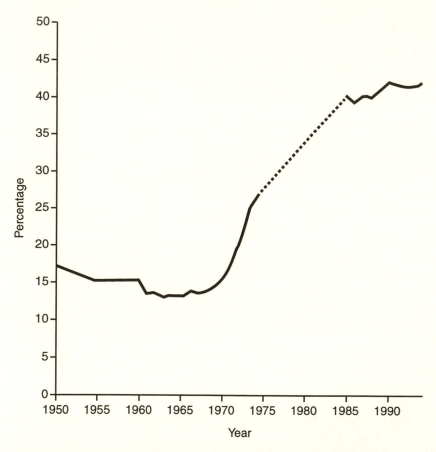

Fig. 5-2. Number of children and adolescents placed in private families as percentages of all out-of-home placements calculated on a specific day of the year, 1950–1994. Figures for the period 1976–1984 are excluded due to uncertainty of methods of calculation. *Source:* Danmarks Statistik in Christoffersen, 1993, p. 16.

Table 5-1. Type of Placement, Rate per 1,000 Children, 0–19 Years Old

Placement	1980	1983	1986	1989	1992
Private family	4.01	4.08	4.69	4.74	4.45
Residential institution	4.00	3.24	3.26	3.04	2.64
Boarding school and the like	2.61	1.94	2.43	2.12	2.20
Own room and the like	0.84	0.79	1.26	1.22	1.22
Total	11.46	10.05	11.64	11.12	10.51

Source: Annual Statistical Series from the Central Statistical Office of Denmark (1994).

clined by more than 10%. As noted in Table 5-1, during that period the overall rate of out-of-home placements declined from 11.5 to 10.5 per 1,000 children.

Finally, between 1960 and 1991 there was a change in the age composition of children and adolescents placed outside their homes. In 1960 0–6 year olds constituted about 20% of placements; now they only constitute about 10% of placements (see Fig. 5-3). During the same period the percentage of 15–17 year olds increased from about 33% to almost 50% of all placements. (These noticeable differences in age composition of placements cannot be explained by differences between small and large birth cohorts).

Current Issues and Directions

Forcible Placements

It is a characteristic feature of the Danish system that there are very few forcible out-of-home placements. Only about 5% of out-of-home placements of children and adolescents are involuntary. As stated above, one of the main principles of legislation in this field is that public support and protection of children and adolescents should take place in cooperation with the parents. Yet when the Social Welfare was being revised in 1992 one of the criticisms raised was that the requirements for parental consent were too vague. Some observers thought these requirements established a "gray zone" in which parental consent did not constitute a genuine willing agreement, but rather voluntary consent given under the threat of force (Andersen, 1989; Betaenkning No. 1212, 1990).

In contrast to professionals' concerns that sometimes voluntary parental consent might be subtly coerced, others are apprehensive that the law—and practice—express a too one-sided support of parents' interests at the expense of children. This concern is fueled by practice that has resulted in many "swinging door children" who move back and forth between multiple placements and their home.

Ertmann (1994) describes how research on out-of-home placements seems to be rooted in two contradictory attitudes on how to intervene when parents let down their children. One attitude emphasizes the child's right to grow up in stable and secure conditions with parental figures who show affection to the child even though they may not be the natural parents. The other research

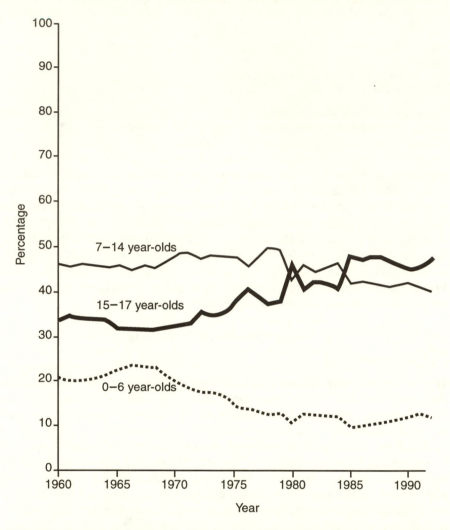

Fig. 5-3. Age composition of 0–17-year-old children and adolescents placed out of home. The numbers are for 0–6 year olds, 7–14 year olds, and 15–17 year olds as percentages of all 0–17 year olds place out of home, 1960–1991. Due to varying numbers of children born in different years, some general changes of the relative age composition between 0–6 year olds and 15–17 year olds have occurred. Therefore the rise in 1986–1991 of the number of 0–6 year olds in placement as compared to the number of all 0–17 year olds in placement is due to the rise in the number of 0–6 year olds in that period. *Source:* Danmarks Statistik in Christoffersen, 1993, p. 17.

tradition focuses on the relation between child and parents, emphasizing that a child's natural ties with parents never can be substituted. Danish legislation and practice are based in principle on this approach, which supports the relation between child and parents, including the period during out-of-home placement.

Continuity

The importance of insuring the continuous relation between children and parents is expressed in the work of the Committee on the Legal Framework for Efforts to Support Children and Adolescents, which drafted the 1992 law. In the committee's deliberations, continuity is defined as "continual belonging together" and reference is made to those circumstances that should be considered essential for healthy development of the personality. Continuity involves external conditions, especially stability in contact and attachment relations. As noted in the White Paper, *Legal Framework for Efforts to Support Children and Adolescents* (Bataenkning No. 1212, 1990) these conditions support the internal developmental aspect of continuity, which contributes to the child's formation of an identity. In efforts to promote continuity the Social Welfare Act emphasizes the need to maintain connections between parents and children during out-of-home placement.

A number of studies document the importance of continuing relations between children and parents after out-of-home placement. Christoffersen's (1993) investigation into the course of life of children who were placed out of home reveals a connection between adolescents' vulnerability as adults and a severed relationship with parents. The study also shows that a higher proportion of the children and adolescents placed in family care experienced more limited contact with their parents during the period of placement than children in a residential institution.

Ertmann's (1994) research on forcibly removed children and adolescents in Copenhagen in 1990 indicates that there were often extensive restrictions on parents' contact with their children placed out of home (before the 1992 amendments to the Social Welfare Act). The author found that parents seem to experience restrictions of their right to contact their children as being more radical and more offensive than the actual forcible removal of their children.

The 1992 amendments set out in more detail than before the rules for maintaining relations between parents and children. Among other things, the law is explicit in emphasizing that the authorities have an active obligation to ensure that relations between parents and children are maintained during the period of placement and that family rights in this area are respected. Family rights to continuous relations include the right to mutual visits and the right to contact by letter and telephone. In certain instances, however, the local authority can decide to regulate and even to terminate relations between children and parents. A decision that restricts parent-child visits to less than once every month is comparable to a decision of termination. Such decisions may only be taken by the Child and Adolescent Committee.

As further safeguards to family rights in the placement process the revised legislation also includes a series of procedures that involve consultation with parents and children. Before a decison is taken to make an out-of-home placement, whether voluntary or forcible, the authorities are required to prepare an action program that describes the aim of the placement, its expected duration, and special circumstances connected to the case in question. An important feature of the action program involves the procedural requirements for informed consent that must be met if placement is to be carried out voluntarily. The requirement was introduced on the assumption that informed consent will make parents feel more bound by their agreement and therefore more motivated to cooperate.

The law also requires that children be involved in the placement process. Irrespective of age, the child's attitude toward the action program must be taken into consideration. This means that the child or adolescent must be informed of what measures are planned for the family. All reports on investigations and recommendations of forcible placement, therefore, must include details from the standpoint of the child or adolescent with regard to any measures planned.

The requirement to incorporate the views of children takes into consideration the age and maturity of the child. Those who have reached the age of 12 years have a mandatory entitlement to be heard, which means that an interview must be held with the child prior to any decision on the initiation of measures. Although children this age must always be offered an interview, they have the right to decide whether to accept the offer or not. Children under 12 years of age, depending on the child's maturity and the nature of the case (which are assessed on an individual basis), also have the opportunity to state their views.

Children who have reached 15 years of age are given independent status to exercise their own rights as a party to the case in a number of instances. For example, placement of the adolescent outside the home can only take place on a voluntary basis if the adolescent consents. In cases in which the adolescent refuses to give consent, access to legal assistance is provided. Furthermore, with the adolescent's consent, under less stringent conditions those who have reached the age of 15 years can be placed out of home even though the parents oppose such placement. To safeguard the parents' legal rights, the decision must be made by the Child and Adolescent Committee according to the rules for compulsory enforcement of measures. On their own initiative adolescents may lodge a complaint against decisions made by the Child and Adolescent Committee regarding their cases.

Conclusion

In recent years Danish legislation has focused on support of children, adolescents, and families with children with special needs. The government initiated extensive committee work in 1988 that resulted in the 1990 report, *Legal Framework for Support of Children and Adolescents* (Betaenkning om de retlige rammer for indsatsen over for børn og unge, 1990). The proposals in this report stimulated comprehensive amendments to the Social Welfare Act in 1992, the implementation of which took effect on January 1, 1993. These extensive reforms promote new developments that seek to protect the rights and well-being of children and families. However, it is too early to judge the effectiveness of these measures. As the new policies are being designed, the questions remain: To what extent will they be implemented? What new problems will they uncover? How well will they balance the needs and interests of children and parents? An empirical evaluation of this comprehensive law reform will be conducted during the years 1996 and 1997.

References

Andersen, B. H. (1989). *Anbringelsesforløb — En registerundersø-gelse af børn og unge anbragt uden for hjemmet.* Copenhagen: The Danish National Institute of Social Research.

Betænkning om de retlige rammer for indsatsen over for børn og unge. (1990). *Afgivet af udvalget om de retlige rammer for indsatsen over for børn og unge.* Betænkning No. 1212.

Børnekommissionens betænkning. (1981). Social-ministeriet. Betænkning No. 918.

Christensen, E. (1991). *Trængte familier.* Copenhagen: The Danish National Institute of Social Research.

Christensen, E. (1992). *Omsorgssvigt? En rapport om de 0-3-årige baseret på sundheds-plejerskers viden.* Copenhagen: The Danish National Institute of Social Research.

Christoffersen, M. N. (1988). *Familieplejen — En undersøgelse af danske plejefamilier med 0-17-årige plejebørn.* Copenhagen: The Danish National Institute of Social Research.

Christoffersen, M. N. (1993). *Anbragte børns livsforløb. En undersøgelse af tidligere anbragte børn og unge født i 1967.* Copenhagen: The Danish National Institute of Social Research.

Clark, R. E., & Clark, J. F. (1989). *The encyclopedia of child abuse.* New York: Facts on File.

Ertmann, B. (1994). *Tvangsfjernelser. En analyse af samtlige tvangsfjernelser i København Kommune 1990.* Copenhagen: Kroghs Forlag a/s.

Gelles, R. J. (1987). What to learn from cross-cultural and historical research on child abuse and neglect: An overview. In R. J. Gelles & J. B. Lancaster (Eds.), *Child abuse and neglect: Biosocial dimensions.* New York: Aldine de Gruyter.

Grinde, T. V. (1989). *Barn og barnevarn i Norden.* Oslo: Tano.

Grinde, T. V. (1993). *Kunnskapsstatus for barnevernet.* Oslo: Tano.

Grønhøj, B., & Pruzan, V. (1974). Idealer og praksis. Om anbringelse af børn i familiepleje. Copenhagen: The Danish National Institute of Social Research.

Jørgensen, P. S., & Nissen, M. (1990). *Det usynlige omsorgssvigt.* Copenhagen: The Danish National Institute of Social Research.

Leth, I., & Stenvig, B. (1988). Sexuelle overgreb mod boern og unge. Omfang og karakter. *Nordisk psykologi, 40*(5), 383–393.

Merrick, J. (1984). *Omsorgssvigt. En bog om boernemishandling.* Copenhagen: Hans Reitzels forlag.

Michelsen, N., Christensen, E., Ovelund, Merrick, J., & Weicher, I. (1985). *Boern*

   i noed I. Handling og behandling — Den konkrete virkelighed. Copenhagen:
      Mentalhygiejnisk forsknings institut, Mentalhygiejnisk forlag.
Vestergaard, J. (1993). *Afskaffelse af "revselsesretten." Om betydningen af den saerlige
      bestemmelse i ML§7 stk. 2.* Kriminalistisk Institut, Koebenhavns universitet,
      Aarbog 1993. ("Abolition of the right to inflict corporal punishment on chil-
      dren," The Institute of Criminology, University of Copenhagen, 1993).

6

Finland

Child Abuse as a Family Problem

TARJA PÖSÖ

The debate about child abuse is relatively new in Finland. Prompted by discussions of child abuse in the United States and Great Britain, in the 1970s and early 1980s opinion polls were taken and predictions were made, following estimates and models borrowed from abroad, about the extent of child abuse in Finland. *Child Abuse,* by Ruth S. Kempe and C. Henry Kempe (1981) was translated into Finnish in 1981. In Finland, too, it was mostly medical professionals and researchers who initially published articles and expressed their worries about child abuse (Korpilahti, 1981, p. 62).

It is important to note that concerns about child abuse in Finland emerged at the same time that the problem of wife battering was gaining recognition, also stimulated by debates that were being carried on abroad. Contrary to their international and even Nordic counterparts, however, feminists in Finland did not initiate the discussion about wife battering. Rather it was the activists working in the areas of social and health care who were responsible for raising public consciousness about this problem. The similarities between child abuse and wife battering were emphasized as they both usually took place in the homes of the victims and in both cases the abusers were people the victims knew well and were dependent on. Linking these problems by emphasizing their similarities placed child abuse and wife battering within the common framework of "family violence." Thus the efforts to explain and treat these private forms of violence focused on the family as a unit of emotional, social, and interactive ties.

In terms of wife battering, the framework of family violence ignores the gendered nature of the problem as the family system is considered more the focal point of intervention than individual actors within the family (even though it is the individual actors, mainly males, who are the abusers). This family-oriented framework however has not been criticized to any great extent.

143

This was also the case with child sexual abuse, awareness of which emerged in the late 1980s partly in response to the growing awareness of this problem abroad, especially in other Nordic countries. As before, the activists were mainly authorities in social and health care; sexual abuse was treated as a family problem requiring family-centered interventions and therapeutic programs, which were introduced nationwide.

Child abuse remains a marginal topic for academic research in the social sciences. Most of the limited materials published in this area are articles and books for social and health care professionals, either presenting general guidelines for treatment of the victims of abuse (e.g., *Miten auttaa lasta,* 1993; Sundholm, 1989; Taskinen, 1982, 1986, 1994) or analyzing current professional practice (Antikainen, 1994).

Several attempts have been made to estimate the extent of child abuse in Finland. Sariola and Uutela (1992) report estimates made in 1988 based on questionnaires answered by a random sample of 9,000 school children, age 15 years. According to this relatively large study, 72% of the respondents reported mild violence (such as hair pulling, slapping, beating with a birch twig) and 8% severe violence (such as hitting with an object, kicking, threatening with a knife or gun) experienced at the hands of their parents. Overall the frequency of violence toward children in Finland appears significantly lower than in the United States. Comparisons with Sweden show a somewhat similar level of child abuse (Sariola & Uutela, 1992). In the same study 7% of the female respondents and 3% of the males reported sexual abuse (the criteria for which included experiences involving coercion or violence in which the adult's or child's genitals were touched while the person was either fully dressed or naked and occurrences of sexual intercourse or sexual contact without penetration) (Sariola, 1990). These findings revealed the existence of more abuse than had been expected, which alarmed the public. In 1993 a sample of 1,015 parents was surveyed about child-rearing practice; 38% of them said that they used corporal punishment from time to time as a part of their methods of upbringing (Sihvola, 1994, p. 25). Again the results were discussed in the press with a degree of moral apprehension.

Beyond these few studies, child abuse as such has not received significant attention in professional debates and is not seen as a problem for extensive interventions. The health and social welfare authorities, for example, do not, except in very rare cases, count child abuse (apart from sexual abuse) as a statistical category when they make reports about their clients. The lack of statistical information about abuse places certain limits on the analysis of this problem in Finland. Much of the information in this chapter is drawn from a case study of child welfare reporting and administrative practices in Tampere, the country's second largest city.[1]

Definitions of Abuse

Legal Definitions

In criminal law regarding assault, since 1866 parental punishment of children has been considered a legal violation if it caused severe bodily harm. This meant that corporal punishment was accepted if it caused only mild bodily harm. That was changed, however, in 1969 when conditional acceptance of parental corporal punishment vanished from the criminal law and was treated as any other kind of physical assault (Mattila, 1984, p. 93; Taskinen, 1982, p. 6). Thus after 1969 parents did not have a right to inflict even mild forms of corporal punishment on their children. If they misuse the parental position by employing physically assaultive behavior, the legal system treats the parents as any other abuser.[2]

In 1983 physical punishment of children was explicitly forbidden by the Child Custody and Right of Access Act, which prohibited corporal punishment and any treatment that would hurt or oppress children. The act did not however specify the criteria for the definition of maltreatment of a child, and neither did the new Child Welfare Act, also introduced in 1983.

The 1983 Child Welfare Act descended from the Child Welfare Act of 1936, which entitled children to protection by the state. Under the act of 1936 — the first of its kind in Finland — the state assumed the right to intervene in the family and to suspend parental rights if children were neglected or their asocial behavior caused harm to society or to themselves. State intervention could involve taking the child into custody, in which case the parents' right to raise and educate their children was temporarily or permanently abrogated and the municipal social welfare authorities assumed the duties that were necessary for this purpose. Custody ended through a reevaluation of the case by the social welfare authorities or when the child turned 16 years old. The Child Welfare Act of 1936 did not define the rights and duties of child welfare interventions with great precision (Rauhala, 1978, pp. 144–145). It did however list the official grounds for taking a child into custody as follows:

a) his parents have died or have rejected him;
b) he requires special care and education outside the home, which his parents cannot give him by their own means and which cannot be procured for him otherwise, owing to his physical or mental illness or retardedness, defective sight or hearing or other physical disabilities;
c) his parents do not give him the care and education he needs owing to their illness, lack of understanding, drunkenness or other such reason, or he is otherwise not receiving the necessary care and education;
d) he is abused or his life, health or morals are otherwise endangered at home;
e) due to his own fault or that of his parents, he has employment unsuitable for his or her age, fails to attend school as stipulated in the Compulsory Education Act, or has broken school rules and is not amenable to school discipline. (pp. 145–147)

The Child Welfare Act identified child abuse as one of the categories for legitimizing child welfare interventions for children under 16 years of age. The category covered when a child was abused in his or her home as well as situations in which his or her life, health, or virtue were threatened. The "threatened" child was often used in professional language to describe the work done in child welfare, and it also functioned as a statistical category when child welfare interventions were presented in numerical terms. This changed when the new Child Welfare Act was introduced in 1983.

Contrary to the initial act in 1936, the 1983 legislation tried to avoid an extensive categorization of the problems of children. The earlier categorization was criticized as being based on a mechanical list of the child's and family's symptoms (Kivinen, 1989). A wider view was preferred. Therefore a skeleton law was introduced that focused on the child's healthy development rather than the risks of mistreatment. For the first time children's rights to care and protection were to be the guiding principle for interventions.

This view was accompanied by a broader conception of public responsibility for child welfare that expanded to include not only the municipal social welfare boards that still have a definite duty to act in cases of concern, but all the public agencies with services that are related to the needs and interests of children.[3] Instead of responding to the problem areas categorized in the earlier act, the municipal social welfare boards are now asked to intervene when children's living conditions are unsafe or threaten their health and development and when the children's behaviors are harmful to their own health or development. The determination of unsafe and threatening conditions is based on the judgments of professional social workers. Although children may be taken into public custody if there is reason to suspect serious threat or harm to themselves or their development, the law does not specify any further what kind of criteria should be met to legitimize the action. Thus child abuse per se is not explicitly defined as a formal reason for child welfare interventions.

Professional Definitions

In implementing child welfare legislation, social and health care professionals base their work not only on legal definitions, but also on concepts and guidelines developed in the professional literature on child abuse.

In Finland guidelines for professional practice have been influenced by several documents, beginning with a booklet about the nature and treatment of child abuse that was widely distributed in 1982 to workers in the social and health care systems. This booklet was published by the National Board of Social Welfare and the National Board of Health Care (Taskinen, 1982). The aims of this work were to give background information about child abuse and neglect, improve the skills of the professionals to help and support children and families, and emphasize the essential role of cooperation when working with families at risk. The aims were, in other words, very high, and the booklet was perceived as offering the best practice guidelines in the field.

In the 1982 booklet (Taskinen, 1982), the discussion of child abuse included not only physical abuse, which was the most emphasized, but also sexual and chemical forms of abuse. In the definitions of abuse, the difficulty in determining when "abuse really is abuse" was given much thought. The boundaries between active physical abuse and passive abuse in the form of neglect, as well as between "normal" corporal punishment and "real" physical abuse, were discussed. Finally an attempt was made to specify the signs of child abuse, which were identified as follows: physical damage and signs of maltreatment pertaining to the body of the child (bruises, broken bones, undernourishment, sicknesses left untreated, etc.), long-term psychological problems, fears and anxieties of the child, and a hostile, extremely labile, and indifferent attitude of the parent toward his or her child.

This view was expanded in 1986 when the next general guideline booklet on child abuse was published by the same organizations, this time focusing on sexual abuse (Taskinen, 1986). This work aimed to give general information about sexual abuse and, more than the previous booklet, emphasized the importance of cooperation among different authorities. The definition of sexual abuse was broad, ranging from sexually provocative behavior to actual sexual intercourse, not only between the child and the parent but between adults and children generally. This time discussion focused on the boundaries between accepted forms of physical expressions of parental tenderness and sexual abuse. The author noted that it was dangerous to identify all signs of tenderness as sexual exploitation. Since sexual abuse is a particularly sensitive and difficult issue (as are other problems in the area of sexual behavior) for social welfare professionals to deal with, specialized training and supervision was recommended for treating sexual abuse cases.

Later, in 1993, a collection of articles concerning the treatment of child abuse was published by the Central Organization for Child Welfare (*Miten auttaa lasta,* 1993) to assist professionals in their practice. Unlike the first two booklets, this work was published more on a commercial basis. It presented a broad view of child abuse that covered the physical, psychological, and sexual forms of abuse from the point of view of health, social, education, and juridical professionals. The section by Taskinen (1993, pp. 15–16) specifying the definition of child abuse identified six categories of abuse (physical, chemical, psychological, sexual, socioeconomic, and sociostructural) and divided them into active and passive forms as follows:

1. Physical abuse
   1.1. Active: for example beating, kicking
   1.2. Passive: neglect of care
2. Chemical abuse
   2.1. Active: the misuse of drugs, medicine etc.
   2.2. Passive: neglect of diet or medical treatment
3. Psychological abuse
   3.1. Active: cruel treatment, humiliation, scaring, mockery
   3.2. Passive: invalidating, not paying any attention
4. Sexual abuse
   4.1. Active: abuse of sexual organs, forced sexual intercourse and other hurt of bodily integrity
   4.2. Passive: attempting sexual activities, offering sexual material, introducing to prostitution
5. Socio-economic abuse
   5.1. Active: misuse of accommodation, financial blackmail
   5.2. Passive: abandonment
6. Structural violence
   6.1. Active: hierarchic systems, oppression

6.2. Passive: any norms and regulations which do not pay any attention to the child's right to growth, protection and security. (pp. 15–16)

Throughout the book (*Miten auttaa lasta,* 1993), sexual abuse again received more attention than other forms of abuse. What was new in the definitions of abuse was the situational approach: One part of the book was devoted to violence at school, in institutions, in multicultural families, and the like. Also the definition of abuse was expanded more than ever before to include not only the obvious signs of physical and psychological maltreatment (typical in the discussion of the early 1980s), but any oppressive public regulations that might be regarded as abusive against children in the 1990s.

Despite variations in the scope of definitions, the analytic framework for examining child abuse has remained much the same through all these guidebooks for professionals. In these works the explanations of child abuse have three levels: social, familial, and individual. Social and economic deprivation are seen as connected with child abuse as well as the individual experiences of abuse and maltreatment in the abuser's childhood (the circle of violence). Professionals are therefore advised to focus their work on cooperative measures with families and other professionals, as well as on preventive action. In practice however work with families has been delineated in the most concrete terms and receives the highest priority.

Changing Trends in the Definitions of Child Abuse

Generally two trends mark the development of child abuse definitions since 1975. First, from a legal perspective, although corporal punishment and other abusive behaviors have become explicitly prohibited, in child welfare legislation the definitional focus has shifted since 1983 from specific concerns about abusive behavior to more comprehensive (and vaguer) concerns for ensuring the child's health and development. This means that child abuse as a special category for interventions by child welfare authorities has become more abstract and indefinite than it was under the earlier child welfare legislation. Second, in the professional debate, a very broad definition of child abuse and its causes has recently been narrowed down to a focus mainly on sexual abuse with physical or emotional abuse, for example, increasingly ignored.

Among the different forms of child abuse, concerns about sexual abuse are emerging as the most dominant issue for the near future. In assessing the implementation of the Convention of Children's Rights in Finland, the Working Group on the Rights of Children voiced strong concerns about sexual abuse and the exploitation of children and youth (*Lapsen oikeuksien,* 1994, p. v). These concerns were not only about sexual abuse in families and close relationships, but also about the commercial exploitation of children for sexual purposes (emerging in the 1990s in the Finnish context). Among other issues, child prostitution and sex crimes against children were identified for closer examination and stricter regulation by law and social policy.

Filing of Reports

Child Welfare and Other Authorities

The municipal child welfare board is the central organization that in principle should know about every case of child abuse in a municipality. The Child Welfare Act requires every authority working for social and health care agencies, the educational system, police, and church to inform the child welfare board of cases of abuse.[4] The crucial feature here is that these authorities are supposed to act automatically whenever a case of child maltreatment or neglect is uncovered: The duty to report is beyond any case-bound consideration. In addition every citizen is entitled to inform the child welfare board if they have any doubts or concerns about the well-being or the quality of care of any children.

The various public authorities play a highly visible role in identifying the needs for child welfare interventions. In the early 1980s, the Committee on Child Welfare noted a tendency toward the declining role of parents and community members in reporting problems and claimed that public authorities were becoming the most important catalysts in detecting the need for child welfare. However a statistical analysis of all the child welfare cases in Finland in 1987 revealed a different picture: An equal number of reports to child welfare services had been made by the parents of the children and by the authorities, which together accounted for 80% of all reported cases. The reports initiated by parents usually expressed their concerns about family conflicts, problems in upbringing, and their own psychiatric problems. The reports made by social welfare, health care, education, and police authorities tended to involve cases of child neglect, cases in which the parents had psychiatric and family problems, and cases in which there were difficulties at school and crimes committed by the youngsters. Overall few reports were initiated by relatives, other community members, and the children themselves (Kivinen, 1994, p. 72; Kivinen & Heinonen, 1990, pp. 21–22). A striking finding of this study is that child abuse was mentioned very rarely as a motive for a contact. Indeed, based on the categorization system used, child abuse made up only 1.3% of all cases referred to the municipal child welfare board (Kivinen & Heinonen, 1990).

The legal requirement to report suspected cases of child abuse is apparently neither well known nor widely complied with by the authorities. The lack of compliance is sometimes excused by referring to legal norms. The concern about breaching confidentiality in professional relations with clients is often noted as a reason for the reluctance of authorities to report incidents of abuse to child welfare services. It is assumed that the confidentiality of the client relationships is harmed if any information is passed to outside authorities. In addition to issues of confidentiality, the lack of compliance with mandatory child abuse reporting regulations occurs because the standards of evidence for reporting are often misunderstood. Although many workers think that there ought to be definite proof of child abuse before the municipal child welfare organization is informed, the law requires that a report be filed when the worker suspects the likelihood of child abuse, even if there is no firm proof at the moment.

Currently there is no registration system that gathers and stores all the reports and contacts regarding child welfare cases in Finland. Drawing on data from several social welfare offices, a recent study by Tarja Kivinen (1994) notes the absence of systematic recordkeeping procedures for reports made to a municipal child welfare organization; the study also found that such reports did not necessarily lead to an investigation or other actions. This study reveals that information from different sources about a case is often stored in the memory of the social worker, particularly when the case involves cooperation with other authorities. Some child welfare offices have special report forms to collect the information reported on children in need, but the researcher found that the information on these forms was not used by social workers in any systematic way to assist their practice.

According to the law every case reported to the municipal child welfare organization should be checked in one way or another. However, in professional everyday practice, the pattern of response is somewhat irregular. Response to reports is according to the social worker's sense of emergency, based mainly on whatever previous information the social worker has about the case. Kivinen (1994) concludes that systematic procedures need to be introduced for gathering and utilizing child welfare reports so that the social workers' judgments will be informed by more than professional intuition and random information.

An examination of how the reporting system functions in Tampere (the second largest city in Finland) reveals a striking absence of reports of child abuse. In interviews with regional social workers in charge of child welfare in Tampere, the respondents had difficulty recalling any reports made to them concerning cases or suspected cases of child abuse. The social workers indicated that in their individual case loads there are normally at most a couple of child abuse reports a year, usually made by day care personnel, school teachers, and the health nurses of the maternity and child welfare clinics. These reports are usually based on observations of bruises on a child or the continuous tiredness of the mother. The neighbors, police, hospital, or health center were not mentioned as informants, nor were children younger than teenagers. Other family members made reports only of sexual abuse; these reports occurred mainly in the context of divorce and conflicts over guardianship. Similar to Kivinen's (1994) findings, the interviews in Tampere indicate that personal knowledge about the reported case more than the details of the current report guided the social worker's decisions about the interventions needed. In Tampere, however, every report led to some kind of action, most often gathering more information from other authorities. Direct contacts with the child or the family were made only in cases for which there was a considerable amount of proof about the likelihood of abuse.

In Tampere it appears that child abuse is used as a category for intervention by the child welfare authorities only if a doctor can prove that physical (or sexual) abuse occurred. Thus, for purposes of intervention, child abuse is defined by medical examination; moreover it is used only to cover specific circumstances. If child abuse takes place as a part of general violence in the family or the parents suffer from alcohol problems, for purposes of intervention the problem is more likely to be defined in the categories of "family conflicts" or "parental drinking problems" than as child abuse. This explains why child abuse is so rarely identified as the reason for child welfare interventions, having only been used in a handful of cases of care orders during the last years as shown in the general statistics.[5] It also helps to clarify why the municipal child welfare authorities receive so few reports of child abuse. As long as child abuse is diagnosed mainly as an indication of some type of family crisis and the authorities responding to these problems intervene along the lines of family work, child abuse as a distinctive issue "disappears" from the professional systems of social and health care.

For the most part the reporting system fails to treat children as individual victims of abuse (even though it recognizes and responds to violence in families), with one important exception — cases of sexual abuse. Sexual abuse has a distinct status as a special social — and family — problem: It is diagnosed as such and it is treated as such. Moreover, separate reporting systems and cooperative networks have been created to receive reports and to deal with cases of sexual abuse. In Tampere there is a team of workers, consisting of members from the municipal social welfare organization, child guidance clinics, child psychiatric clinic, and police, that collects all the cases of sexual abuse and discusses the best ways of treating them. Every social welfare office has a social worker designated as a special "sexual abuse representative" to whom all cases or suspected cases of sexual abuse are directed. This worker contacts the network group to discuss sexual abuse cases and how to treat them. Since it was organized in the late 1980s this reporting structure has identified a relatively large number of sexual abuse cases relative to other types of child abuse in the Tampere area.

In general the child welfare reporting systems tend to perceive different types of child abuse differently. Psychological abuse, well recognized as a category in the child abuse literature, is not distinctly conceptualized as a form of abuse for purposes of reporting. This is also the case for physical abuse as long as it does not become medically diagnosed. Sexual abuse is also defined largely by doctors, but the reporting systems recognize it as a distinct problem that demands immediate and specialized treatment.

The municipal child welfare authority is the organization initially informed about cases of abuse and in charge of dealing with them. Other authorities get involved more or less indirectly. The police are supposed to be informed in any case of abuse when the victim is below the age of 15 years, but in practice this is rarely done. According to the police, the social welfare and health care authorities are extremely reluctant to bring cases of child abuse into the legal system except in instances when the abuser is someone outside the child's family (Kokko, 1993). Therefore the police deal with cases of abuse that are somewhat different from those that come to the attention of the social and health care authorities. On the other hand, the police in Tampere had not reported any cases of abuse to the child welfare board as far back as the individual police interviewed could remember (each having served for 15 years or so). Neither had the police registered any house calls due to child abuse, but they had responded to many cases of family violence.[6]

In hospitals doctors focus on medical care of the symptoms caused by abuse and then refer the case to hospital social workers when they suspect that abuse occurred. This leads to underreporting for several reasons. First, cases handled this way are rarely registered. According to the mandatory reporting laws it is not the social workers in the hospital who should be informed, but the social workers in the municipal child welfare authority (Kivinen, 1994). In addition findings from Haikonen's study (1984) and my interviews with hospital social workers in Tampere suggest that doctors do not always refer suspected cases of abuse to the social workers. An overload of work and the intimacy of the problem are offered as reasons for the doctors' underreporting of cases. According to Pirjo Haikonen (1984) the likelihood of reporting increases with the level of social problems in the family and the seriousness of the harm suffered by the child.

The near disappearance of child abuse as a diagnostic category is more than an issue of definition; it can lead to a failure to protect children. Interviews with several authorities in Tampere revealed the following contradiction: At the same time that the child welfare system was receiving very few reports of physical child abuse and the medical doctors and police were not being confronted with abuse either, professionals working for more therapeutically oriented organizations such as child psychiatric clinics or child guidance clinics recalled many cases of violence in the family directed toward children. In long-term therapy relations the therapists were told about many incidents of violence their clients had experienced in their homes but that until then had remained family secrets.

At the end of the 1980s the social and health care authorities in Tampere were reorganized into independent, self-governing regions, as had been done in many other Finnish towns. A strong argument in favor of this major organizational change was that it would enhance cooperation between the social welfare authorities and other authorities in the region; this regionalization would also bring the authorities closer administratively to the inhabitants they served and thereby provide better ways of doing preventive and investigative social work, for example, with children and families at risk. In 1995 the new forms and advantages of the regional approach were still taking shape, and its impact on the reporting of child abuse remains to be seen.

Inhibition of Reporting by Family-Centered Work

One of the major obstacles to child abuse reporting is due more to the nature of professional intervention in the social and health care services than to the regulations and structure of the reporting system. Since the 1980s, family-centered work—or family work—has been the main approach in most social work practice, as well as services in maternity and child welfare clinics. Although the family is seen as the main target of intervention, in concrete terms it is most often only women and children who become clients of family work in the social welfare system (Forsberg, 1994; Kuronen, 1994, pp. 68–71). In this approach to practice the family is seen as a source of support and as a solution to the problems. Therefore social workers need to develop a good relationship and a trusting atmosphere to gain the families' cooperation.

The social workers interviewed in Tampere observed that the need to gain the family's cooperation makes it difficult to discuss even vague suspicions of child abuse. In a similar vein, Marjo Kuronen (1994) found that the health nurses in maternity and child welfare clinics tried to avoid discussions of child abuse with their clients as much as possible in order to maintain a supportive relationship with the mothers. Only very clearly defined problems, connected mostly with the physical development of the child or the tiredness of the mother, were discussed in the health care clinics. Other research reveals a similar pattern of behavior among social workers in social welfare offices (Forsberg, 1994) and in residential child welfare services (Pösö, 1993). In social welfare offices family problems were discussed by the workers only if the problems were urgent (such as in cases of definite neglect of the child) or if they were discovered "naturally" in long, well-established client relations (Forsberg, 1994). These ethnographic studies of professional practice in the social and health care services reveal that child abuse was never introduced as a topic for family work with clients even though in some cases the workers strongly suspected that abuse had occurred.

Professional efforts to gain cooperation in work with client families foster an obvious tendency toward nonspecific definitions of the problems in order to avoid stigmatizing diagnoses. On legal grounds this tendency is supported by the definitions of child welfare in the Child Welfare Act of 1983 and the formal procedures linked with it. In terms of professional practice, there has been strong criticism against taking too narrow a view of social problems. In many cases families are seen to be suffering more from a collection of problems ("multiproblem families") (Rajavaara, 1992) than from a highly specific problem (temporary financial problems excepted). Katja Forssen (1993) describes a typical family served by child welfare as belonging to the working class with an overrepresentation of single mothers; these families often experienced problems such as poverty, alcoholism, helplessness, and unbalanced family life. The picture of child welfare families as multiproblem families is found in other studies of the clients of child welfare (Kähkönen, 1993; Rauhala, 1978). There does not seem to be any change in this pattern during the last 20 years (Bardy, 1989).[7]

From the multiproblem perspective, physical violence or child abuse in the family is seen as too narrow a category that emphasizes the symptoms of the problem more than the basic causes and stigmatizes or blames the perpetrator too easily. These problems, it is argued, should be seen in the context of "family conflicts" instead.

A concrete example of the nonspecific approach to problem definition comes from an interview with a health nurse in a child welfare clinic. The nurse observed that she often encounters families who have conflicts in their marriage, and the mother needs support in order to cope with the conflicting situations. When asked for an example, she referred to a case in which the husband had been physically abusing the child in order to force the wife to do things in the way he wanted. This problem was neither perceived nor labeled as child abuse; from the nurse's perspective is was categorized as a case of family conflict. Instead of informing the child welfare authorities the nurse proceeded to offer the psychological support she believed the mother needed.

Reporting and Placement Trends

The period from 1970 to 1994 was a time of great changes in child protection, the landmark being the Child Welfare Act of 1983.[8] This act not only redefined the categorization of the needs for child welfare interventions (as noted above), but opened a whole new approach to child welfare. "A child is entitled to a secure and stimulating environment in which to grow and to a harmonious and well-balanced development. A child has a special right for protection." These are the first words of the act, which divides child welfare into two main areas: preventive measures that have to do with children's living conditions and general welfare services and family-oriented and individual child welfare interventions. The former deals broadly with children's interests and the latter deals with assistance to individual children in their natural living surroundings (the term *open care* is used here to describe activities such as professional guidance and advice, intensified family/home help, financial help, assistance in finding a job or accommodations, organizing lay help for the child or the family, temporary substitute care), taking the child into care and substitute care (in other words, a formal care order by the child welfare board is required for substitute care), and after care (guidance and financial support for child welfare clients up to 21 years of age).

Concerning interventions in the lives of children at risk, supportive measures have been emphasized, with prevention and open care highly valued. At the same time, care orders and out-of-home placements are avoided as far as possible and, if necessary, made on a short term basis. Although the number of children and young persons receiving child welfare services has been approximately 20,000 per year during the last few decades, the number served in open care has increased. In 1971 there were 12,600 children placed outside their own home and 6,000 children and young persons in open care or after care. Between 1971 and 1987, there was a decrease of 4,200 children placed outside their own home, whereas the number of children and young persons in open care or after care increased by nearly 6,700. More often than before, the child welfare interventions have been partly overlapping. During a year, children may both be placed outside their home and also receive assistance in open care or after care. One client might have also experienced different types of placement as had 12% of the children (Child Welfare, 1993, p. 64; Kivinen & Heinonen, 1990). These child welfare client and placement trends are illustrated in Table 6-1. It should be noted that the data in Table 6-1 include all

Table 6-1. Child Welfare Clients 1970–1991

	1970	1975	1980	1983	1987	1991
Child welfare clients	18,577	18,992	21,305	21,294	18,288	—
Children in open or after care	5,993	8,066	12,028	12,571	12,645[a]	—
Children placed out of home	12,584	10,926	9,177	8,723	8,395	8,724
Rates of clients of child welfare per 1,000 children (under 18 years of age)	13	14	18	18	16	—
Rates of female clients of child welfare	38%	37%	38%	41%	53%	—
Rates of clients placed out of home per 1,000 children (under 18 years of age)	9	8	8	7	7	7
Rates of girls of the children placed out of home	44%	46%	46%	47%	47%	48%
Type of out-of-home placement[b]						
Family care	5,476	5,378	4,917	4,724	4,645	4,346
Institutional care	7,108	5,548	4,260	3,999	3,750	3,691
Voluntary placements	95.3%	94.5%	92.9%	91.9%	92.3%	90.4%

[a]Due to the new Child Welfare Act, the figure also includes, unlike the previous years, temporary out-of-home placements done as part of open care.

[b]These figures list all the instances of placement during one year. One child might have had two or more placements.

Source: Child Welfare, 1993; Suomen virallinen tilasto: Sosiaalihuoto (1970, 1975, 1980, 1983).

child welfare clients, only a small fraction of whom (as shown in Table 6-2) were specifically identified as victims of child abuse.

Nationally, as Table 6-1 shows, among the types of out-of-home placement family care has increased relative to institutional care over the last 20 years. Placements in family care are more often made in smaller rather than bigger municipalities, and they are more often intended to be longer placements than institutional placements (Kivinen & Heinonen, 1990).

Table 6-2. Child Abuse as a Specified Reason for Child Welfare Interventions 1970–1987

	1970	1975	1980	1983	1987
Child abuse cases registered	91	118	182	186	256
Neglect-of-care cases registered	1,048	887	1,583	1,615	2,835
Out-of-home placements of the registered child abuse cases	75%	81%	56%	55%	46%
Out-of-home placements of the registered cases of neglect of care	87%	98%	69%	67%	53%
Percentage of child abuse of all out-of-home placements	—	0.9%	1.1%	1.2%	1.4%

Source: Child Welfare, 1993; Suomen virallinen tilasto: Sosiaalihuolto (1970, 1975, 1980, 1983); Kivinen & Heinonen (1990).

Although the vast majority of placements continue to be made on a voluntary basis, the proportion of involuntary placements has increased since 1970. This can be partly explained by the fact that today, in addition to the child's custodian, the child's own wishes and views are given more weight in decisions on voluntary placement (Child Welfare, 1993, p. 64).

Another recent trend in child welfare interventions involves the increase in the number of girls. This very likely reflects the change in the registration practice of the crimes committed by youngsters. As most juvenile crimes are committed by boys and as they are registered in the child welfare systems less often than before, the proportion of boys has also decreased. Meanwhile, the age of the clients has changed, too. The proportion of children served below school age has increased since the early 1980s, and the proportion of teenagers has decreased (Kivinen & Heinonen, 1990, 13–14). The low average age of the clients marks Finnish child welfare practice as different from that of other Scandinavian countries (except Norway).

Most of the reasons for child welfare activities are now found in the difficulties parents have in coping with their parenthood. In 1987 one fifth of all the children had been placed out of their homes due to the parents' abuse of intoxicants. This, together with neglect of care and the parents' mental problems, explained 48% of all the out-of-home placements that year.

Detailed information on cases in which child abuse was specified as the reason for child welfare interventions is difficult to obtain. The data in Table 6-2 convey a picture of child abuse as being a rare occurrence, which (as noted above) reflects reporting practices that tend to categorize instances of abuse in terms of other problems. Although the numbers are relatively small, the data indicate that registered cases of child abuse have increased by almost 300%, and registered cases of neglect more than doubled between 1970 and 1987. During this period, the proportion of out-of-home placements in the cases of child abuse and neglect of care declined following the general placement trend for all child welfare clients (Kivinen & Heinonen, 1990, p. 26).

How are abused children served? As child abuse remains so often hidden and unnoticed in the reporting and categorization practices, social work interventions in the lives of abused children take various forms beyond out-of-home placements. Child welfare workers interviewed in Tampere, for example, mentioned a range of interventions that included installing locks on the doors of the room (in order to protect the teenage girl from the violent parents and their visitors), running a series of sessions of network therapy (in order to find supportive systems for the family in which abuse had taken place), and taking the child into care (which was rarely done). Concrete family supports in the form of home help and public day care for the children were preferred very often as interventions to deal with abuse, even cases of obvious physical abuse, neglect, and psychological abuse.

The expansive public day care system (kindergartens and family day care) was quite important as a mechanism that provided continuous monitoring of the situation. Kindergarten teachers and nurses were asked to report any changes in the behavior or condition of the child, which, one assumes, they were able to do quite well as they met the child and at least one of the parents daily. At the same time, these programs guaranteed that the child was well looked after during the daytime. According to social workers, the public day care arrangements were essential in supporting troubled families and protecting children at risk. Older children, on the other hand, were looked after by the education authorities at school. In addition the health care workers in child welfare clinics and at school were consulted as informants about possible signs of danger and risks toward the children.

Thus, cases of child abuse are most often cared for and monitored through the general service provisions of the welfare state; these provisions are well trusted by social workers and tend to be given the first priority in the overall Finnish service culture. Specific child welfare interventions such as direct professional support or out-of-home placement, as a matter of fact, are only a fraction of the interventions made in the lives of the abused children.[9]

As the data in Table 6-1 indicate, there has been a growing tendency to avoid out-of-home placements in the child welfare system. Since the end of the 1980s child welfare workers have been rather critical of residential care, which is seen as too expensive and not in the best interests of children and their families. The central argument was that the families in trouble needed intensive support, not accommodations. Residential care offers accommodations, but not enough support. Therefore a new system was needed to help the families in their homes (Tuurala, 1992). Thus residential workers (e.g., in Tampere) were trained to do family-centered work in the homes of the families, and the children were taken out of their homes only in extreme cases.

Interventions with children who have been sexually abused are somewhat different from those employed to deal with other forms of abuse. The most important difference — always mentioned by the Tampere social workers interviewed — is that child sexual abuse cases are immediately referred to the special sexual abuse authority network, which is in charge of dealing with this type of abuse. In cases of sexual abuse children placed out of the home were most likely to be put into psychiatric care. More than offering protection by placing children for part of the day into day care, as is the practice in non-sexual abuse cases, psychiatric therapy is an important part of intervention in cases of child sexual abuse. This marks the sharp distinction between the intervention systems for cases of sexual abuse and other forms of child abuse: Sexual abuse is seen to require specialized treatment by service providers who base their knowledge mainly on psychiatry.

As the municipal child welfare agency and the public health care services (child psychiatry) together with other public institutions are the main sources for the treatment of child abuse, the costs of treatment are mainly covered by public funds. There is however an increasing number of private services that the public system uses through purchase of service contracts. As the market for private services is still relatively new, public agencies have not yet developed sophisticated procedures to monitor the quality of care provided by private services.

In the child welfare system, the most common services purchased from private sources involve family home placements. Under this arrangement a family that can show that at least one of the adults is qualified in social service work offers their home as a place for a child to live. Some family homes are small, caring for 2 to 3 children; others can take 8 to 10 children.[10] The municipal child welfare agency can place a child in a private family home as assistance to open care or based on a care order; in either case, the child welfare agency pays for the child's living and subsistence costs. The fact that purchase of private services has focused on family homes reflects the general tendency toward child welfare placements in family care either in the child's home or at somebody else's home except in the treatment of sexual abuse cases.

Issues

One of the main issues surrounding child abuse in Finland concerns the low administrative visibility of this problem in the welfare state service system. As noted above, child abuse is rarely defined as a problem either for official registration with public authorities or for child welfare interventions.

In Anglo-Saxon research on child welfare, child abuse has long been a central topic of concern. In Finland research on child welfare has been limited. The tradition of child welfare research is generally much weaker here than, for example, in Sweden (Forssen, 1993, p. 8). The professional literature on child abuse has focused largely on prevalence surveys and general practice guidelines for the professionals. This may partly explain why child abuse has not become an important topic for social welfare and health care practitioners.

A more important reason, however, is the somewhat undifferentiated approach taken by social work professionals to problems occurring in the private area of family life. As noted above, many social problems such as wife battering, child abuse, drug abuse, and delinquency are only recognized in the broad diagnostic category of family problems.

This familistic approach to social problems can be traced to the philanthropic work at the turn of the century, which was further modified in the population policy of the 1940s, when the state introduced several financial subventions to the families (Takala, 1992). Moreover, professional social work in postwar Finland combined the different traditions of German and American social work, both sharing a deep (but different) interest in family (Satka, 1994). Today professional practices in social work and in other helping professions have emphasized the importance of family work to such an extent that, in a small country such as Finland, it has become the principal method for treating a variety of problems that occur in the families.

The dominance of the familistic approach hides the individual in the family. Curiously enough, there have been only limited pressures to develop more woman-friendly or feminist approaches to practice, which would recognize women as individuals and not just as family members.[11] However demands are currently increasing for more child-centered practices in all the service programs of the welfare state (e.g., *Lapsen oikeuksien,* 1994). One of the main objectives is to empower children to play a more active role in determining how interventions might best serve their interests.

Whether the demands for a new child-centered approach will be realized remains to be seen. The potential impact of this new approach might not, after all, do much to improve the detection of child abuse. In legal terms, children above the age of 12 years are supposed to be heard in child welfare decision-making processes and in negotiations over guardianship. This is the group on whom the child-centered approach might focus its efforts for empowerment. Empowering children below the age of 12 years is more difficult as very young children are not capable of expressing their needs for protection directly.

Efforts to improve the detection of child abuse will rely heavily on the functioning of child welfare authorities. At the moment the status of the municipal child welfare authorities has become rather blurred. This is reflected in the practices of other public agencies, which usually ignore their legal duty to report cases of abuse to child welfare authorities. Moreover, when a child abuse case is uncovered, the child welfare authorities deal with it as a general family/social problem, which is referred to other social service providers for treatment. Professionally, social work practice under the auspices of child welfare authorities does not have any independent status in handling cases of child abuse. The medical profession is relied on for diagnosing physical and sexual abuse. Child psychiatry has been mainly interested in treating sexual abuse. Psychological and emotional abuse are seen largely in terms of general family problems. In this context the municipal child welfare services have a vague role in identifying and treating cases of child abuse. This institutional role needs to be clarified.

The reassessment of the role of municipal child welfare authorities as a child protection institution rather than an organization offering and organizing psychosocial services to families in trouble might be one way to go. This would require a shift in professional perceptions from seeing the child as a dependent part of the family unit to recognizing the child as an individual needing, in some cases, protection from his or her family. Movement toward change in this direction however is likely to encounter several objections. First it might be said that many problems of children could be alleviated through intensive support to their families (especially to parents); after all, situations for which protection is really needed constitute only a small fraction of all child welfare cases. This viewpoint assumes that there is a full range of welfare services available (a view that might be undermined by the present financial cutbacks in welfare services). Second the protective approach might be seen as reintroducing old, paternalistic child welfare practices that have long been criticized. Even now child welfare becomes a media issue most often in regard to "unnecessary" care orders—cases in which the child welfare authorities are blamed for interfering with the rights of the families. Although recently the media has expressed some concern about the role of child welfare services and their coverage, there have not been any media reports in Finland criticizing child welfare authorities for failing to act in child abuse cases. In the current cultural climate, a shift in child welfare practice toward as a protective service that promotes children's rights is very unlikely to take place.

One cannot however forecast the implications of the decreasing welfare services resulting from the years of recession in the early 1990s in Finland. The expansive network of services is not so readily available anymore and therefore the generalist approach to dealing with child welfare problems might also have to be put into question. General support to the families and surveillance at a distance of the children at risk will not work without a wide service and professional network. Due to the diminishing resources and services in child welfare, more specific detection and treatment of children's problems might be needed. This naturally involves many risks. The broader and socially aware view of problems of abuse might be replaced primarily by a clinically and therapeutically oriented approach. The present view on sexual abuse might, in the worst case scenario, support that kind of development as the problem is currently diagnosed and treated as such by the psychomedical professionals. On the other hand, if the combination of the present social and clinical approaches to child abuse succeeds, the outcome will hardly be detrimental to the welfare of abused children.

In summary, this analysis of the institutional response to child abuse in Finland reveals a child welfare system in which child abuse as such is seldom reported or diagnosed as a specific problem for treatment. The exception is sexual abuse, for which a distinct reporting and treatment network has been created. Although the municipal child welfare authorities and the social workers employed by them should function as the central mechanism for the referral and treatment of child abuse cases, this rarely happens. Instead the orientation to practice prevalent in social and health care perceives problems in the family as family problems amenable to general and supportive welfare services. From this perspective, it is difficult to identify child abuse as a separate problem requiring special treatment.

Notes

1. As comprehensive statistical information about child abuse is missing on both the national and local levels, my decision was to gather material about child abuse reporting systems by conducting a case study of the town of Tampere, the second largest town in Finland, with about 160,000 inhabitants. The data are based on interviews with authorities in social and health care, the police, and the justice system. The attempt was to interview authorities who actually encounter clients in their daily work and who have to make assessments of possible child abuse, as well as to interview administrative social and health authorities who are in charge of developing the organization services. The material consists of 25 interviews carried out in January–April 1994 and guidelines and reports made by the local authorities. National reports, data, and research have been used as much as possible.

2. Physical abuse against a child under 15 years of age, as well as parental sexual abuse, are publicly prosecuted but other forms of abuse are mainly offenses for which the prosecution rests with the plaintiff.

3. In Finland the municipalities have the practical responsibility to provide adequate welfare services in their area. Child welfare is the responsibility of the communal welfare boards. The people working for child welfare are mainly trained social workers, whereas municipal welfare board members are political appointees named by the municipal council. The Child Welfare Act of 1983 commits local authorities to keeping a watch on the environment in which children grow up, rectifying any defects in the environment, or preventing such defects from happening. The main purpose of child welfare services is thus to ensure a good environment of growth and assist a child's parents (or custodians) in bringing up the child (Virtanen, 1994, pp. 14, 31). In child welfare legislation, by "child" is meant a person below 18 years of age.

4. This also includes the members of the municipal welfare boards.

5. Ever since 1990 the municipal social welfare authorities in Tampere have used a computer-based system to follow the work done in child welfare. At the moment the information gathered is quite general and is not much trusted by the social workers to give any proper picture about child welfare practice. Unfortunately, the statistics did not contain much information for the purposes of this study.

6. As the police do not keep any statistics about the victims of crime, neither is there any information available about the cases of child abuse they have with which they have dealt. The experiences of the Tampere police about the invisibility of child abuse in their work are however generally shared (see, e.g., Kokko, 1993).

7. Race is not an important matter in this context as Finland is ethnically one of the most homogeneous countries in Europe. There are only two well-defined ethnic minority groups in Finland: the Gypsies and the Samic Lapps, who combined constitute 2 per 1,000 of the population. Finland has adopted a very strict policy toward refugees and migrant workers from other countries. Ethnic issues have not so far been in the forefront of Finnish consciousness. How many children with a minority background are child welfare clients is not known or registered. However social workers have recognized some problems in dealing with the families from different ethnic groups, especially in work with refugees (also there have been problems in terms of using punishment as a part of the upbringing of children), and therefore this issue might become topical in the coming years.

8. The early 1980s was a period marked by strong changes in social legislations, including child legislation. Since the 1970s and 1980s, the main principle of the Finnish social welfare and health care legislation has been the unity of values — in other words, consistency — in order to provide integrated services for the population in general and children and youth at risk and their families in particular. This was done through the Social Welfare Act of 1982 (which took effect in 1984) and the Planning and the State Subsidies for Welfare Act (1992), which guaranteed state subsidies to municipal social welfare and health care equally for up to 31–64% of the establishment, operating, and administrative costs of the welfare services in the municipalities (Virtanen, 1994).

9. The profile of the child welfare system as a coordinator of different types of follow-up systems of abused children can be, however, a cause for some doubts. As shown in the previous section, the reporting system of child abuse does not function satisfactorily due to many reasons. If the general service system does not identify the first signs of abuse through a contact and a report to the municipal child welfare system, is it really to be trusted that the situation of the threatened child is taken care of adequately after the child welfare system has categorized the child as a risk case and asks for follow-up?

10. In the child welfare institutions, the maximum size for a ward is 8 children. The emphasis is on small institutions, normally housing about 20 children at most.

11. There are, however, certain national pressure groups that want to improve the position of fathers. It is stated that the welfare state service system does not welcome men as clients and especially not as fathers fully aware of the situation of their children. The professionals are therefore asked to increase their father friendliness.

References

Antikainen, J. (1994). *Lasten seksuaalinen hyväksikäyttö* [Sexual abuse of children — Professional challenges and orientations of work]. Helsinki: Sosiaali — Ja terveysalan tutkimuslaitos. Tutkimuksia 46.

Bardy, M. (1989). *Uhkat, uhrit ja arjen sankarit. Lastensuojelu tutkimuksen valossa* [Threats, victims and heroes — Child welfare from the point of view of research]. Helsinki: Sosiaalihallituksen julkaisuja 2.

Child Welfare, 1987, 1991 (1993). Helsinki: National Research and Development Center for Welfare and Health. Social Security 1993:1.

Forsberg, H. (1994). *Yksi ja monta perhettä* [One and many families]. Tampere, Finland: Julkaisematon lisensiaatintutkielma. Sosiaalipolitiikan laitos.

Forssen, K. (1993). *Suojaverkon lapsiperheet* [Families with children in the safety net]. Turku, Finland: Sosiaalipolitiikan tutkimuksia. Sarja A:2.

Haikonen, P. (1984). *Uhanalainen lapsi* [A threatened child]. Helsinki: Mannerheimin Lastensuojeluliiton lapsiraportti A 47.

Kähkönen, P. (1993). *Vanhemmuuden murtuminen* (The breaking of parenthood]. Julkaisematon psykologian lisensiaatintutkimus. Jyväskylä, Finland: Psykologian laitos.

Kempe, R. S., & Kempe, C. H. (1981). *Lasten pahoinpitely* [Child abuse]. Helsinki: Lastensuojelun Keskusliitto. (Original work in English published 1978)

Kivinen, T. (1989). *Viimeinen pari verkosta ulos. Selvitys lastensuojelun tilasta ja kehityksestä* [The state and development of child welfare]. Helsinki: Sosiaalihallituksen julkaisuja 11.

Kivinen, T. (1994). *Valikoituminen lastensuojelun asiakkaaksi* [Becoming a client in child welfare]. Julkaisematon lisensiaatin tutkimus. Helsinki: Sosiaalipolitiikan laitos, sosiaalityö.

Kivinen, T., & Heinonen, P. (1990). *Lastensuojelu vuonna 1987* [Child welfare in 1987] (Väliraportti 28.2.1990). Helsinki: Sosiaalihallituksen raporttisarja 11.

Kokko, P. (1993). Poliisi ja rikoksen uhriksi joutunut lapsi [Police and the child as a victim of crime]. In *Miten auttaa lasta* (pp. 93–104). Helsinki: Lastensuojelun Keskusliitto.

Korpilahti, M. (1981). *Lasten pahoinpitelyt ja niiden käsittely Suomessa ja Ruotsissa* [Child battering in Finland and Sweden]. Helsinki: Oikeuspoliittinen tutkimuslaitos. Julkaisuja 46.

Kuronen, M. (1994). *Lapsen hyväksi naisten kesken* [For the best of the child, between women]. Helsinki: Sosiaali — Ja terveysalan tutkimus — Ja kehittämiskeskus. Tutkimuksia 35.

Lapsen oikeuksien työryhmän raportti 24.2.1994. [The report of the Working Group on the Rights of Children]. (1994). Helsinki: Ulkoasianministeriö.

Mattila, H. (1984). *Lapsioikeuden pääpiirteet* [The outlines of the Children's Law]. Helsinki: Juridica.

Miten auttaa lasta [How to help a child]. (1993). Helsinki: Lastensuojelun Keskusliitto. Julkaisu 89.

Peltoniemi, T. (1984). *Perheväkivalta* [Family violence]. Helsinki: Otava.

Pösö, T. (1993). *Kolme koulukotia* [Three reformatory schools] (Ser. A., Vol. 388). Tampere, Finland: Acta Universitatis Tamperensis.

Rajavaara, M. (1992). *Tavallisesta perheestä tapaukseksi* [From an ordinary family to a social case]. Helsinki: Lahden koulutus – Ja tutkimuskeskus.

Rauhala, U. (1978). *Huostaanotto* [Taking into custody]. Helsinki: Suomen virallinen tilasto. Sosiaalisia erikoistutkimuksia 33:54.

Sariola, H. (1985). *Lasten seksuaalinen hyväksikäyttö* [Sexual abuse of children in Finland]. Helsinki: Lastensuojelun Keskusliitto. Julkaisu 79.

Sariola, H. (1990). *Lasten väkivalta – Ja seksuaalikokemukset* [Children's experiences of violence at home]. Helsinki: Lastensuojelun Keskusliitto. Julkaisu 85.

Sariola, H., & Uutela, A. (1992). The prevalence and context of family violence against children in Finland. *Child Abuse & Neglect, 16*, 823–832.

Satka, M. (1994). *Making social citizenship.* Jyväskylä, Finland: University of Jyväskylä, Publications of Social and Political Sciences and Philosophy.

Sihvola, S. (1994). *Lapsen terveys ja lapsiperheiden hyvinvointi* [Children's health and the well-being of families with children]. Helsinki: Mannerheimin Lastensuojeluliitto.

Sundholm, S. (1989). *Insesti* [Incest]. Helsinki: Gaudeamus.

Takala, P. (1992). Kohti postmodernia perhettä – Perhepolitiikan muuttuvat käsitykset [Toward a postmodern family – The changing attitudes in family policy]. In O. Riihinen (Ed.), *Sosiaalipolitiikka 2017* (pp. 577–600). Helsinki: Wsoy.

Taskinen, S. (1982). *Lasten pahoinpitely ja hoidon laiminlyönti* [Child abuse and neglect]. Helsinki: Sosiaalihallituksen julkaisuja 1 & Lääkintöhallituksen tutkimuksia 24.

Taskinen, S. (1986). *Lapsen seksuaalisen riiston ehkäisy ja hoito* [The prevention and treatment of child sexual abuse]. Helsinki: Sosiaalihallituksen julkaisuja 13 & Lääkintöhallituksen julkaisuja 87.

Taskinen, S. (1993). Väkivalta on vallan väärinkäyttöä [Violence is misuse of power]. In *Miten auttaa lasta* (pp. 13–25). Helsinki: Lastensuojelun Keskusliitto.

Taskinen, S. (1994). *Lapsen seksuaalisen riiston selvittäminen ja hoito* [Prevention and treatment of sexual abuse of children]. Helsinki: Sosiaali – Ja terveysalan tutkimus – Ja kehittämiskeskus. Oppaita 23.

Tuurala, T. (1992). *Avautuva laitos* [Opening institution]. Helsinki: Suomen kaupunkiliitto.

Virtanen, P. (1994). *Services integration for children and youth at risk and their families. The case of Finland.* Helsinki: National Research and Development Center for Welfare and Health. Themes 4.1994.

III

Family Service Orientation — Nonmandatory Reporting

7

Belgium

An Alternative Approach to Child Abuse Reporting and Treatment

CATHERINE MARNEFFE

PATRICK BROOS

Belgium is a small European country of 10 million inhabitants composed of three linguistic communities (French, Flemish, and German). Although small, the country is very divided, which makes it rather complicated for an outsider to understand. Our research examines child abuse and neglect policies during the period between 1986 and 1992. Belgium has no mandatory reporting system for cases of child abuse and neglect. Since the mid-1980s, 17 specialized centers for the prevention and treatment of child abuse and neglect have been established by decree in Wallonia and by resolution in Flanders (two of the country's three major regions). The centers are organized around three functions.

First, the centers offer direct assistance and management of abused children and their families. This means that children are protected in the family and remain with the family whenever possible. Even if a safe place has to be found outside the family, the parents are involved in the decision making.

Second, the centers offer support, supervision, and counseling for professionals confronted with child abuse. Help for the families indeed necessitates help for those who work with them.

Finally, the centers' more general function is preventive. The focus is more on changing public opinion than trying to change the family because child abuse and neglect cannot be reduced to a problem of bad or pathological parents.

The Belgian reporting system is very flexible since people are encouraged, but not legally obliged, to report cases of child abuse to these centers. Current issues facing the Belgian system are expressed in the following questions: Is solidarity a better answer than repression in cases of child abuse, especially child sexual abuse? Is maltreatment an isolated problem, or do we have to place it in a broader social and psychological context? How efficient is the system? Is the emphasis too much on coordination of help and registration of cases rather than on the quality of the help delivered? This chapter tries to answer these questions through the analysis of child protection work in Belgium. We begin with an overview of the legal context.

Legal Context

The first act in Belgium concerning child protection was passed on May 15, 1912 (Belgisch Staatsblad, 1912). It stated that offenses committed against children under the age of 16 years were to be severely punished. It also provided for specific protective measures for these children. However many problems concerning abused children and their families were not addressed by this law. For instance, abusive parents could be punished, while the underlying causes remained untreated. Moreover, the judge needed hard evidence to be able to prosecute the abuser so that the child almost had to be beaten black and blue before any legal action could be taken. The 1912 act did not include preventive measures.

It was only in 1965 that a new law was adopted with a broader mandate. The act of April 8, 1965 (Belgisch Staatsblad, 1965) concerning youth protection provided for a whole range of preventive measures to reduce the dangers to which minors (those younger than 18 years) might be exposed.

Before 1980 two authorities, each having a specific role, dealt with youth protection: the Youth Committees, offering "social protection," and the juvenile courts, guaranteeing "legal protection." The committees could be asked to intervene when the child was in danger. However they did not possess any legal power and could therefore only intervene when help was refused by caretakers. The committees had to inform the attorney about the infringements for the sake of the physical health or the morality of the minor; they also were expected to cooperate with the attorney if the minor was "in danger."

After 1980 Belgium was divided into regions (Flanders, Wallonia, and Brussels), which resulted in a French and a Flemish Youth Protection Committee to serve the major linguistic communities in these regions. In Flanders as well as in Wallonia and Brussels, critical responses to the 1965 law resulted in a reorganization of child protection work. During the 1980s the Flemish government took several legislative initiatives (among which the decree of June 27, 1985, is the most powerful) coordinated in the 1990 decree (Belgisch Staatsblad, 1985, 1988, 1990). The committees are now called Committees for Special Youth Care and have to work on a voluntary basis with a clear separation from the juvenile court. Children have to be heard and must be kept as long as possible in their family. In line with these objectives a Mediation Commission was established to resolve family conflicts and to reduce interventions by the juvenile judge (Decock, 1991).

In Wallonia the evolution was slightly different and was more centered around the Convention for Children's Rights. The committees in Wallonia, called Services for Help to Youngsters, are comparable to the Flemish committees though they are closer to juvenile court. Their director is also the contact person with the juvenile court. When families disagree with the director's decision for help (e.g., placement of a sexually abused child), the director is obliged to report the case to court. Still the director can take measures to influence the court decision; for example, if the court decides the child has to be placed in an institution, the director can propose a foster family, but cannot decide that the child can remain home (Belgisch Staatsblad, 1991). Since March 1988 the French Community also has had a mediation organ that consists of one person who protects the rights of children and defends them in court. On November 1, 1991, a National Delegate for the Rights of the Child was nominated for the defense of children (Boermans, Lampo, & Marneffe, 1988; Eliaerts et al., 1990; Lelièvre, 1993).

The juvenile courts and the juvenile courts of appeal possess legal power and are responsible for the legal protection of youth. While the courts can take protective legal measures for children, these measures are not necessarily punitive.

In Belgium the juvenile courts are qualified to consider

1. Criminal acts: The juvenile judge can officiate in cases of minors (less than 18 years old in Belgium) who commit an act considered a crime; these cases are described in the law on youth protection of 1965 as those of a "child in danger," which means that children who commit crimes (e.g., robbery, willful injuries, etc.) are victims of their education. Measures that may be taken include reprimand, supervision, placement, psychiatric treatment, and jail as provisional measures.
2. Problematic educational situation: Educational directives to parents or guardians of the child, placing children under supervision for short or longer periods.
3. Measures toward parents: Supervision of payment, dismissal of parental authority.

Although the 1965 Youth Protection Act (Belgian Law, 1965) was passed four years after Henry Kempe introduced the "battered child syndrome," (Kempe et al., 1962) this term is never mentioned in the text. In fact the law does not specify the restraint of violence against children. Even though the intent of the lawmakers in 1965 was to protect children against their caretakers, the law failed to consider that punitive action in cases of child abuse or neglect probably does not provide the best solution.

The conflict between a "general referral" and "professional secrecy" often interferes with the treatment of child abuse and neglect. The general referral, mentioned in the penal code (Strafwetboek van Strafvorderingen, 1994), compels citizens who witness an assault (art. 30 of the penal code) or civil servants who have knowledge of a criminal offense (art. 29 of the penal code) to report these to the proper authorities. Failure to report these acts can be punished by a prison sentence of up to a maximum of six months (art. 422 bis of the penal code). Since child abuse can be interpreted as an assault, one might argue that (because they are citizens) doctors, social workers, and other professionals are obliged to report such cases. At the same time doctors, social workers, and other professionals recognize that infringements on their professional secrecy can also be sanctioned by the penal code (art. 458). These conflicting obligations make it difficult for health professionals to help and for the abusive parents to ask for help (Decock, 1991; Eliaerts et al., 1990; Lelièvre, 1993). Since 1976 members of Parliament have introduced 13 bills to resolve this conflict in cases of child abuse; these bills recommended either to abrogate the privilege of professional secrecy in cases of child abuse or to create special services (like the Confidential Doctor Centers) to deal with problems of child abuse and neglect (Boermans et al., 1988).

In 1979 four research projects were initiated by the Ministry of Social Welfare to examine the extent of child abuse in Belgium and to analyze how child protection work should be organized to prevent child abuse. The studies were developed under the auspices of Kind en Gezin (K & G, meaning Child and Family) in Flanders and the Office de la Naissance et de l'Enfance (ONE, Office of Birth and Infancy) in Wallonia. K & G and ONE both are medicosocial organizations that are active in the field of birth and motherhood counseling to parents with young children. A free network of nurses functions all over the country. They visit new parents at home weekly to give advice, to support the young families, and to abet the healthy development of the newborn. They also help young parents with their babies' care and education and provide necessary vaccinations.

Starting in the autumn of 1979, the studies lasted four years and were conducted in collaboration with universities in Brussels, Louvain, Liège, and Antwerp. The findings of these studies revealed

1. That child abuse and neglect existed in Belgium
2. That once professional teams were sensitized to the problem many cases were discovered
3. That in 80% of the cases the children could stay with their parents after family therapy was applied (Clara, 1983; Kempe & Kempe, 1978; Marneffe, 1990; Soumenkoff et al., 1982)

These results led to a decree of the French Community in 1985 implementing 11 multidisciplinary teams for the prevention and treatment of child abuse and neglect, called SOS-Enfants' centers (Belgisch Staatsblad, 1985). The Flemish Executive followed in 1987 with a resolution installing 6 multidisciplinary teams based on the same model in Flanders. Thus Belgium has 17 multidisciplinary teams for 2,316,488 children (less than 18 years old) or one center for each 136,264 children. These child- and family-oriented teams all function on the basis of the same broad principles: The centers have multidisciplinary teams offering support and coordination of professionals as well as help to the abusive families in an anonymous neutral environment. Emphasis is on treatment and not on investigation. However there are differences, for cultural, philosophical, and conceptual reasons.

First, Flanders is influenced by the Netherlands, where progressive solutions are sought to social problems, while Wallonia is influenced by France, where repression plays an important role in solving social problems. The tendency of the Flemish teams to collaborate with judicial authorities, especially in cases of sexual abuse, is somewhat minimal (3–7% of the cases), while this rate is higher in Wallonia (40%) (Bontemps & Binot, 1993; Willems & Buysse, 1992).

A second difference is linked to the implementation of the team efforts within a medical structure. Six teams are clearly directed by a medical doctor and integrated within university hospitals for children. This increases the reports of the most vulnerable children (babies less than 1 year old) and gives immediate access to the abusive parents, who will come anyway to the hospitals with their injured children. Anonymity of the parents is also protected by the hospitals, while this is not the case for centers located in a child protection center on the street. Everybody knows why parents visit that kind of center, but not why they come to the hospital.

Third, in 11 centers, collaboration with other services is utilized more than direct, immediate help to families. The referral of families to other services is often motivated by the idea that abusive families should be given help by the universal child welfare services in place. However in practice abusive families are already known by an average of five professionals when reported to the centers (Willems & Buysse, 1992). Moreover, families tend to reduce their efforts in seeking help when they are sent to different agencies for their different problems. Too much coordination and too many round table conferences also include the risk of a dilution of responsibilities, as well as the risk of losing sight of the child and the family. The six teams directed by doctors take into account the need to collaborate with different existing structures, but they first provide immediate help for the child and the family. It is only afterward that other professionals are involved at the convenience of the parents.

Definitions Used in Daily Practice

In practice Walloon and Flemish centers use a broad definition of child abuse that can be compared to Gil's (1978) definition:

> Child abuse is any act of commission or omission by individuals, institutions or society as a whole, and any conditions resulting from such acts or inactions, which deprive children of their equal rights and liberties and/or interfere with their optimal development, constitute by definition abusive or neglectful acts or conditions.

This definition is specific enough to identify physical and emotional abuse and neglect resulting from acts of parents and other individual caretakers, as well as institutions such as schools, juvenile courts, detention centers, child welfare homes, and so on. It also covers abuse and neglect tolerated or perpetrated by society collectively, such as malnutrition of children and expectant mothers, substandard housing, and inadequate educational, recreational, and cultural measures and so on.

The centers commonly categorize child abuse into four groups: (i) physical abuse, (ii) neglect, (iii) emotional abuse, and (iv) sexual abuse.

Physical abuse involves all forms of nonaccidental trauma to children by their caretakers. As described in medical literature, clinical signs of the battered child syndrome include a spectrum ranging from bruises, welts, lacerations, abdominal injuries, ocular damage, burns, scalds, and bone fractures to death (Ajoub & Pfeifer, 1979; Caffey, 1946; Cooper, 1978; Gornall, Ahmed, Jolleys, & Cohen, 1972). Skull fracture and the presence of subdural hematoma have been frequently reported (Caffey, 1946; Silverman, 1953). Any bruising of a baby not yet mobile is very suspect (Cooper, 1978). Shaking an infant may cause injury to the child's neck, bleeding within the skull, and brain injury that may be associated with early death (Caffey, 1972). Frequently the diagnosis of severe child abuse is supported by the simultaneous presence of new injuries to bone and soft tissue and by signs of previous trauma, detected on physical examination or on X-ray film. The instruments used to inflict harm on children vary from bare hands or feet to belts, sticks, electric cords (Showers & Bardman, 1986), boiling water, and pokers (Ajoub & Pfeifer, 1979; Lenoski & Hunter, 1977), with a total of 95 different implements being reported in one survey (Johnson, 1985).

A recently recognized form of child abuse is Munchausen's syndrome by proxy, a psychiatric illness in which the parent creates a physical illness in the child in order to gain attention and medical treatment. The children described by this syndrome have parents who, by fabrication, have caused innumerable harmful medical procedures. They injure the child by simulating episodes of bleeding, neurological abnormalities, rashes, fevers, and abnormal urine through injection of water or fecal material, substitution of contaminated urine samples for the child's own urine, or poisoning the child with medication (Meadow, 1977, 1982).

Neglect can be a very insidious form of maltreatment and if there is no contact with a doctor or nurse, it can persist unnoticed for a long time. Neglect implies the failure to provide shelter, hygiene, medical care, education, or supervision. Victims of neglect show a scaly and dirty skin, matty and sparse hair, sunken eyes, an aged face, and look particularly apathetic, sad, and anxious. This form of abuse is felt to be the most common form of child maltreatment reported, accounting for almost two thirds of identified cases (Cantwell, 1980). The "failure-to-thrive" syndrome has been associated with neglect of children. It is a potentially life-threatening condition in which weight, height, and often head circumference of the child fall below the third percentile of children their age. Neurologic and psychologic growth also slow, and there are no signs of organic illness to account for these symptoms.

Emotional or psychological abuse of children refers to detrimental treatment of a child by a caretaker. This covers the whole spectrum from consistent negative attention such as verbal harassment, criticism, and belittlement to complete lack of attention through, for example, withdrawal, rejection, or denial of the child's existence. This type of abuse is the most value laden and the most difficult to evaluate; it is also probably the most prevalent form of abuse in families. Garbarino (1979) has proposed the following definition: "the willful destruction or significant impairment of the child's competence" (p. 88). Emotional injuries may be more disabling than some physical injuries and inflict just as much damage on the developing personality (Garbarino & Gilliam, 1980). The problems of defining the term, the difficulty in predicting outcomes for such children, and the untested efficacy of therapeutic intervention may explain why professionals feel so powerless to help and tend to remain passive when confronted with emotional abuse.

Sexual exploitation of children has received increasing attention in the past 10 years. Kempe and Kempe (1978) define sexual abuse as "the involvement of dependent, developmentally immature children and adolescents in sexual activities that they do not fully comprehend, to which they are unable to give informed consent, or that violate the social taboos of family roles" (p. 60). This type of abuse can involve fondling, exhibitionism, or sexual intercourse mostly by acquaintances or family members of the child and also by strangers.

Reporting and Placement Trends

Reporting and Substantiating Child Abuse

Collecting data in Belgium is very difficult. Information before 1986 is nonexistent. Social services are new and started registration mostly in the mid-1980s. Police stations started registration in 1990, and results were only released in 1995. Trends in placement can be discerned since 1986. Before that any problem child was called handicapped, delinquent, or not educable and was placed in an institution.

In the period between 1989 and 1992 when registration was made obligatory for all Centers, 19,098 abused children were referred to all Belgian Centers. The majority of abused children were between 3 and 6 years old. Cases of abuse that appeared least often were Munchausen syndrome by proxy, sexual abuse by mothers, and abuse of children older than 15 years of age. In Flanders 57.9% of the abused children in 1992 were female.

More than one third of the cases are referred by the parents or close family members, others are referred by schools, hospitals, or external professionals. This was not the case before 1986 when Centers worked in collaboration with judicial authorities; for example, initially only 3% of self-referrals were made to the Brussels Center.

In 1992 only 8% of the children reported to the Flemish centers needed intervention by the judicial authorities. Extrafamilial cases are included, of which an exact number is not available. One can presume though that extrafamilial violence is a substantial part of this total number (Willems & Buysse, 1992).

An overview on reported children per 1,000 is given in Table 7-1. The data consist of all the registered abused children reported in the specialized centers (SOS and CDCs) in 1986, 1989, and 1992. In 1986 the Committees for Special

Table 7-1. Rate of Child Abuse Reports per 1,000 Children

Type of Abuse	1986	1989	1992
Physical abuse	0.23	0.39	0.31
Neglect	0.84	0.37	0.21
Sexual abuse	0.08	0.27	0.70
Emotional/psychological	0.03	0.24	0.14
Other (at risk)	0.02	0.51	0.21
Categories unavailable	0.59	0.24	1.34
Total per 1,000	1.79	2.02	2.91
(N)*	(3,988)	(4,405)	(6,800)

*N = total number of children reported each year (i.e., 3,988 reported in 1986).

Youth Care also registered abused children. The data given in Table 7-1 are complete. The system in Belgium is organized so that practically all abused children are reported directly to the centers.

Most of the children reported are between 0 and 15 years old. The rate per 1,000 was calculated for children between 0 and 17 years old (18 years is majority). This underestimates the reporting rate because the group of abused children between 15 and 17 years old reported to the centers is relatively small. Often this group of children consults other (adult) centers.

Cases reported per 1,000 children are given by category, but some centers do not have the time and resources to separate the data into categories. This is especially the case for the Walloon centers. Therefore the category in which type of abuse was not specified ("categories unavailable") was included. In addition to the categories of physical abuse, neglect, sexual abuse, and emotional abuse, there is an "other" category that includes high-risk families, instances of Munchausen syndrome by proxy, and institutional maltreatment. High-risk families are the largest group in this category, with Munchausen syndrome by proxy and institutional maltreatment accounting for only a small fraction of the cases.

Discussion and Trends

As to trends, an important change over the years involves reporting data on sexual abuse. Sexual abuse was and still is taboo, but now people accept that it exists. Thus between 1986 and 1992 the reported rate of child sexual abuse increased almost ninefold. Children reported before 1992 for physical abuse or neglect often were sexually abused. Emotional abuse also increased from 1986 to a high in 1989 after which it has declined as professionals have learned to make better distinctions among the categories. The rate of neglect was very high in 1986; this was due to reports from Committees for Special Youth Care, which tend to work more with people of low socioeconomic status. Questions have been raised about the accuracy of data in this category.

Overall, since 1986 the data show an increase in the reports of abused children. There are several reasons for this increase. CDCs have become better known to the population. People are more aware of the deliberate help that is offered in these centers to both children and abusive parents, which makes it easier to report problems. Offering help instead of referrals to court also increased the number of self-reports. These factors suggest that the increasing rate of child abuse reports does not necessarily reflect a higher occurrence of child abuse. However one must recognize that the European economic crisis has resulted in more problems and greater strains for low-income families, which may affect abusive behavior.

In approximately 90% of the cases the abuse is substantiated because the system is based on voluntary help offered to the families. The diagnosis of child abuse is nearly always confirmed for three main reasons:

1. One of the parents or family members reports to the centers with the demand to recognize child abuse by his or her partner. Identification of the abuse is strengthened by assessment of the child as well as interviews of both parents.
2. The abusive parent asks for help for his or her violent behavior. The basic reason for a high level of substantiation is the absence of the threat of judicial intervention. However substantiation in sexual abuse cases is lower because 20% of these reports are made in the context of divorces. Substantiation is then very difficult because it concerns younger children torn between parents, who are supported by lawyers. Once there is the risk of judicial intervention, it seems logical that perpetrators will not talk and that substantiation becomes more difficult.
3. In cases of reports by professionals, the diagnosis is confirmed after an honest discussion with both parents and all professionals involved and a thorough examination of the child.

In 1992 42.9% of the total number ($N = 2,669$) of children reported to the centers were reported by the family members of the child, 22.9% came from health care, 13.1% from social care, 12.7% from schools, 3.1% from forensic services, 3.1% from special youth care, 0.9% from preschool services, and 1.4% from anonymous sources.

In addition to the reports to CDCs the most severe and threatening cases of child abuse are reported to the police. The figures of Table 7-2 represent the number of cases of child abuse reported to the police that went on to prosecution in the courts.

Table 7-2. Complaints of Child Abuse (of Children 0–15 Years) that Go to the Prosecutor (Rate per 1,000 Children)

	1992	Substantiation
Willful blows and injuries	0.126	58%
Homicide	0.005	36%
Rape	0.110	16.5%
Total	0.241	36%

Trends in Out-of-Home Placement

Complete figures for out-of-home placement are available since 1988 and only for children in institutions and foster care. Out-of-home placements of children are subsidized by the government (Wallonia, Flanders, & Brussels) and can be required by court or voluntarily decided on by parents or caretakers with the help of a social service such as the Committee for Special Youth Care, Service for Help to Youngsters, Kind en Gezin, Office de la Naissance et de l'Enfance, and Public Center for Social Welfare. Funding goes to institutions, which are roughly divided into medical pedagogical boarding schools, child psychiatric residences, family homes, and group homes.

Table 7-3 gives an overview of the total number of children placed in institutions and foster care families, excluding the Child Psychiatric Clinics. Institutional placements are divided into two categories, those that provide for the handicapped and those that serve minors in problematic educational situations.

As the data here indicate, in the last few years the placement of handicapped children has remained practically the same, but there is a clear decrease in the number of children placed in institutions for educational problems. Foster care has increased and is used more as an alternative to institutional placement, especially in Wallonia. Foster care is often an alternative for adoption since a child can only be adopted in Belgium when relinquished by his parents for at least one year or by decision of the juvenile judge by transfer of parental authority to a tutor, who can adopt the child. This means that not many (3%) Belgian children are adoptable. Adoption overseas is a more attractive option since the waiting periods are relatively shorter (Senaeve, 1995). Of the placements, 75% are imposed by a court, with only 25% voluntary placements.

The total number of out-of-home placements has decreased. This reflects a tendency to recognize that the family of origin is often the best place for children and that parents have to be helped with their child's education instead of removing children from their homes. Services for Care at Home (Thuisbegeleidings-diensten) were implemented in Flanders. These services offer help at home mostly to multiproblem families referred by the Committees of Special Youth Care or juvenile court (Ghesquière, 1989). In 1992 120 families referred by juvenile court and 140 families referred by the committees were

Table 7-3. Children in Belgium Placed Out of the Home in Institutions and Foster Care (Rate per 1,000 Children)

	1989	1992
Institutions — problems	4.4	2.6
Institutions — handicapped	3.7	3.6
Foster care	2.2	2.8
Total	10.3	9.0

assisted at home. Another reason for the decrease is the very high cost of out-of-home placement in a time of fiscal crises.

Beyond the placement rates there is relatively little information on abused children placed in out-of-home settings. The available data indicate however that the percentage of maltreated children placed in foster care is higher than for those placed in residential homes, there is virtually no adoption of maltreated children, and the average stay in foster care is four years compared to two years in residential institutions. More than 80% of the children in residential care are older than six years.

Issues: The Case for An Alternative Approach

From the earliest attempts to deal with the issue of child maltreatment, differences in concept and philosophy arose between the judicial approach to child rescue and the social work approach to protection and protective services. Despite these fundamental conflicts regarding the correct approach to child protection, ideological controversy on this issue of child abuse is not really in the foreground. The bulk of literature in the field of child maltreatment and protection throughout the world tends to focus on better methods of assessment; investigation; reporting systems; therapeutic programs for the perpetrators, which assumes they are deviant; and descriptions of out-of-home care facilities for the victimized children, which assumes they are better off without their (even abusive) parents.

Emphasis is not on analysis of the broader social context in which child protection is organized in our modern societies. Evidently it is not easy to think about the context of the child protection work in day-to-day practice because there are so many overwhelming practical problems to be solved. This explains probably why decriminalization of child maltreatment is not yet possible, why responses based on social control are implemented so easily, and why the prevalent intervention is still—at least in regard to sexual abuse—a legal one. Mandatory reporting of abused and neglected children using a strategy of legal or social coercion toward the perpetrators is still considered as the way society will overcome this difficult problem.

Therefore alternate forms of intervention, based on a new concept and practice of child protection work, are to be understood as alternatives to the traditional paradigm. Comprehension and compassion, the offer of noncoercive services and support by one agency for those who fail in their familial relationships, are put forward instead of scandal, reporting, and the obligation to visit a specific agency for those who are labeled child abusers. This nonpunitive response to child abuse and neglect was developed simultaneously in several western European countries in the early 1970s. The Confidential Doctor Bureaus were the first ones to be created in 1972 in the Netherlands (Koers, 1981), Kind in Nood ("Child in Need") in Belgium (Marneffe, Lampo, Proost, & Boermans, 1987), and the Fifth Province in Ireland (McCarthy & Byrne, 1988) followed, reflecting the same background philosophy as introduced by Reinhart Wolff (Wolff, 1991) in the Berlin Child Protection Center in 1975.

This new model of child protection work was derived from three main lines of analyses:

1. Analysis of child abuse in a broader socioeconomic and political context
2. Analysis and comparison of traditional judicial and medicopsychosocial models of intervention
3. Analysis of the costs and benefits of traditional interventions for the child and the child's family

Structural Analysis of Child Abuse and Neglect

As Gelles (1979) pointed out 20 years ago, child abuse and neglect amounts to a social construction. Of course children were injured, abandoned, or tyrannized before people began to call this problem "child maltreatment." Child abuse is described as a pathology or a crime, in other words, as an individual qualitative problem. Child abuse differs not in quality from other human relationships, but in quantity. Exploitation, rejection, indifference, and aggressiveness are daily reactions of all of us. Child abuse is an extreme expression of these reactions and cannot be considered without taking into account the social context in which it is enacted. Child abuse has thus been created as a social problem — it is not just there, it is a discourse.

This may sound irresponsible in regard to child abuse since children experience very real problems when they are hit, burned, yelled at, or ignored. This does not mean that there is no violent behavior on the part of parents toward their children, that there are no families in need of services, or there are no abused and neglected children. This means that objective statements are impossible because they are inherent to the social context in which these problems arise. The areas of medicine, law, social work, and psychotherapy have generated different responses to the problem of violence in the family and various "constructions of reality." This is also true for the family: Each family member will have to understand their own construction of the reality to be able to change it, to adapt a new behavior, and to eliminate or at least diminish dysfunctional patterns underlying child abuse and neglect. When a child is hit, is it abuse, a way to educate the child, or the expression of rage or powerlessness? Is it necessary for the child's upbringing, or is it the result of parental failure? Do the parents share their ways of seeing the same facts? How does the child experience what occurs to him or her, as a cruel act from his or her parents or as a well-deserved reaction to his or her bad behavior? Parents indeed have to be encouraged to talk about why they want to harm each other, they have to acknowledge their involvement in the family disputes, and they have to be brought to develop a new understanding of their children and their relationship with them — in other words they have to reconstruct reality (Wolff, 1991).

The tendency to describe violence as merely an aggressive act on the part of an individual (i.e., the "illness" model) still dominates the understanding of child abuse. Child maltreatment is not yet understood as a sociopsychological, cultural, political, and gender problem. That is, anybody could become a child abuser depending on the specific relational and societal circumstances (Wolff, 1991). Child abuse and neglect differ only in quantity and not in quality from the usual attitudes of adults toward children and also from violent behavioral patterns that are obvious and even highly praised on other levels in our society.

On the one hand western state economies emphasize individual freedom, opportunities, and responsibilities. This individualism goes together with the tendency to attribute "blame" for unfortunate life events to the victims of misfortunes (Muller, Caldwell, & Hunter, 1993). Those at the bottom belong there because they lack virtue, merit, and talent (Keniston, 1979). They are the "undeserving poor" (Katz, 1989). On the other hand the same society expects parents not to behave as competing individuals using their power in order to educate their weaker children, but as a family of related people moved by each other's well-being and preoccupied by the fate of the smallest. Although individualism suggests that those who suffer financial, social, or moral problems are to blame for their condition, it becomes suddenly intolerable when parents blame their children for their failures. This does not mean that parents should be allowed to exploit their children. It means that behavioral patterns in abusive families to some extent mirror societal attitudes.

Moreover, child abuse cannot be isolated from the larger social and cultural institutions that unwittingly encourage it (Gil, 1975). Most settings such as day care centers, schools, courts, child care agencies, and welfare departments generally tend to inhibit children's spontaneity and creativity and to promote conformity rather than critical, independent thought. How many professionals would indeed leave their children for more than one day in the care of the institutions they so warmly recommend? Worse though is the legally sanctioned, massive abuse of children denied the benefits of comprehensive welfare systems or of children living in foster care or institutions (Gil, 1978). They are condemned to conditions of existence under which physical, social, emotional, and intellectual developments are likely to be severely handicapped (Gil, 1975).

Many social scientists (Garbarino, 1977; Gil, 1975; Pelton, 1978; Wolff, 1991) have discouraged fragmentary therapeutic efforts aimed at one or another cause of child abuse. Instead they propose fundamental changes in social philosophy and value premises, in societal institutions, and in human relations. The changes are centered on the elimination of social inequalities such as poverty, unemployment, and bad housing rather than on altering the behavior of abusive and neglectful parents. Today more than ever it is clear that these types of basic changes are not going to come about immediately. Even in western Europe where comprehensive public welfare seemed to be highly valued, along with some degree of equality, this fundamental right is threatened by the increasing economic crisis.

However, by focusing on only this broad social transformation, one could lose sight of the daily reality of damage to children, the misery of their parents, and the isolation of many professionals. In the absence of broader changes Garbarino (1977) recommends that smaller steps can be taken. Even in contemplating these smaller steps one must bear in mind the social construction of child abuse, the continuous interactions between individuals and society, and the economic context. Current interventions have to go beyond the unidimensional psychiatric approach, which considers child abuse the result of understandable and predictable patterns in parent-child interactions that are basically determined by the way parents were cared for in infancy themselves. Societal frustration and stress are important variables associated with violence, as is the past history of abusive parents.

Current Interventions: Judicial Versus Medicopsychosocial Models

Considering child abuse as a crime or as a result of a family dysfunction determines the reactions of society to child maltreatment. At the core of the controversy about the proper role of justice in family violence is the question: To what extent does child abuse represent a violation of criminal law? By 1874, for example, the New York Society for the Prevention of Cruelty to Children (SPCC), which was organized as a result of the famous Mary Ellen Wilson case, was given police powers that are still in place to this day (Shepard, 1987). The Massachusetts SPCC, established in 1878, became known as "the cruelty," suggesting the recognition and fear of its function, mainly centered on the removal of children, after judicial intervention (Gordon, 1988).

In the judicial model abuse and neglect of the child by the child's parents may be considered a criminal offense, and the first solution is to punish and penalize the abusers. This corresponds with a violent disapproval of a deviant attitude and assumes that not to punish these parents amounts to giving them the right to harm their children. Although legal sanctions regulate the conflict between the perpetrator of an offense and society, they neither solve the more complex underlying problems of family dysfunction nor alleviate the victim's lot. That the sanction thus hits the perpetrator but does not heal the victim's wounds is a leitmotiv in the child abuse literature (Eisenberg, 1981; Gil, 1978; Kempe & Kempe, 1978; Wolff, 1991).

Moreover the punitive approach is often disastrous to the child's situation. The child is separated from his or her family, which the child considers as a punishment and blames himself or herself for what happens to his or her parents. The existing tensions in the parent-child relationship certainly will not be alleviated by this measure. Although the child is now protected from further mistreatment, without help the child is likely to feel guilty for what happened and feel abandoned and punished. The child's parents, who were often marked by their past lives, are now exposed to yet more social and familial stigmatization. As a result they experience more isolation, more tensions, and more reasons to feel bad about themselves and thus more risk that they will lose control and attack their children without seeking help. Their distrust of society is confirmed by its repressive intervention (Koers, 1981).

In addition, from the judicial perspective intervention might be warranted only when abuse results in serious harm to a child. This is illustrated by a survey on court disposition of 71 abusive families referred to a treatment program: 96% (25 families) of the court-ordered referrals involved physical evidence of abuse compared to 20% (46 families) of those not court ordered.

Moreover court-ordered referrals comprised 73% of all cases in which the child had clear signs of physical abuse, and voluntary referrals comprised 27% of such cases (Wolfe, Aragona, Kaufman, & Sandler, 1980).

Other forms of judicial interventions have emerged, aimed more at the protection of children and the support of the family as a whole than at the sanction of the parents' inadequate behavior. Judicial protection became the way to set up guidance or to promote counseling to the abused child, the abusive family, or both. Some authors suggest that threatening maltreating parents with prosecution encourages them to accept treatment (Crivillé, 1983; Deltaglia, 1976; Larter, 1979; Rosenfeld, 1979; Wolfe et al., 1980).

The medicopsychosocial model assumes that child abuse and neglect is understood as the result of a family dysfunction. Both the abuser and child are perceived as victims influenced by broad sociological and psychological factors beyond their control (Gelles, 1979). The parents have to be helped to normalize their relationship with each other and with their children. Protection of the abused child is a priority, but the child is more often maintained in the child's family together with the provision of services to support the parents and help them cope (Kempe & Kempe, 1978).

In the medicopsychosocial model the approach to child abuse is frequently subjective or intuitive. For practitioners the clinical "feeling" that a family is under stress or needs help or that a child is "at risk" is enough to intervene; in contrast the legal model is unwilling to accept conclusions or impressions lacking empirical corroboration (Newberger & Bourne, 1978). However the offer of therapy does not necessarily mean that parents consent to proposed interventions. When parents resist the offer of counseling, professional clinical interventions often become like judicial inquiries: inquisitive, moralizing, sometimes stigmatizing (even though they are supposed to be free of any judgment and based on the offer of help to families with difficulties) (Drew, 1980). Such attitudes result in efforts at social control, with the threat to report the parents to the judicial or administrative authorities, without the procedural guarantees offered by the courts (Somerhausen, 1979).

Many professionals have questioned the wisdom of trying to function as both an agent of social control and a helper (Drew, 1980; Wolff, 1983). While child welfare agencies should offer their assistance to violent families, they are in fact often functioning as the disguised deputies of justice (Somerhausen, 1979).

Both systems, the judicial and the medicopsychosocial, are thus difficult to differentiate. Judicial authorities that are supposed to implement social control are often proposing therapeutic solutions, and social services are often too controlling and not therapeutic enough. There is a confusion of roles with practitioners often using justice as "the big stick," taking the place of the judge, and magistrates sometimes hesitating to make decisions and trying to replace the failing or absent therapists.

Moreover, independent of the chosen model, findings in three American studies (Besharov, 1985; Drew, 1980; Meddin & Hansen, 1985) show that in a majority of cases of child abuse services are not provided because of the huge allocation of resources for investigation. Besharov (1985) recognizes that mandatory reporting results in too many reports, too many unsubstantiated reports, and too many intrusive investigations with deleterious consequences for the child and the child's parents, while the children in danger are not really helped. However, Besharov does not question the system itself, which emphasizes reporting and investigation above tolerance, compassion, and the real desire to help children and parents in their difficult relationships (Solnit, 1980).

Currently, because of the urgency of investigatory functions, social workers are forced to spend the majority of their time conducting investigations and completing the accompanying forms. The result is that little time and resources are left for the therapeutic role. Many children are not better off. This in turn provokes the critique or even scapegoating of social workers.

Placement is the most frequently provided service, but only one third of these placed children receive any clinical services (Shepard, 1987). To protect the abused child and the child's family through the offer of help is generally seen as a less important goal than is the need to protect the child through reporting, investigation, and separation, even against the child's will.

Under the traditional system even when therapy is available it is often infused with retributive aspects (Illich, 1975). The less "curable" the abuser — that is, the more vindictive and independent the abuser — the less treatment will be offered and the more punitive will society's response appear (Newberger & Bourne, 1978). Socioeconomically marginal individuals are more likely to be defined as deviant than others since characteristics frequently identified with the battered child syndrome are associated with poverty (Kempe & Kempe, 1978). Under the traditional system professionals perform an intricate process of selection, finding facts to fit the label, defining aberrant behavior as a medical problem or a legal problem, and providing treatment or court action. The conflict inherent in fulfilling the two responsibilities of social control and therapeutic support seriously hampers the establishment of a positive helping relationship with the family (Drew, 1980; Gordon, 1988; Wolff, 1983). "Helping" services are inadequate in most communities, with the standard of professional action so low and the consequences of incompetent intervention for the family so distressing that a new philosophy in child protection work is needed.

A New Approach to Child Protection Work

The philosophy underlying a new approach to child protection work consists of offering help instead of punishment, respecting confidentiality instead of implementing control, emphasizing solidarity instead of reporting, mobilizing the family's own resources instead of maintaining their passivity, and encouraging collaboration among professionals instead of competition. Activating the clients' resources is emphasized because denying families the opportunity to participate actively in problem resolution amounts to denying their right to self-determination (Meddin & Hansen, 1985).

The system of services includes crisis intervention and telephone counseling; child, couple, and family therapy; a high-quality residential structure attached to an ambulatory unit; professional training and supervision; research activities; and teaching. Services to families are offered without control or sanctions: Police and criminal court action are not sought. Services aim to consolidate strengths in families and children for the promotion of health rather than the treatment of disease through collaboration with a multidisciplinary team and other concerned professionals the families know and trust. This approach requires the voluntary participation of the family and not their submission under the threat of court action.

A clear separation from the judicial system is necessary to establish a trustful relationship with the families. Successful psychotherapy depends in part on an assurance of privacy and a sense of trust, which permit the most open and intimate expression of thoughts and feelings. Confidentiality is an essential aspect of the therapeutic interaction (Green, 1979; Steele, 1986). Therefore parents with difficulties or who have endangered their children should be able to come of their free choice and spontaneously to places they know they will get help without the risk of social or judicial control. To diminish their fear of being depreciated or judged, services have to be offered without delay and free of charge with a guarantee for anonymity.

The aims of this new child protective care are to relieve the family immediately of an actual crisis situation, to guarantee the well-being and security of an abused or neglected child, to offer educational and therapeutic help to work through the conflicts that led to the abuse, and finally to develop a sound perspective for the child and its family.

It is the deficit of options for early voluntary assistance that leads to later needs for mandatory reporting and coercive interventions, "services" that can be characterized as "too late" (Solnit, 1980). As illustrated by epidemiological data, only 10% of abusive parents are considered impossible to treat (Jones & Alexander, 1987; Kempe & Kempe, 1978). Coercive interventions that breach the privacy of the family should only be permitted when there is an urgent need to implement a decisive, often emergency life-saving, intervention in cases of serious bodily injury or abandonment. Moreover the specific grounds for coercive intervention should be well known in order to provide advance warning to parents and to set the boundaries for restraint of the state's power to inquire and intervene into family affairs (Solnit, 1980). Once well informed, it is the abusive parent who must decide between coercive and voluntary help.

Judicial authorities certainly have a role to play in the legal protection of children, especially when parents do not see the utility of treatment. Though Goldstein, Freud, and Solnit (1973) introduced the concept of the psychological parent and urged court decisions based on children's needs, interests, and time perspectives, the decision to replace biological parents with other psychological parents is extremely rare in the new approach to child protection. When judicial intervention is necessary, instead of reporting the abusive parents to the attorney, the social worker should accompany and support the parents in their choice of judicial protection rather than medicosocial protection of the child. This happens especially when parents are unwilling or unable to question their own behavior in regard to their children's upbringing. These parents are drug addicts, mentally handicapped, or psychotic and untreatable; they often have too many difficulties in their own lives to be able to take care of their children. In these cases the professional should accompany the parents to take the necessary legal steps, instead of reporting them like criminals, to find other psychological parents for their children.

A multiprofessional team approach is emphasized. Fragmentation and competition among professionals (identifying with mother, father, and child and thus reproducing family conflicts by proxy) can be avoided by involving them in the decision making concerning the family if the family agrees. Although social workers and nurses seem best able to conceptualize the familial and social context of problems of violence, they are least paid, most overworked, and as a rule have minimal access to the decision prerogatives of medicine and law (Newberger & Bourne, 1978). If they are to function better in respect to families and their problems, they have to be treated with appropriate respect and support. An effort in this direction has been made at the Brussels Confidential Doctor Center, where the work has been organized under the leadership of a social worker.

In essence the alternative model of child protection is based on the idea that child abuse and neglect differ only in quantity and not in quality from the usual attitudes of adults toward children or powerful people toward the weakest. This model aims to provide universal services based on the principle of need, with services accessible to everybody. Organizations built on the model, such as the multidisciplinary Child Protection Centers in Germany and the Confidential Doctor Centers in Holland and in Belgium, are likely to be most successful if they are embedded in a welfare state system under which they can draw on services ranging from general health insurance to low-cost public and private day care and schools, from low-cost counseling to free infant and mothers' health care, and from social assistance for people in need to family services and family aids. As Wolff (1991) puts it: "This social welfare structure greatly reduces the chance of having environments with a large amount of poverty and deprivation and thus contributes to having fewer and less severe cases of child maltreatment" (p. 5).

The Brussels Confidential Doctor Center Kind in Nood decided to apply this new child protection model in 1986. Practically, direct assistance and management of abused children and their parents have been organized around four major steps:

1. Direct or indirect contact between the abusive family and the center
2. Assessment of the abused child and protective measures if necessary
3. Offer of help to the child and the child's family
4. The child remains at the center or returns to his family

The first step concerns the first contact between the abusive family and the Center. Families are encouraged to come when something goes wrong with their child, when the situation grows worse, when they are worried about their child's development, when they often quarrel about their child, when the child upsets them, when they think only hitting can help, when their child has been ill-treated in the past, when they have been abused in their childhood, or when they need advice or support. The Brussels Center Kind in Nood does not support reporting campaigns, believing civilians should not function as the "eye of the state." Instead of making a report of the neighbor, maybe one could think of what can be done to help. The act of reporting should be transformed into an act of solidarity. Information concerning high-quality treatment programs, rather than the promotion of massive reporting campaigns, is thus provided through the media for all families in difficulty, motivating them to ask for help in confidentiality. Therefore professional services have to be as accessible as possible for abusive parents and their children. Effective reporting of child abuse depends on the accessibility and readiness of the helping system, which is based on

1. Offered help is free, 24 hours a day, seven days a week
2. Guarantee of anonymity for both referrer and abuser
3. Clear distinction of judicial authorities

That this was a successful initiative is proven by comparison of data before and after 1986 (see Table 7-4) (Lampo, Broos, Marneffe, & Deneyer, 1994; Marneffe, 1990).

The fact that referrals by the abusive parents themselves increased from 2% to 38% shows that when services are adapted to encourage abusive parents, they bring their children and ask for help. Moreover, high-quality care centered on the parents decreases the risk for reinjury or fatality of the child.

The second step consists of the diagnosis or evaluation of risk once the parents and the child have arrived in the center. The parents' first interview always happens in the presence of the child immediately after the report. The overall principle is to establish a trusting relationship with the parents from the start. Even though the first interview is used to gain the parents' confidence and is less centered on the child, this does not imply that the observation of the child's attitude, play, and relationship with parents and the interviewer are not used to help evaluate the possibility of further danger. One cannot emphasize enough how important it is to make a diagnosis of child abuse and neglect only after a complete assessment, which consists of a physical and psychological examination of the child, an interview of the parents and of the parents and the child, and a meeting with all the professionals involved, always with the agreement of the child and parents. A thorough examination of the abused

Table 7-4. Comparison of Data Within Traditional and New Child Protection Work

	1979–1986	1986–1994
Reported children	374	3,956
Reinjuries	58	26
Death	1	1
Reports by abusive parents	2%	38%

child without danger for the child often requires a temporary hospitalization. One indeed needs time to evaluate the situation seriously, without supplementary risks for the child. Hospitalization in high-quality conditions appears as a better means than out-of-home placement to protect the child for a short period without endangering the child's further long-term relationships, that is to say, the child's further life within the family.

The third step consists of the offer to help the child and the child's parents. Practically, therapeutic sessions include all family members, which does not mean that each person cannot be seen individually. The adult needs help for the same things the child does and to a certain extent the therapy of the adult is similar to that of the child, being basically a "reparenting process" (Green, 1979). Abused children especially need to have their separate therapist, whom they can trust, before they can be brought to trust their parents again. Meanwhile, parents are encouraged by another practitioner, who works closely with the child therapist, to think about themselves, about their own childhood, and about their sorrow as children and the same sorrow they provoked for their own children. Children as well as parents are brought to recognize first their anger toward their abusive parents, their sadness, and finally their wishes. Only then exists the hope for a new type of relationship following the model of the open professional relationship that was offered to the family.

It must be clear that a positive attitude to abusive parents does not mean that decisions cannot be made against parents on the behalf of their children if the children are in danger. Even if one has to go through this process of separation, it is most important for the child and parents to do it in close and continuous contact with each other, even if they reject the professional.

Reporting to or collaboration with the judicial authorities regarding the families is unthinkable if a trusting relationship is to be established with families for confidentiality is an essential aspect of the therapeutic intervention. When judicial authorities are necessary because abuse is severe and no agreement is possible with the parents, a referral is made to the juvenile court with the parents' knowledge and never behind their backs. This happens in 7% of the cases reported to the Brussels center.

The fourth and last step consists of the reintegration of the child in the child's family. There are no rules. Each case needs an individual approach, and decisions about the child are taken progressively and together with the parents. This can avoid poor and hasty decisions regarding the child's future. When there are signs of improvement, it should be explored to determine whether they reflect real improvement, which can happen quickly in a relatively less damaged personality, or whether it is evidence of a lifelong ability to deny the self and adapt very quickly to the expectations of the environment without any real internal change taking place. When the child is in care one must question whether the therapy has produced real change in the parents' attitudes, or the improvement has been related to the fact that the problem child is no longer in the family.

So far 81% of the children reported between 1986 and 1994 returned into their families. As shown in Table 7-4, although one child died under guidance, and only 26 were reinjured and brought back to the center by their parents, and even if the death of a child is dramatic, one can still consider that one dead child for 4,000 reports is very low compared to the 10% deaths one can expect without care (Kempe, Silverman, Steele, Droegemuller, & Silver, 1962). Follow-up of families is facilitated in Belgium because it is a small and crowded country supported by a well-organized public welfare structure in permanent contact with nearly all families with children.

Conclusion

Violence toward children is not the exclusive characteristic of some marginal parents, but is part of society, culture, a daily lifestyle, and a way of thinking. One cannot expect parents not to be violent with their children when society has nothing to offer but exclusion. Poverty, unemployment, and inaccessible health care and education are the roots of violence. It thus makes no sense to organize modern child protection systems if they are not embedded in a comprehensive public welfare structure. Prevention and treatment of child abuse and neglect thus consist of overcoming repression and punitive attitudes not only in families but in the wider context.

Perhaps to start, professionals should be asking: Are the child protection agencies philosophically and materially ready to approach this delicate issue without provoking more misery than already exists in these families? Are clinics and services really equipped to offer a safe environment and ideas that the abusive families can use to grow and develop their own understanding and self-esteem?

Although excessive use of the medical profession is certainly not to be sought, it is a reality that most distressed parents turn to their private doctor or to a hospital-based service when they are concerned about their children's health or strange behavior. Doctors, pediatricians, psychiatrists, and social workers thus have to create places within their practice or hospitals where people harming their children would not be afraid to come, where parents and children would be able to talk about what happened, where they can show the darkest parts of their souls without threat or fear of criticism, and where especially doctors would not react to them as the worst abusive parents react to their children, by ignoring, rejecting, threatening, or moralizing without asking the child what the child thinks and what the child would like to happen. Successful therapeutic responses to child abuse and neglect are thus possible if a new model in child protection is offered based on empathy, trust, and encouragement for those who fail in raising their children instead of offering the traditional approaches based on mandatory reporting, control, judgment, and sanctions.

References

Ajoub, C., & Pfeifer, D. (1979). Burns as a manifestation of child abuse and neglect. *American Journal of Diseases of Children, 133,* 910–946.

Algemene folder Kind en Gezin can be obtained at Centrale Administratie, Dienst vorming & voorlichting, Hallepoortlaan 27, 1060 Brussels.

Belgisch Staatsblad. (1912). Wet van 15 mei 1912, betreffende de Kindermishandeling.

Belgisch Staatsblad. (1965). Wet van 8 april 1965, betreffende de Jeugdbescherming.

Belgisch Staatsblad. (1985). *Décret sur la reconnaissance de services SOS-enfants, 29 avril 1985.* 12.06.

Belgisch Staatsblad. (1988). *Besluit van de Vlaamse Executieve houdende de vaststelling van de voorwaarden van erkenning en subsidiëring van centra voor hulpverlening inzake Kindermishandeling—8.7.1987.* 15.01, pp. 540-541.

Belgisch Staatsblad. (1990). *Decreet van 28.03.1990 tot wijziging van het decreet van 27.06.1985 inzake Bijzondere Jeugdbijstand.* 07.04.90, pp. 6644-6655.

Belgisch Staatsblad. (1991). *Besluit van de Vlaamse Executieve houdende de wijziging van het besluit van de Vlaamse Executieve van 8 juli houdende vaststelling van de voorwaarden van erkenning en subsidiëring van centra voor hulpverlening inzake Kindermishendeling—19.02.1990.* 22.02, p. 3507.

Besharov, D. J. (1985, November–December). An overdose of concern—Child abuse and the overreporting problem. *AEI Journal on Government and Society,* 25-28.

Boermans, E., Lampo, A., & Marneffe, C. (1988). *Child abuse and child protection in Belgium.* Brussels: Confidential Doctor Center Kind in Nood.

Bontemps, C., & Binot, M. L. (1993). *Evaluation quantitative et qualitative à moyen terme, de l'action de prévention secondaire et tertiaire face à l'enfance victime de la maltraitance.* Namur, Belgium: FUNDP.

Caffey, J. (1946). Multiple fractures in the long bones of infants suffering from chromic subdural hematoma. *American Journal of Röntgenology Therapy & Nuclear Medicine, 56,* 163-173.

Caffey, J. (1972). On the theory and practice of shaking infants: Its potential residual effects of permanent brain damage and mental retardation. *American Journal of Diseases of Children, 124,* 161-168.

Cantwell, A. B. (1980). Child neglect. In Ch. H. Kempe & R. E. Helfer (Eds.), *The battered child* (3rd ed., pp. 193-197). Chicago: The University of Chicago Press.

Clara, R. (1983). Kindermishandeling en kinderverwaarlozing. *Tijdschrift voor Kindergeneeskunde, 39*(9), 543-553.

Cooper, C. E. (1978). Child abuse and neglect. Medical aspects. In *The maltreatment of children* (pp. 9-69). England: MPT Press.

Crivillé, A. (1983). Rôle mobilisateur du mandat d'autorité et du placement dans l'intervention sociale pour les enfants maltraités. *Child Abuse and Neglect, 7,* 451-458.

Decock, G. (1991). *De decreten inzake Bijzondere Jeugdbijstand. Algemene en Artikelsgewijze Commentaar.* Brussels: In opdracht van de Gemeenschapsminister van Welzijn en Gezin, Jan Lenssens.

Deltaglia, L. (1976). *Les enfants maltraités* (Dépistage et interventions sociales, Eds.). Published at E.S.F., 1970, Paris, France.

Drew, K. (1980). The role conflict of the child protective service worker: Investigator-helper. *Child Abuse and Neglect, 4,* 247-257.

Eisenberg, L. (1981). Cross-cultural and historical perspectives on child abuse and neglect. *Child Abuse and Neglect, 5,* 299-308.

Eliaerts, C., Gerlo, J., Verhellen, E., Ballet, D., Wylleman, A., & Cappelaere, O. (1990). *Van Jeugdbeschermingsrecht naar Jeugdrecht?* Antwerpen: Kluwer Rechtswetenschappen. Arnhem: Gouda Quint B.V.

Garbarino, J. (1977). The human ecology of child maltreatment. *Journal of Marriage and the Family, 39,* 721–735.

Garbarino, J. (1979). The abusive crime of emotional abuse. *Child Abuse and Neglect, 3,* 88–89.

Garbarino, J., & Gilliam, G. (1980). *Understanding abusive families.* Massachusetts: Lexington Books.

Gelles, R. J. (1979). The social construction of child abuse. In D. G. Gill (Ed.), *Child abuse and violence* (pp. 145–157). New York: AMS Press.

Ghesquière, P. (1989). Multi-problem gezinnen. Eigen-aardige cliënten vragen een eigen-aardige hulpverlening. *Tijdschrift voor Orthopedagogiek, Kinderpsychiatrie en klinische Kinderpsychologie, 14*(4), 157–170.

Gil, D. G. (1975). Unraveling child abuse *American Journal of Orthopsychiatry, 45,* 345–356.

Gil, D. G. (1978). *Violence against children, physical child abuse in the United States.* Cambridge, MA: Harvard University Press.

Goldstein, J., Freud, A., & Solnit, A. J. (1973). *Dans l'intérêt de l'enfant* (Vers un nouveau statut de l'enfance, Eds.) Published at E.S.F.

Gordon, L. (1988). Child abuse, gender and the myth of family independence: A historical critique. *Child Welfare, 64*(3), 215–225.

Gornall, P., Ahmed, A., Jolleys, A., & Cohen, S. B. (1972). Intraabdominal injuries in the battered baby syndrome. *Archives of Disease in Childhood, 47,* 211.

Green, A. H. (1979). Expanding psychiatry's role in child abuse treatment. *Hospital and Community Psychiatry, 17,* 356–371.

Illich, I. (1975). Het medisch bedrijf: Een bedreiging voor de gezondheid, Ned. uitgave, Het Wereldvenster, Baarn, 32–72.

Johnson, C. F., & Showers, J. (1985). Injury variables in child abuse. *Child Abuse and Neglect, 9,* 207–215.

Jones, D. P. H., & Alexander, H. (1987). Treating the abusive family within the family care system. In R. E. Helfer & R. S. Kempe (Eds.), *The battered child* (4th ed., pp. 339–360). Chicago: University of Chicago Press.

Katz, M. B. (1989). *The undeserving poor. From the war on poverty to the war of welfare.* New York: Pantheon Books.

Kempe, R. S., & Kempe, C. H. (1978). *Child abuse.* London: Fontana Open Books.

Kempe, C. H., Silverman, F. N., Steele, B. F., Droegemuller, W., & Silver, H. K. (1962). The battered child syndrome. *Journal of the American Medical Association, 181,* 17–24.

Keniston, K. (1979). Do Americans really like children? In D. G. Gill (Ed.), *Child abuse and violence* (pp. 274–285). New York: AMS Press.

Koers, A. (1981). *Kindermishandeling.* Rotterdam: Donker.

Lampo, A., Broos, P., Marneffe, C., & Deneyer, J. (1994). Annual Report, Confidential Doctor Center Brussels, Free University of Brussels (to be obtained from authors).

Larter, D. (1979). Social work in child abuse: An emerging mode of practice. *Child Abuse and Neglect, 3,* 889–896.

Lelièvre, C. (1993). *Rapport annuel, 1er novembre 1992–31 octobre 1993. Le Délégué général aux droits de l'enfant et à l'aide à la jeunesse.* Brussels: Editions Jeunesse et Droit asbl.

Lenoski, E. F., & Hunter, M. D. (1977). Specific patterns of inflicted burn injuries. *Journal of Trauma, 17,* 842–846.

Marneffe, C. (1990). *The use of psychotherapy during pregnancy as a means to prevent child abuse and neglect.* Unpublished doctoral dissertation, Free University of Brussels, A.Z.-V.U.B. (Can be obtained from the author.)

Marneffe, C., Lampo, A., & Proost, G. (1989). It shouldn't hurt to be a child. Edited on the occasion of the Second European Conference on Child Abuse and Neglect, organized by the Confidential Doctor Center Kind in Nood, Brussels.

Marneffe, C., Lampo, A., Proost, G., & Boermans, E. (1987). *It shouldn't hurt to be a child* (Confidential Doctor Center Brussels: Free University of Brussels, Ed.).

McCarthy, I. C., & Byrne, N. (1988). Mis-taken love: Conversations on the problem of incest in an Irish context. *Family Process, 27,* 181–199.

Meddin, B. J., & Hansen, I. (1985). The service provided during child abuse and/or neglect, case investigation and the barriers that exist to service provision. *Child Abuse and Neglect, 9,* 175–182.

Meadow, R. (1977). Munchausen syndrome by proxy: The hinterland of child abuse. *Lancet, 2,* 343–345.

Meadow, R. (1982). Munchausen syndrome by proxy. *Archives of Diseases in Childhood, 57,* 92–98.

Muller, R. T., Caldwell, R. A., & Hunter, J. E. (1993). Child provocativeness and gender as factors contributing to the blaming of victims of physical child abuse. *Child Abuse, 17*(2), 249–261.

Newberger, E. H., & Bourne, R. (1978). The medicalization and legalization of child abuse. *American Journal of Orthopsychiatry, 48*(4), 593–607.

Pelton, L. H. (1978). Child abuse and neglect: The myth of classlessness. *American Journal of Orthopsychiatry, 48*(4), 608–617.

Rosenfeld, A. A. (1979, October 19). The clinical management of incest and sexual abuse of children. *Journal of the American Medical Association, 242*(16), 1761–1764.

Senaeve, P. (Ed.) (1995). Actuele vraagstukken van Interlandelijke en Inlandsd Adoptie en van Verlatenverklaring. Leuven, Belgium: Acco.

Shepard, J. R. (1987). Law enforcement's role in the investigation of family violence. In R. E. Helfer & R. S. Kempe (Eds.), *The battered child* (4th ed., pp. 392–401). Chicago: University of Chicago Press.

Showers, J., & Bardman, R. L. (1986). Scarring for life: Abuse with electric cords. *Child Abuse and Neglect, 10,* 25–31.

Silverman, F. N. (1953). The röntgen manifestation of unrecognized skeletal trauma in infants. *American Journal of Röntgenology, Radium Therapy and Nuclear Medicine, 69,* 413–427.

Solnit, A. J. (1980). Child abuse: Least harmful, most protective intervention. *Pediatrics, 65*(1), 170–171.

Somerhausen, C. (1979). Les réactions: Contrôle social formel et informel. In *Aspects criminologique des mauvais traitements des enfants dans la famille* pp. 87–134. Quatrième Colloque Criminologique du Conseil de l'Europe. Brussels: Council of Europe.

Soumenkoff, G., Marneffe, C., Gerard, M., Limet, R., Beeckmans, M., & Hubinont, P. O. (1982). A coordinated attempt for prevention of child abuse at the antenatal care level. *Child Abuse and Neglect, 6,* 87–94.

Steele, B. F. (1986). Notes on the lasting effects of early child abuse. *Child Abuse and Neglect, 10,* 283–291.

Willems, G., & Buysse, B. (1992). *Kindermishandeling in Vlaanderen, Registratie bij de centra voor hulpverlening inzake kindermishandeling, rapport 1992.* Brussels: Kind & Gezin, Studiedienst.

Wolfe, D. A., Aragona, D., Kaufman, K., & Sandler, J. (1980). The importance of adjudication in the treatment of child abusers: Some preliminary findings. *Child Abuse and Neglect, 4,* 127–135.

Wolff, R. (1983). Child abuse and neglect: Dynamics and underlying pattern. *Victimology: An International Journal, 8,* 105–112.

Wolff, R. (1991). Child protection in Germany. *Violence update, 2*(3), 4–6.

8

The Netherlands

Responding to Abuse — Compassion or Control?

MARIAN A. S. ROELOFS
HERMAN E. M. BAARTMAN

In this chapter we describe the child abuse and neglect reporting system and the methods of intervention used in the Netherlands. First we discuss some recent developments concerning public awareness of child abuse and neglect. To make these developments understandable we have to place them in a historical context that illustrates how the attention paid to child abuse since the beginning of the 1970s relates to a tradition of child protection, which goes back to the turn of the century. Second we discuss the meaning of the concept of child maltreatment, especially with regard to its judicial implications. Third the Dutch system of reporting cases of child abuse and, more specifically, the Dutch Confidential Doctor Offices (*Bureau Vertrouwensarts*) and their strategies are described. Fourth we describe some recent trends in reporting child abuse and in the policy of placements. Finally some current dilemmas with regard to child abuse policies are discussed.

Recent Developments

At the end of the 1960s articles about child abuse and neglect were published in Dutch journals. Some Dutch pediatricians and social workers, stimulated by Kempe and colleagues' (Kempe, Silverman, Steele, Droegemueller, & Silver, 1962) classic article, started to respond to signals of child abuse. Their efforts led to the formation of the Dutch Society for the Prevention of Cruelty to Children (*Vereniging tegen Kindermishandeling*) in 1970 and the establishment of four Confidential Doctor Offices in 1972, two in the urban conglomeration of western Holland, one in the northern region, and one in the eastern part. This organization gives doctors the opportunity of reporting cases of child abuse to colleagues without violating professional confidentiality. The Confidential Doctor Offices were seen as a way of offering the help abusive parents needed because child abuse was seen as a symptom of family problems. However, in spite of this organization's medical affiliation, in 1983 and 1993 respectively, 93% and 81% of the reports did not come from doctors or medical institutes. In 1993 43% came from the child's immediate surroundings (e.g., family members and neighbors) and 17% from schools, to name the most important other sources.

The Society for the Prevention of Cruelty to Children pursues the prevention of child abuse by providing information and education, improving professional expertise, and offering advice on policy development. Besides a coordinating bureau there is a national network of 12 prevention teams that, operating on a regional basis, carry out the main tasks of the society. (In 1988 the society established a special chair in child abuse and neglect at the Free University in Amsterdam that is held by the second author.) Publicity by the society about child abuse and about the function of the Confidential Doctor Offices has greatly contributed to the annual increase in reports to these offices.

Child Protection and Child Abuse

The establishment of the Confidential Doctor Offices in 1972 was a remarkable initiative. The Child Care and Protection Boards[1] have been functioning as part of the Ministry of Justice since 1905 and can be compared with the social services departments in the United Kingdom and the child protective services in the United States. Cases of child abuse can be reported to Confidential Doctor Offices as well as to the Child Care and Protection Board. For a clear understanding of the Dutch situation we must give a brief explanation of the history of both institutions.

In contrast to the Confidential Doctor Offices, the Child Care and Protection Board has the statutory authority to investigate the situation of abused and neglected children and to ask the court to restrict or terminate parental rights. Since 1905 it has been the central agency to which both professionals and laypersons can report cases of child abuse and neglect. In the late 1960s when the awareness of child abuse in the Netherlands began to grow, the Child Care and Protection Board was, generally speaking, the obvious agency around which to expand protective functions in the interests of abused children.

Why were the Confidential Doctor Offices established? Montfoort (1993b, 1994) offers three reasons for this development. First the Child Care and Protection Board concentrated traditionally on neglected children who were defined from the outset as children in danger of moral downfall. Thus child protection in the Netherlands implied "societal protection," too, because it "connected the endangered child with the dangerous child" (Montfoort, 1994, p. 272) against whom society had to be protected. Second, in the late 1960s the child protection system was vehemently criticized, partly because it associated the dangerous child with the endangered child. Critics of the system perceived child abuse and neglect as symptoms of dysfunctional families; these families were thought to be in need of help and help seemed to be incompatible with strategies of controlling children and families. Third, the international movement against violence toward children — later connected with the women's liberation movement, which started in the 1960s — was supported by the medical and social work professions, while the older movement for the protection of neglected children in the Netherlands rested for the most part with lawyers.

Thus the movement against violence toward children was led by another group of professionals who claimed to be fighting a new problem that differed from that addressed by the older movement for neglected children. This different problem required the establishment of a new institution, the Confidential Doctor Office. By reacting — as all new movements do to older and kindred ones — against the judicial approach of the Child Care and Protection Board, the Confidential Doctor Offices consolidated their position and developed their own identity.

In general the goals of the Confidential Doctor Offices and the social workers involved in this movement were to understand the parents and their problems and to influence family functioning in an effort to reinforce the parent-child bond. The Confidential Doctor Offices operate with a general preference for a "compassion strategy" rather than a "control strategy" (see Rosenfeld & Newberger, 1977). Only in exceptional cases of imminent danger is placement of a child recommended in addition, if necessary, to a child protection order.

In the midst of the 1980s, child sexual abuse started attracting public and professional attention. This problem became a major focal point of concern in the domains of child care and the judiciary. The 1972 annual report of the Confidential Doctor Offices did not include any figures on sexual abuse. In 1973 sexual abuse was identified as a problem in 10.7% of the cases reported by the Confidential Doctor Offices involving girls and 0.7% of the cases involving boys. These figures remained almost constant through 1978 (when 0.8% of reported cases involved sexual abuse of boys and 8.6% involved sexual abuse of girls). In 1984 these percentages rose to 3.2% for boys and 6.5% for girls, respectively. In 1993 they were 8% for boys and 18.5% for girls, respectively.

In contrast to the strategy of compassion employed in cases of physical abuse and neglect, punishment of the perpetrator was called for — especially by former victims who placed sexual abuse on the public agenda — in cases of child sexual abuse. Criminal prosecution made it clear that child sexual abuse is the full responsibility of the perpetrator; it was handled as a crime rather than as a family problem. Handling it as a family problem according to principles based on systems theory would mask the perpetrator's responsibility — something at which he or she was already adept — and would make the child, as a member of the family system, responsible for being a victim. Besides these objections in principle to a strategy of compassion, there is a practical reason for the difference in preferred strategies concerning physical abuse and neglect on the one hand and sexual abuse on the other hand. Most parents are willing to admit that they have physically abused or neglected their child, and this opens the way to help. However denial is the rule and admittance the exception among perpetrators of child sexual abuse. This blocks the way to help and makes a judicial investigation often necessary.

Currently, public attention, influenced by the media which is devoted to reporting the most sensational cases, is particularly focused on child sexual abuse. As a consequence physical abuse seems to fade into the background, at least in the media.

Recent Affairs

During the last few years sensational cases have made the Dutch headlines, for example, the Oude Pekela case. In May 1987 in Oude Pekela, an industrial village of 8,000 inhabitants in the northern region of the country, about 70 children were suspected of being victims of extrafamilial sexual abuse. The police investigation team could not produce any incriminating evidence such as admissions by the offenders, photographs, or videotapes, although children reported being involved in filming activities. About 50 children gave statements of sexual victimization. Nevertheless this case remained unresolved. According to some people there were indications of ritual abuse. The case received international attention when it was discussed in *Child Abuse and Neglect* (Jonker & Jonker-de Bakker, 1991) and later included in a book about "the backlash" (Pyck, 1994).

The so-called Bolderkar affair was another example, occurring in the autumn of 1988 and the spring of 1989, one year after the Cleveland case in the United Kingdom. The staff of the Bolderkar — a medical day care center for children (ages 3 to 7 years) — suspected that 15 (25%) of the total children at the center had been sexually abused by their fathers and organized an outplacement for 9 of them, 7 following a juvenile court order. In some cases the sexual abuse could not be proved legally. The accused parents challenged the decision of outplacement. Some fathers who had previously admitted abuse withdraw their admission after contacts with their lawyer. The press presented fathers, mothers, and children alike as victims of a witch hunt. Newspapers were full of letters sent in by all kinds of professionals attacking the Bolderkar staff and defending the parents, even before an investigating team had begun to conduct its inquiries. The media accused the staff of making nonprofessional diagnoses, although the report by the investigating committee was far more balanced in its comments (for a detailed discussion see Edwards & Soetenhorst-de Savornin Lohman, 1994; Lamers-Winkelman, 1994).

The Bolderkar affair had a serious impact on social and care workers, increasing their concerns about "false positives" to the point that they began to outweigh the fear of "false negatives" in cases of child sexual abuse. The results of this affair illustrate that outplacement of children can include great risks not only to the well-being of children and their parents, but also to the professional reputations of social workers and their agencies.

The most recent affair in the Netherlands is the so-called Epe incest case

(Epe is a small town). In this case a woman accused her parents and numerous other parties (e.g., neighbors, friends, relatives, and general practitioners) of sexually abusing her and her younger sister over a period of many years. She accused several policemen who were involved in the investigation of the case. The girls claimed their parents forced them to undergo illegal abortions. Furthermore they accused their parents of the murder of two or three newborn babies conceived as the result of incest. The incest and illegal abortions were proven, and the parents were sentenced to jail. The other horrible facts could not be substantiated. This sensational case received a great deal of public interest. The victim, Jolanda from Epe, became a TV personality. The case became well known and as a result two groups formed: a group of believers and a group of nonbelievers.

At the same time that the Epe incest case dominated the media (between summer 1993 and summer 1994) a related issue also attracted public attention: the ritual abuse of children. Publicity surrounding charges of ritual abuse induced the state secretary of the Ministry of Justice to establish a task force to investigate this issue. The task force was assigned to define ritual abuse and to map the scope of this problem by listing and examining reported cases. One of the task force's conclusions was that "the possibility that the stories told by alleged victims of ritual abuse are entirely true, must be considered very small."

All the publicity surrounding child maltreatment, particularly in regard to sexual abuse and incest, has had several consequences. First, these problems have become well known. The public, local authorities, and professionals' heightened awareness of child maltreatment partly explains the annual increase in reports. Second, cases like Oude Pekela and particularly the Bolderkar case led to a turning point in the public debate. Until the Bolderkar case concerns about the fate of abused children, especially sexually abused children, dominated public debate and professional strategies. Child protection and child care professionals were criticized for being too passive. Following the Bolderkar case the risk of false accusations received greater attention and parental rights came to the fore as child protection and child care workers were criticized for being too active. By the mid-1990s a movement had evolved, with participants consisting mainly of parents who claim to be the victims of overzealous and prejudiced professionals; this group forms the Dutch counterpart of organizations such as VOCAL (Victims of Child Abuse Laws) in the United States, PAIN (Parents Against Injustice) in the United Kingdom, and other organizations in Germany, Sweden, and New Zealand.

Definitions of Child Maltreatment

Too Broad or Narrow?

The way child abuse and neglect are defined forms the cornerstone of a Confidential Doctor Office. The National Foundation for the Confidential Doctor Offices (*Landelijke Stichting Bureau Vertrouwensarts inzake Kindermishandeling,* LSBVK) defines child abuse and neglect as "every non-accidental form of physical or emotional violence or neglect which happens to a child by parents or caretakers, which provokes or threatens to provoke emotional or physical damage to the child" (Koers, 1981). This definition leans heavily on Gil's definition of physical abuse:

> Physical abuse of children is intentional, non-accidental use of force, or intentional, non-accidental acts of omission, on the part of a parent or other caretaker in interaction with a child in his care, aimed at hurting, injuring, or destroying that child. (Gil, 1979, p. 177)

The Dutch definition is even broader than Gil's; it includes all types of child maltreatment: physical and emotional abuse, physical and emotional neglect, and sexual abuse. In 1972 the Confidential Doctor Offices chiefly concentrated on the physical abuse of young children, in line with the focus of Kempe's (Kempe et al., 1962) classic article on the battered child syndrome. Later older children and other types of maltreatment (emotional abuse, physical and emotional neglect, and sexual abuse) were included.

The Dutch perspective on child abuse thus includes harmful situations and risks that are difficult to define precisely such as "emotional damage," "a threat to provoke," and "emotional abuse and neglect." In 1992 and 1993, 43% and 46%, respectively, of all substantiated reports concerned emotional abuse and/or neglect. This rather vague concept runs the risk of becoming a "container concept" that attracts an increasing number of reports by embracing all situations not beneficial to the development and well-being of the child.

Judicial Aspects

According to the Dutch penal code, physical child abuse is a criminal offense punishable by a maximum of 2 years imprisonment or a fine. Excessive premeditated physical abuse resulting in the death of the victim carries a maximum penalty of 15 years. These penalties can be increased by one third if the victim is a relative. However the law does not define physical abuse; it equates physical abuse with "intentionally damaging someone's health." Physical neglect can be covered by sections of the penal code that concern "abandoning the needy." Emotional abuse or neglect is not an issue in criminal law, although a proposal to make it a punishable offense was advanced by Clemens Schröner (1956) in her doctoral thesis on emotional abuse.

The penal code does not contain the term *child sexual abuse*, although adults who have had sexual contact with a child can be criminally prosecuted. Besides the nature of the sexual act, the victim's age and relation to the perpetrator contribute to determining the level of the sentence. If the victim is under 12 years of age, sexual contacts are always a punishable offense and suspects can be prosecuted; an official complaint filed by the victim or the victim's legal representative is not required.[2] If the victim is between 12 and 16 years old sexual acts are punishable, but prosecution is only possible if a formal complaint has been filed by the victim, the victim's legal representative, or the Child Care and Protection Board. Sexual acts between parents and their children or stepchildren are considered as punishable offenses until the children have reached the age of majority, and the filing of a formal complaint by the victim or the victim's legal representatives is not necessary.

Until recently the limit of liability for crimes like sexual child abuse was in most instances 12 years from the date the crime was committed. For many young victims of sexual abuse this meant that by the time they wanted to file a formal complaint against the perpetrator, the right to prosecution had expired (because the alleged sexual abuse took place more than 12 years ago). Under a new amendment to the criminal code, the term of limitation for sexual child abuse now ends 12 years after the victim has reached the age of majority.

Despite the criminal sanctions available, in practice the preferred approach to child abuse is usually to seek solutions outside the legal system except in cases of sexual abuse. In cases of child physical abuse the medical confidants try to keep the child at home and to organize family support. If necessary the juvenile court appoints a family guardian who is responsible for assisting the parents in the child's upbringing. In serious cases the child can be placed outside the home on a voluntary basis or, if necessary, in combination with a child protection order.

In cases of sexual abuse, however, the criminal law is applied more frequently, first with a view to fact finding and second to coerce the perpetrator to admit his (or in some cases her) responsibility and to recognize the status of the victim officially. From statistics it is difficult to tell the rate of prosecutions; that is, we do not know the number of all (alleged) cases of child abuse reported to the police. Recent research (Montfoort, 1993a) indicates that 53% of all reports of sexual abuse to the police lead to a report by the police to the public prosecutor, and 49% of the cases that have reached the public prosecutor lead to a conviction. In contrast prosecution in cases of physical abuse is fairly exceptional; 10% of all reports reach the public prosecutor, and 8% of these cases lead to a conviction.

Functioning of Reporting Centers in the Netherlands

Here we first describe the procedures followed by the Confidential Doctor Offices and by the Child Care and Protection Board and then compare the approaches of these two public agencies.

The Confidential Doctor Offices

Confidential Doctor Offices employ a team consisting of two or more part-time confidential doctors (family doctors or pediatricians), two or more social workers, and one or more administrative aides. In 1995 the number of centers had increased to 12, organized nationwide. The number of child abuse reports received by the offices increased from 430 in 1972 to 13,220 in 1993. From 1972 to 1985 the offices came under the authority of the Ministry of Health, Welfare, and Cultural Affairs, but were denationalized in 1985; in 1992 administrative functions were transferred from this ministry to the local authorities.

The Confidential Doctor Offices are charged with the following functions:

- Registration of reports of child abuse made by professionals (e.g., physicians, teachers) and laypersons (e.g., members of the family, neighbors).
- Verification of these reports through confidential information from professionals who are in contact with the family (family doctors, teachers, district nurses, etc.).
- When necessary, stimulating, organizing, and coordinating assistance to the abusive family (social services, etc.). Alternatively, the Confidential Doctor Offices can also initiate intervention if necessary.
- Organizing the follow-up by regularly contacting organizations that provide assistance to the family.
- Collecting data for research purposes.

In contrast to the situation in Belgium, it is not usual for the Confidential Doctor Offices to give assistance or treatment to abusing families by themselves; the offices engage more in verification, coordination, and data-gathering functions than provision of treatment services, for which they are not equipped. The referee's anonymity is a basic prerequisite of Confidential Doctor Offices. The offices never reveal the identity of a source to the family if the referee does not want it. This basic principle was intended to encourage potential referees, and it works very well.

In the Netherlands there is no system of mandatory reporting. From time to time this issue comes under discussion. The debate has two sides: The police, the Child Care and Protection Board, lawyers, and women's groups support a mandatory system, while doctors and social workers hesitate to implement such a system. It is unlikely that a law that obliges professionals to report will soon be introduced; mandatory reporting seems to be incompatible with Dutch culture, moreover there is the practical fear that a system of mandatory reporting would inhibit abusing parents from voluntarily coming forth to seek help.

Before the 1970s reports could only be made to the police and to the Child Care and Protection Board. With the establishment of the Dutch Society for the Prevention of Cruelty to Children in 1970, a new reporting center was temporarily available. This was a new phenomenon: a private organization that collected reports of child abuse and neglect from the public and professionals and then aimed to help parents and children by seeking solutions inside the family. The four Confidential Doctor Offices founded in 1972 worked toward the same goal. One of the aims was to receive reports about child abuse and neglect and consequently collect national data about child maltreatment.

These days the majority of reports concerning all types of child maltreatment seems to be made to the Confidential Doctor Offices. However it is difficult to compare the numbers of reports received by the Confidential Doctor Offices to those received by the Child Care and Protection Board. Not only do both use a different registration system, but the label "child abuse" as employed by the Confidential Doctor Offices is defined more broadly than the term used by the board. According to Montfoort's (1993a) analysis the board receives 5,000 to 6,000 reports, which are comparable with the type of reports received by the Confidential Doctor Offices, of child abuse concerning 8,000 to 9,000 children yearly. The Child Care and Protection Board receives another substantial number of reports, generally concerning more severe cases of physical and sexual abuse. This is the consequence of a strategy that gives priority to voluntary help. When this strategy is not successful and the child is in need of protection, the case is given to the Child Care and Protection Board; therefore the board generally receives the more severe cases. A minority of reports is made to the police.

When the Confidential Doctor Offices receive a report, an investigation is started. In this phase professionals who are in contact with the family and the child (e.g., a primary health care nurse, a family doctor, a teacher, a professional of the day care center, or other involved professionals) are asked if they can substantiate the report. If at least two other independent sources concur with the report, it is considered to be substantiated. The parents generally have not been informed about the report at this stage because of concerns that the family will isolate itself and hinder any attempts at assistance. However this practice is at odds with legislation on privacy and openness toward parents of children in youth care. A guideline (Rÿksplan Jeugdhulpverlening, 1994) recently set down by the government states that parents who have been reported must be informed of such reports within at most 6 weeks after a report has been filed. Currently there is a tendency to inform the reported families about the Confidential Doctor Offices' activities when it is believed that this information will cause no risk to the child.

After substantiation possible assistance to the family is planned and started, or assistance already in place is alerted to the abuse. Almost all families reported to the Confidential Doctor Offices are enmeshed in numerous other problems apart from the child abuse. The range of difficulties includes the child's individual problems, the parents' current psychological problems or own unhappy childhoods, the parents' marital problems, general communication problems inside the family, socioeconomic stress, and problems with social support and child rearing. Depending on the nature of these problems and on the level of abuse, the Confidential Doctor Offices refer the case to a specialized agency, which provides treatment to the family. Treatment strategies range from moderate to extensive family interventions. Relatively moderate strategies include the school doctor or the family doctor talking to the parents about the child and offering advice on child rearing, the regular visits of a social worker to the home to offer support to the parents, individual therapy for a parent or child, and family therapy. More extensive intervention strategies involve the out-of-home placement of the child on a voluntary basis or on the basis of a child protection order.

In cases for which service is entered into on a voluntary basis the Confidential Doctor Offices organize a follow-up about 6 months after the treatment begins. This is to check if the treatment has been accepted by the family, if progress has been made, and if the child abuse has ceased. If no progress has been made, a new strategy may be planned. Again the Confidential Doctor Offices follow up on this new treatment. If the social workers or therapists serving the family are of the opinion that the treatment is beneficial, the Confidential Doctor Offices can close the file.

In recent years special awareness of the problem of drug-addicted mothers and their babies has also developed. The Confidential Doctor Offices, together with other agencies, are very concerned about these children, who are considered to be at high risk of abuse or neglect. In many urban areas the Confidential Doctor Offices cooperate with specialized drug assistance teams, and reports of child abuse or neglect involving drug-addicted parents are commonly given to the medical confidant.

The Child Care and Protection Board

If a family is reported to the Child Care and Protection Board, there is a statutory obligation to inform the parents of the report and the identity of the reporter. The Child Care and Protection Board initiates an inquiry into the situation of the child and the family. Depending on the outcome of an inquiry the board can use its statutory power to obtain a child protection order from the juvenile court.

Dutch civil law has two main types of child protection orders. The first and most frequently used is a court-ordered supervision (COS), which means that the parents have to share their authority with a family guardian. The legal ground for this order is that the child is in danger of moral or physical downfall. It is comparable to a supervision order in the United Kingdom. The family guardian supports and guides the parents in bringing up their child and informs the juvenile court about the child's development and the parent's child-rearing activities. The parents are obliged to take the guardian's recommendations into account. When an out-of-home placement is ordered in combination with a COS, the family guardian can act as an intermediary between the parents and the child in the children's home or foster family. If the family guardian and the juvenile court judge the treatment to be successful, the child may return home and the limitation of parental authority can be terminated. If circumstances do not change or have not sufficiently improved, limitation of parental authority can be continued until the child's coming of age. The second order, comparable to a care order in the United Kingdom, implies a termination of parental authority and is always combined with the out-of-home placement of the child.

A Comparison of Agencies

The Confidential Doctor Offices and the Child Care and Protection Board have a number of similarities. Both agencies aim to protect children against physical and emotional abuse and neglect and sexual abuse. Children at risk must be defended. Both agencies examine the situation of child and family but do not themselves offer treatment and direct assistance. Both agencies focus on the borderlines between medical care, social work, therapy, and law.

The most notable differences between the agencies are the following. The central position of the medical profession within the Confidential Doctor Offices can be contrasted to the position of social workers and jurists at the

Child Care and Protection Board, although the majority of work is done by social workers and not by doctors or jurists. The Confidential Doctor Offices withhold the reporter's identity from the family, whereas the Child Care and Protection Board is obliged by law to inform parents of the reporter's identity. The Confidential Doctor Offices' nondisclosure of information about the report to the reported family in a considerable number of cases diverges from the Child Care and Protection Board's practice of disclosure to all families, which is required by law. There is probably also a difference with respect to the characteristics of the populations reported to these agencies: the Confidential Doctor Offices receive reports on all types of cases, the less severe as well as the very serious ones; the most serious cases will often be given to the Child Care and Protection Board, which will bring them to the attention of the courts. For this reason the Confidential Doctor Offices have an important preventive task.

The public images of these agencies are also different. In brief the Confidential Doctor Offices are associated with compassion, while the Child Care and Protection Board is associated with control. Recently the Child Care and Protection Board and Confidential Doctor Offices pleaded for more integration of both institutions while retaining their separate advantages. Experimental efforts to increase integration and cooperation are planned for the near future, but the government wants the agencies to remain separate. Finally, although the Confidential Doctor Offices seem to occupy a central position concerning reports of child abuse, they are a relatively small agency with only 74 full-time positions compared to the Board with its over 1,200 full-time positions (Montfoort, 1993b).

Reporting and Placement Trends

Since 1970 there has been a growing awareness of child abuse. This awareness is dynamic, drawing on developments in the way the concept has been defined, reporting practices, and therapeutic and judicial reactions. Consequently it is difficult to compare figures and practices concerning different periods, even within a relatively small span of 25 years. For example the registration system of the Confidential Doctor Offices, which is the most important source for gauging amounts and types of reports, has changed since 1989. Since then, in principle only one type of child abuse — the most serious — was registered for each case, while previously numerous types of abuse could be registered for one case. The forms of abuse registered, ranging from the least to the most serious, include "emotional abuse and/or neglect," "physical neglect," "physical abuse," and "sexual abuse." Thus, in cases of sexual abuse no other types of abuse are registered, in cases of physical abuse without sexual abuse no other types are registered, and so on.

In our opinion this hierarchy of forms of abuse is rather subjective. Since 1989 emotional abuse and emotional neglect — the above-mentioned container concept — were combined into one category, emotional abuse and/or emotional neglect. Furthermore Confidential Doctor Offices keep a specific registration system of reports of child abuse concerning child protection orders. These data provide the best insights into fluctuations over time. Unfortunately these systems of data on forms of abuse and child protection orders function separately and cannot be interlinked. Nevertheless we try to sketch some trends and developments concerning reporting trends together with protection orders and placement trends.

The annual reports of the National Foundation for the Confidential Doctor Offices (LSBVK), are the basis for reporting trends. Data from the Department of Justice (Mertens, 1993) are used as a basis for observations on different trends. We also refer to research by Montfoort (1993a) concerning the Child Care and Protection Board.

Reporting Trends

The total number of reports to the Confidential Doctor Offices rose from 430 in 1972 to 13,220 in 1993. Table 8-1 presents fluctuations over the years 1973, 1978, 1983, 1988, and 1993. It presents total amounts of reports, percentages of types of reported abuse within the total of reports, and substantiation rates. As mentioned these figures are confined to the Confidential Doctor Offices. Comparable figures for the Child Care and Protection Board are not available, mainly due to a totally different system of registration.

Of course there is a difference between the total amount of reports and the amount of substantiated reports. The proportions of types of abuse noted in Table 8-1 are based on substantiated cases. The registration system differs between types of reports: cases in need of advice and cases that require investigation by the Confidential Doctor Offices. Due to the yearly increase in reports and the decrease in the organization's workforce, the practice has evolved of handling as many reports as possible demanding advice. In 1993 the offices classified 5,957 reports as demanding advice and 7,263 as demanding investigation. Substantiation rates in this table concern only reports demanding investigation. The registration system counts a reported case of child maltreatment as the report of a family, not of a single child. Thus one case report can include more than one child. For example the 13,220 reports received in

Table 8-1. Numbers of Reports and Substantiation Rates

	1973	1978	1983	1988	1993
Total number of reported cases	628	2,796	3,179	7,492	13,220
Cases reported per 1,000 children	0.1	0.59	0.86	2.1	3.5
Physical abuse (%)	56.1	57.2	37	36	20
Neglect (%)	15.3	37.4	22.5	13	8
Sexual abuse (%)	5.5	4.5	7.2	20	16
Girls (%)	95	91	86	87	75
Boys (%)	5	9	14	13	25
Emotional abuse/neglect (%)	8.3	41.4	29.5	26	46
Other types (%)	0.7	1	1	5	10
Substantiation rate (%)	86	74	82	79	85

1993 concerned 18,404 children. The data on cases reported per 1,000 children in Table 8-1 are based on the assumption that a report concerns 1 child. Therefore the figures reported in this category underestimate the actual rate of cases per 1,000 children.

The data of Table 8-1 have to be interpreted carefully. They are drawn from annual reports that are not always based on the same figuring system and the same conceptualization of different types of abuse. The types of abuse in the reports of 1973 and 1978 were not mutually exclusive; thus, for example, a child suffering emotional abuse and physical abuse would be counted twice, once in each category. Nevertheless some trends are clearly noticeable.

Over the two decades between 1973 (a year after the Confidential Doctor Offices first opened) and 1993, the number of reported cases increased enormously from 628 to 13,220. The largest increase occurred between 1977 and 1978, during which time the number of reports rose by 57.6%. The authors of the Confidential Doctor Offices annual report in 1978 partly explained this increase as a result of a national campaign, organized by the Dutch Society for the Prevention of Cruelty to Children, that alerted the public and drew the professionals' attention to child abuse and to the Confidential Doctor Offices. Similarly more recent increases in reporting rates are attributed to a large-scale public campaign carried out between 1991 and 1992 that sought to stimulate children to talk to a person they trusted about their "secret." From 1982 until 1992 reports increased by an average of 18%. However in 1992 and 1993 the reporting rate climbed by 25.2% and 36.5%, respectively. It seems reasonable to ascribe these deviations from the normal increase to this campaign (Hoefnagels, 1994).

In 1973 sexual abuse accounted for 5.5% of all reports. This proportion increased to 16% in 1993. The change over 20 years in the ratio of boys and girls within this category is noteworthy. In 1973 5% of all reports of sexual abuse concerned boys; 20 years later this proportion increased fivefold. Reports of emotional abuse, emotional neglect, or both fluctuated between 22% and 46%. As in most other countries, it was the physical abuse of young children that initially stimulated awareness of child abuse. Later the concept of child abuse expanded to cover other types of maltreatment, including emotional violence or neglect. It is unclear why reports of emotional abuse/neglect climbed so steeply between 1973 and 1978. The decline in reports of emotional abuse/neglect between 1973 and 1988 is probably due to the fact that since 1983 in reporting cases for which several forms of abuse might be present only the most severe type of abuse would be counted, contrary to the preceding years. However this does not explain the change between 1988 and 1993, when the rate of cases reported as emotional abuse/neglect rose from 26% to 46%.

Compared to the United States, the Dutch substantiation rates are rather high (Eckenrode, Powers, Doris, Munsch, & Bolger, 1988). As the number of reports rose in the United States the percentage substantiated declined. Thus between 1975 and 1985 the percentage of substantiated reports in the United States fell from 65% to about 40%. Perhaps this difference between substantiation rates in the United States and the Netherlands is connected with the

Table 8-2. Distribution of Types of Child Abuse over Age Groups in 1983

	0–5	6–11	12–17	Totals
Physical abuse	40%	34%	26%	1,026
Neglect	57%	32%	11%	737
Sexual abuse	13%	26%	61%	189
Emotional abuse and/or neglect	43%	41%	17%	1,292
Totals	44%	36%	20%	
	(*n* = 1,402)	(*n* = 1,166)	(*n* = 676)	3,244

absence of a mandatory reporting system in the Netherlands. Though it should be recognized that, as noted, the Dutch substantiation rates refer only to those reports that demanded investigation, about 55% of all reports in 1993.

The broader the concept of child abuse one uses, the higher the substantiation rate will be of course. Unfortunately the way figures are presented by the annual reports makes it impossible to specify substantiation rates per type of abuse. We can only mention the general experience, confirmed for example by Noordhoek-van der Staay and Buffing (1994), that a report of sexual abuse is the type of report most difficult to substantiate.

The data in Tables 8-2 and 8-3 describe the distribution of some types of child abuse grouped by age of the abused in 1983 and 1993. These years were selected for two reasons: Data in the annual reports before 1983 are unsuitable for this comparison because types of abuse often are counted more than once, and the time between 1983 and 1993 is long enough to reveal possible trends within this period.

Among the notable changes the data show that within the category of physical abuse, older children (6 to 17 year olds) were abused more frequently in 1993 than in 1983. In 1993 79% of all physically abused children were 6–17 years old compared to 60% in 1983. Physical neglect was most reported among 0–5 year olds in 1983 but was most reported among 6–11 year olds in 1993. With regard to sexual abuse, public awareness of child sexual abuse was just dawning in the Netherlands in 1983. At that time the dominant idea was that victims of child sexual abuse were mainly girls between ages 12 and 17 years

Table 8-3. Distribution of Types of Child Abuse over Age Groups

	0–5	6–11	12–17	Totals
Physical abuse	21%	40%	39%	973
Neglect	37%	44%	19%	427
Sexual abuse	13%	39%	48%	855
Emotional abuse and/or neglect	24%	44%	32%	2,374
Totals	22%	42%	36%	
	(*n* = 1,040)	(*n* = 1,958)	(*n* = 1,631)	4,629

(61% of the sexual abuse cases reported were in that age group in 1983). Later it became clear that younger children, including boys, could also be victims. An increasing proportion of the sexual abuse cases reported in 1993 were among children under 12 years of age.

A more general and unusual trend is the overall shift of attention from younger children in 1983 to older children in 1993. In 1983 44% of all substantiated reports concerned children from ages 0 to 5 years; 10 years later the proportion of reports in this age group decreased to 22%. The increasing proportion of reports on children over 5 years of age reflects the rising number of reports for emotional abuse and/or neglect within this group. In interpreting this shift in attention toward older children however, we must bear in mind that the figures in Tables 8-2 and 8-3 refer to reports that have been investigated by the Confidential Doctor Offices. As mentioned above, these cases must be differentiated from reports classified as only requiring advice. Indeed the substantiated cases on which these figures are based represent a declining proportion of all reports.

Recent years show an increase in reports needing advice, so it is possible that the increased proportion of older children among investigated reports reflects a tendency to treat cases as advice reports when they concern younger children and to concentrate the organization's own investigations on older children. To examine this issue, we reanalyzed the data to find out if the apparent increase in the proportion of 12–17 year olds represents a difference in report handling — handling cases as requiring advice or investigation — or a growing rate of abuse of older children. Table 8-4 shows the distribution of reports diagnosed as cases for advice or investigation within three age categories in 1991 and 1993. The total number of children represented by the data in Table 8-4 is higher than the number of reported cases of child maltreatment because the registration system counts a reported case of maltreatment as the report of a family, which often includes more than one child. Reports concerning persons older than 17 years are not counted.

As shown in Table 8-4, between 1991 and 1993 the proportion of reports that were treated as a demand for advice increased from 28% to 39%. The data reveal that this increase was fairly constant across the three age groups. This trend reflects a policy response to pressures from the increasing number of reports; treating a report as a demand for advice takes less time than handling it as a demand for investigation.

Table 8-4. Disposition (Percentage) of Reports Within Three Age Categories

Age Group (Years)	1991		1993	
	Advice ($n = 3,440$)	Investigation ($n = 9,327$)	Advice ($n = 6,610$)	Investigation ($n = 11,035$)
0–5	23	77	35	65
6–11	27	73	37	63
12–17	32	68	44	56

The data also indicate that the proportion of reports treated as a demand for investigation rises as the age groups get younger. The tendency to handle reports concerning younger children as a demand for advice is smaller than in the case of reports concerning older children. We cannot explain this difference. Perhaps the situations of younger children are more complicated or youngsters may be considered to be more vulnerable and thus in need of greater protection. In any event, the rising proportion of cases treated as advice reports does not explain the overall increase in the proportion of older children among investigated reports noted in Tables 8-2 and 8-3.

Trends in Placement and Child Protection

As noted above, there are two institutions at which child abuse can be reported, the Child Care and Protection Board and the Confidential Doctor Offices. However the Child Care and Protection Board does not keep a child abuse register. In cases of child abuse it often registers other factors such as "child-rearing problems," "family problems," and sometimes "fornication"; only a few severe cases of physical violence are registered as "physical abuse." Consequently this registration system does not permit a comparative analysis of placement decisions and types of abuse. The Confidential Doctor Offices do keep a child abuse register, but the annual reports give marginal attention to types of intervention in combination with types of abuse.

Nevertheless we can use other sources to say something about placement policies. Montfoort (1993a) analyzed a sample of 915 files of the Child Care and Protection Board for the period 1987 to 1991 to investigate the way cases of physical and of sexual abuse were handled by the board. The period was too short for an analysis of long-term trends, but he was able to compare types of placement decisions and types of abuse over the 4 years. Mertens (1993) described more general changes in civil child protection between 1970 and 1990. These two lines of research offer some information about placement decisions and about trends in civil child protection. In addition we refer to research by Hekken, de Ruyter, and Sanders-Woudstra (1987) concerning trends in residential care between 1975 and 1986. Let us start with Montfoort's findings concerning the board.

The combination of placement decisions and reports of child abuse is complicated because reports are made for a lot of abused children while they no longer live with their parents and the children come back home after interventions as a consequence of the report or they remain away; some are placed after a report and then live away from home for a very long time, and others return home sooner or later after a placement as a consequence of a report. These movements back and forth are reflected in Montfoort's (1993a) finding that 64% of the children reported as abused lived with their parents at the time of the report and 62% did so at the time the handling of the report was ended. Thus between the moment of receiving the report and the moment of closing the file, some children returned home while others left. The findings suggest that the general opinion about the supposed eagerness of the Child Care and Protection Board to snatch children from their parents is not based on fact. More positively formulated, it appears that the board, like the Confidential Doctor Offices, tries to restore the parent-child relationship in many cases. Only 28% of the children who lived with their parents at the moment of report were placed; for 55% of the children who had already left the home, the placement was confirmed formally after the report (this held for 70% of the children in residential care at that time). Furthermore it became clear that the chance of a child being placed out of the home because of reported sexual abuse was greater than for a child reported because of physical abuse. When a stepfather was mentioned as the perpetrator, there was a greater tendency to place the child out of the home than in other cases.

Mertens's (1993) research concerning trends in civil child protection opens a second line of analysis. Between 1960 and 1980 there was a sharp decline (53%) in children with a COS (under which parents must share authority with a family guardian), from 41,820 in 1960 (92 children reported per 10,000 children) to 21,238 children (46 children reported per 10,000 children) in 1980. During this period there was also a decline of 44% in care orders, which involve termination of parental authority. This general decline was especially evident in the 1970s (77 children per 10,000 in 1970) and stabilized again from 1980 until 1985, while we see an upward movement since 1985 (52 per 10,000 children in 1990).

There was a growing reluctance in the 1970s and the first half of the 1980s to intervene in matters of parental authority. The legalistic way the board functioned came under heavy criticism. In many cases a COS was used to enforce a placement. There were several reasons for the increasing resistance to the placement of children in general and to placement in residential care in particular. Cost was a growing concern. Residential care is much more expensive than ambulatory care. The government's policy was that child care had to be as simple as possible, as short as possible, and as near to home as possible — which meant as cheap as possible. A drastic cutback in the amount of available residential beds accompanied this policy. For example the total number of beds under the authority of the Ministry of Justice dropped by 31% between 1975 and 1986, and the total number of beds in Medical Children's Homes fell by 39% (Hekken et al., 1987). The amount of "beds" in day care centers almost doubled during the same period. In addition to cost considerations, ideas were changing about the parent-child relationship, with greater recognition accorded the importance of the quality and continuity of this relationship for the emotional development of the child. As a consequence, disruption of the parent-child relationship was seen as a potential threat to the child's healthy development and the disruption had to be restricted to exceptional cases. Moreover the belief in the therapeutic possibilities and outcomes of residential care, especially for young children, became weaker.

Current Issues in the Netherlands

This chapter ends by reviewing three issues currently on the public agenda in the Netherlands. The first issue concerns the position of the Confidential Doctor Offices within the total context of child care and child protection, particularly in relation to the Child Care and Protection Board. From 1972 until now the legal situation of formal rights and duties of the Confidential Doctor Offices has not been regulated. This means that the offices have to balance the twilight of professional secrecy, rights of reported adults, interests of reported children, and (recently) existing legislation with regard, for example, to the registration of personal data. The offices' policy emphasizes compassion, which allies them to child care rather than to child protection. Both the Confidential Doctor Offices and the Child Care and Protection Board seek to restore the parent-child relationship, but the board employs a control strategy in cases for which a compassionate strategy fails. With different strategies but a similar underlying philosophy it would be possible to integrate both organizations; such integration would resolve the offices' shaky legal base.

However, although in fact the philosophy underlying the work of the board and offices is the same, the board is associated in public opinion (because it has the legal base the offices lack) with legal action. This association could be an obstacle for laypersons as well as for professionals to reporting child abuse. The government recently decided to continue the separate existence of two institutions, the Child Care and Protection Board and another agency, in every region to which child abuse can be reported. In 1994 a task force was established by the state secretaries of the Ministry of Health, Welfare, and Cultural Affairs and the Ministry of Justice with the following assignment: to stimulate and to support the modeling of a regional institute to which child abuse can be reported and to foster the cooperation between this institute and the board on a regional level. The government is in fact charging a task force with a duty that has been neglected since 1972: creating clarity with regard to the position of the Confidential Doctor Offices within the context of child protection, child care, and legislation concerning confidentiality and accessibility of personal data.

The second issue concerns the debate about the desirability and effectiveness of prosecuting incest perpetrators, especially when they are fathers. Under certain conditions it is possible to give a perpetrator the choice of either jail or therapy (in the latter choice, imprisonment can still be ordered if the convicted perpetrator backs out of treatment). Some therapists (Bullens, 1992) claim that the threat of imprisonment is necessary to keep perpetrators in therapy. However, prosecution, the fear of punishment, and other negative consequences may hinder admission of the offense by perpetrators. Besides, prosecution sometimes does more harm than good; it can be damaging for the victim and the family and can obstruct the restoration of the relationship between father and child. Therefore other therapists (Nieskens, 1995) have promised accused persons—mostly fathers—to keep the law at a distance if they will admit having committed the offense. These therapists claim that this bargain stimulates the perpetrator's willingness to admit and opens the way for treatment; the therapists also claim they do not need to involve the threat of imprisonment to keep perpetrators in therapy. However these divergent claims are made in the absence of empirical evidence. The question of which strategy is preferable in which cases remains unresolved.

The last issue relates to the multiethnicity of modern Dutch society. With the influx of immigrants from Morocco, Turkey, Suriname, and the Dutch Antilles during the 1960s and 1970s Holland has become a multiethnic society. This makes the general and academic debate on cultural and normative aspects of the definition of child abuse a compelling issue in daily practice, especially with regard to physical abuse. Subcultures differ in opinions and practices concerning physical violence toward children. From time to time civil law proposals are made forbidding all kinds of violence toward children, as is the case in the Scandinavian countries and Austria (Newell, 1989). Until now the Dutch government has avoided introducing such a provision in civil law and accordingly lacks a possibly important preventive measure. Obviously reluctance to intervene in family privacy and cultural differences temporarily seem to predominate, and children still cannot claim the rights allowed to adults.

Notes

The authors wish to thank Professor J. Doek and A. van Montfoort for their advice.

1. The Child Care and Protection Board is known in the Netherlands as *Raad voor de Kinderbescherming* (RvdK).

2. In general everybody who knows about a crime can inform the police. Depending on the quality of this information, the police may undertake an investigation resulting in the prosecution of the alleged perpetrator. Some crimes (e.g., sexual offenses) can only be investigated and prosecuted if the victim (himself or herself) files a formal complaint with the police. If the victim is younger than 16 years old her or his parent(s) or legal custodian has the right to file such a complaint.

References

Bullens, R. A. R. (1992). Behandeling van incestplegers (Treatment of incest perpetrators). In: H. E. M. Baartman & A. van Montfoort (Eds.), *Kindermishandeling; resultaten van multidisciplinair onderzoek* (Child maltreatment; results of multidisciplinary research). Utrecht: Bruna.

Clemens Schröner, B. L. F. (1956). *Psychische kindermishandeling* [Emotional child abuse]. The Hague: Nijhoff.

Eckenrode, J., Powers, J., Doris, J., Munsch, J., & Bolger, N. (1988). Substantiation of child abuse and neglect reports. *Journal of Consulting and Clinical Psychology, 56,* 9–16.

Edwards, S. S. M., & Soetenhorst-de Savornin Lohman, J. (1994). The impact of "moral panic" on professional behavior in cases of child sexual abuse: An international perspective. *Journal of Child Sexual Abuse, 3,* 145–149.

Gil, D. (1979). Unraveling child abuse. In D. Gil (Ed.), *Child abuse and violence* (pp. 3–17). New York: Ams Press.

Hekken, S. van, de Ruyter, P. A., & Sanders-Woudstra, J. (1987). *Residentiële jeugdhulpverlening, voorwerp van aanhoudende zorg* [Residential youth care, a matter of continuous care]. Rijswijk, Netherlands: Department of Welfare, Health and Culture.

Hoefnagels, C. (1994). *Over praten gesproken . . .* [To mention talking . . .]. Amsterdam: Free University Press.

Hulsenbek, J. et al. (1994). *Rapport van de werkgroep ritueel misbruik* (Report of the taskforce ritual abuse). The Hague: Ministery of Justice.

Jonker, F., & Jonker-de Bakker, I. (1991). Experiences with ritualistic child sexual abuse: A case study from the Netherlands. *Child Abuse and Neglect, 15,* 191–196.

Kempe, H. C., Silverman, F. N., Steele, B. F., Droegemueller, W., & Silver, H. K. (1962). The battered child syndrome. *Journal of the American Medical Association, 181,* 105–112.

Koers, A. (1981). *Kindermishandeling. En wat dan nog?* (Child maltreatment. So what . . . ?). Rotterdam: Ad Donker.

Lamers-Winkelman, F. (1994). Moral panics in the Netherlands? A commentary. *Journal of Child Sexual Abuse, 3,* 145–149.

Mertens, N. M. (1993). *De ondertoezichtstelling en andere maatregelen van kinderbescherming* [Court ordered supervision and other child protection orders]. The Hague: Ministry of Justice.

Montfoort, A. van. (1993a). *Kindermishandeling en justitie* [Child abuse and justice]. Amsterdam: Free University Press.

Montfoort, A. van. (1993b). The protection of children in the Netherlands: Between justice and welfare. In H. Ferguson, R. Gilligan, & R. Torode (Eds.), *Surviving childhood adversity*. Dublin: Social Studies Press.

Montfoort, A. van. (1994). *Het topje van de ijsberg* [The tip of the iceberg]. Utrecht, Netherlands: SWP.

Newell, P. (1989). *Children are people too; The case against physical punishment.* London: Bedford Square Press.

Nieskens, E. (1995). Ervaringen met contextuele hulpverlening (Experiences with contextual treatment). In: H. E. M. Baartman (Ed.). *Op gebaande paden? Ontwikkelingen in diagnostiek, hulpverlening en preventie met betrekking tot seksueel misbruik van kinderen* (Keeping to beaten tracks? Developments in diagnosing, treatment and prevention of sexual child abuse). Utrecht: SWP.

Noordhoek-van der Staay, J., & Buffing, F. (1994). *Kindermishandeling als bijzonder probleem* [Child maltreatment as an exceptional problem]. Amsterdam: Free University Press.

Pyck, K. (1994). The backlash in Europe: Real anxiety or mass hysteria in the Netherlands? A preliminary study of the Oude Pekela crisis. In J. E. B. Myers (Ed.), *The backlash; Child protection under fire* (pp. 70–85). Thousand Oaks, CA: Sage.

Rijksplan Jeugdhulpverlening 1995–1998 (1994). (Plans of the State for youth care, 1995–1998). Rijswijk: Ministeries of Justice, and of Health, Welfare and Sports.

Rosenfeld, A., & Newberger, E. (1977). Compassion versus control: Conceptual and practical pitfalls in the broadened definition of child abuse. *Journal of the American Medical Association, 237,* 2086–2088.

9

Germany

A Nonpunitive Model

REINHART WOLFF

Child Protection in Germany: Historical Background

Modern child protection initiatives in Germany developed early in the 19th century as a reaction to the growing exploitation of children in the expanding industrial system and to widespread neglect of children as a consequence of poverty and family breakup in the early years of capitalism. At the beginning of the 19th century, many Child Saving Houses (*Rettungshäuser*) were established to provide group care for children. In 1829 the first Society for the Betterment of Morally Neglected Children — later to be called Child Saving Association (*Verein zur Besserung sittlich verwahrloster Kinder* or later *Kinderrettungsverein*) — was founded in the small town of Köslin near Berlin.

The society was more concerned with the "demoralization of children" than with the economic and social situation, which produced child labor and poverty that led to a high incidence of child neglect and early child death. It prepared the ground for a moralistic approach that has become prominent in many upper-class-oriented child-saving movements in modern society. With a view of the child as being both endangered and dangerous or morally imperfect, the Child Saving Association typically depoliticized and individualized the problem of child maltreatment. The same conceptual orientation governed the beginnings of institutional child care in the middle of the 19th century; these efforts were dominated by religious movements that sought to save children from the poisonous influence of the growing working class and socialist movements.

At the same time, however, the state, the military, and liberal bourgeois industrialists in Prussia became interested in child protection and pressed for child labor regulations and, at least, a minimal amount of schooling (Bernecker, 1975). In order to reduce the number of frail and sick children, they demanded a curb to "the untimely and excessive employment of young factory workers" (Kuczynski, 1969, p. 91). As a consequence of these concerns the first Prussian Child Labor Law was enacted in 1839 (Wolff, 1996) and amended in 1853, allowing the employment of 10-year-old children for 10 hours. The earliest work-entry age was later raised to the age of 12 years, and it was decreed that 14 year olds could only be employed for 7 hours a day. During this period child protection also meant campaigning for at least a few years of school, which finally led to the introduction of compulsory education in the 1880s. Thus child protectionists in the early days of the movement were labor law activists, school education advocates, and moralistic child "savers"; they were the founding figures of institutional and foster child care, in which maltreated and neglected children were placed, away from their families, sometimes even across the ocean.[1]

In order to understand Germany's response to child maltreatment, we need to bear in mind that by the 1880s Bismarckian social reform acts had already established the foundations of a welfare state. The acts provided social security, health insurance, and sickness benefits and established the first local administrative social work structures. In the course of the 20th century, a full state welfare system was erected on these foundations, with major expansions after 1919 in the Weimar Republic and then, of course, of services, both public and voluntary, after World War II.

At the end of the 19th century, child protection activities, from both state and voluntary agencies like the German Association of Children's Friends (founded in 1897, *Deutscher Verein der Kinderfreunde*) and the Society for the Protection of Children from Abuse and Maltreatment (founded in 1898–1899, *Verein zum Schutze der Kinder vor Ausnutzung und Mißhandlung,* later *Deutscher Kinderschutzverband*) finally coalesced in the establishment of a broad child welfare system. This system encompassed both small local government health and social work departments (mainly responsible for health care, social assistance, and guardianships) and a growing number of voluntary child welfare agencies that provided limited day care and group or institutional care, some counseling, and family education.

Under the 1922 Child or Youth Welfare Act (*Reichsjugendwohl-fahrts-gesetz,* RJWG), public agencies formed the basic child protection structure. Together with private welfare agencies they were responsible for intervening mostly in working-class and sub-working-class families in which children were not always properly educated and child abuse and neglect often occurred. In their child protection work, these agencies relied heavily on a punitive, civil, and criminal law enforcement approach and at the same time they provided services. They used the civil code (*Bürgerliches Gesetzbuch,* BGB) to place a child and terminate parental rights and the penal code (*Strafgesetzbuch,* StGB) to prosecute parents, although prosecution was practically restricted to cases of severe maltreatment, murder, and infanticide. Until the 1960s harsh corporal punishment was a widely accepted practice in Germany; it was rarely considered child abuse and usually did not lead to child protection activities.

Conceptually, since the beginning of the century, the evolving welfare state in cooperation with nongovernment child welfare agencies developed the basic approach that came to dominate child protection activities in this century. This approach combined repressive (categorical) child protection interventions and supportive child and family welfare services.

Interestingly enough, long before C. Henry Kempe (Kempe et al., 1962) rediscovered child abuse and neglect in the 1960s, Germany already had a well-developed field of child maltreatment research in the early 1920s and 30s. These research initiatives were linked to the expanding centers of psychoanalysis (e.g., above all Siegfried Bernfeld and August Aichhorn and the *Zeitschrift für psychoanalytische Pädagogik*) and to early forays in child development psychology in Leipzig and Berlin, with Gertrud Hetzer and the *Zeitschrift für Kinderforschung* (*Journal of Child Research*) as driving forces (Bast, Bernecker, Kastlen, Schmitt, & Wolff, 1975/1995).

It is in this context of educational reform and research that the 1922 Child Welfare Act "enshrined the rights of every young person to fully develop his or her potential with the support of society" (Lorenz, 1991, p. 330) and opted for pedagogical, child-oriented principles, setting standards for child welfare departments (Jugendämter) in every part of the country (Lorenz, 1991).

The Nazi regime centralized this child welfare structure but used it by nationalizing the voluntary social work sector. (The then German Society for Prevention of Abuse to Children by an overwhelming majority voluntarily decided to dissolve itself and be incorporated into the National Socialist People's Welfare Federation, *Nationalsozialistische Volkswohlfahrt,* NSV). The Nazis made child sexual abuse a major propaganda issue ("cracking down" on the "monsters" or *Volksschädlinge*). This form of deviancy control served to advance totalitarian social integration. The Nazis also called for a more punitive line in child protection and introduced a new paragraph into the penal code specially referring to child abuse (art. 223 b StGB, Misshandlung von Schutzbefohlenen) that was meant to make it easier to withdraw parental rights when the state attorney prevailed in a criminal prosecution.

Since the Federal Republic of Germany was established in 1949, a democratic social welfare system has developed with a strong legal grounding in the German Basic Law (the German constitution). The system is organized under a federal structure, with the *Länder*—the states—and the municipalities responsible, together with the voluntary welfare agencies, for providing a wide array of child welfare services.

In the late 1960s and early 1970s, a new concept and practice of child protection developed in Germany. Later this came to be known as the New Child Protection Movement (NCPM). Influenced by the large democratic protest movement of the 1960s and new models of child protection in the Netherlands, Scandinavia, and the United States, the NCPM created an alternative approach to child maltreatment. The 1922 Child Welfare Act was practically reenacted by the 1962 Youth Welfare Act (JWG), which with the Federal Social Assistance Act (*Bundessozialhilfe-Gesetz,* BSHG) served as a legal basis for all services to children and families. This changed in 1991 with the passage of the Child and Youth Welfare Act (*Kinder und Jugendhilfegesetz,* KJHG), which is more comprehensive in scope and orientation than previous legislation. According to Lorenz (1991), "This Act also represents an acknowledgement that German social work practice particularly in relation to children and young people has managed to develop highly creatively and run ahead of the bureaucracy" (p. 339).

The NCPM and grassroots "alternative social work," a broad coalition of voluntary agencies that grew out of the radical opposition movement of the 1960s, influenced the creation and acceptance of the new Child and Youth Welfare Act.

The NCPM was modeled on the efforts of the Berlin Child Protection Center. The center grew out of a research project on family violence at the Free University Berlin in the early 1970s and has widely influenced both the voluntary and the public sectors in the field of child protection and child welfare. Providing direct services to families (without relying on mandatory reporting) and connecting clinical social work programs (family therapy and counseling), crisis intervention, and short-term residential care, it is at the same time a child welfare advocacy, consultation, and continuing education agency. Working from a concept of need, not of control, with the aim of building proactive networks of mutual support, the Child Protection Center became a catalyst for change in the human services.

With the emergence of the NCPM, child maltreatment came to be viewed as a sociopsychological, cultural, political, and gender problem. Attention to the substantial body of new research from the established fields of socialization, child development, psychology, and family studies contributed to revised perceptions of child abuse. Privatization and individualization of the problem did not play a major role in the social construction of child maltreatment, as has been the case in many other countries. On the contrary, a broad contextual definition of child maltreatment and a continuum approach (i.e., it can happen to everybody depending on the specific relational and societal circumstances) are now widely accepted among German child protection workers (Wittenhagen & Wolff, 1980).

A broad contextual view of the problem of course promotes a developmental and conflict-oriented model of child welfare (Hardiker, Exton, & Barker, 1991). It is a model aimed at creating social equality and providing universal services on the principle of meeting need through services accessible to everybody that allow for choice. Such a model emphasizes client friendliness, advocacy, and community participation. From this perspective, there is no place for mandatory reporting or central registers, which elsewhere have led to crisis and disaster, as more and more people have begun to realize (Pelton, 1990; Zellman & Antler, 1990).

In comparing the broader system of child protective services in Germany to those in other countries, three characteristics stand out.

First, in Germany child protective agencies are embedded in the wider context of the whole welfare state service system. German child protection relies mainly on a full-fledged system of services ranging from low-cost day care to free counseling, from infant health care and social assistance (which guarantee a life above the poverty line), to family services and family aides (homemakers), plus a special network of accessible, regionalized services like the multidisciplinary Child Protection Centers.

Second, there is a substantial income transfer to low-income groups in Germany through the legal entitlement to social assistance along with an established tradition of public housing, rent support, a general health insurance system, and widespread low-cost public and private day care institutions. These social welfare provisions have reduced the amount of poverty and deprivation. German society today is less class structured and less violent than, for example, that of the United States. All this contributes to fewer and less severe cases of child maltreatment in Germany than in the United States.

Third, the German model of nonpunitive child protection work and of destigmatizing and decriminalizing, though not overlooking, child maltreatment has influenced other European countries (like Belgium, with the Center *Kind in Nood*; Denmark, Austria, and Italy with child protection centers; and Switzerland, with the *Elternnotruf* in Zurich and a hospital-centered team approach in Bern). However, the approach to child protection in Germany is currently endangered by scandals and paranoid trends that are recurrent features in most modern child protection movements and systems. With the new focus on child sexual abuse, since the early 1980s the German child protection system has begun to develop along more punitive lines. With a growing number of false allegations and "child abuse errors" that have caused heated public debates and even violent actions against authors and workers who are actively engaged in deescalating the debate, the overall climate in child protection work resembles an ideological battlefield in which harsh controversies over philosophies, methods, programs, and agencies have developed (Rutschky, 1992; Rutschky & Wolff, 1994).

Development and Assessment of the Problem

Since the turn of the 20th century, child maltreatment has served to fuel the development of child welfare services. However, the new awareness regarding problems of child abuse and neglect that emerged in Germany (as in many other countries) in the 1960s reflected wide social, technological, scientific, and cultural changes. In the course of a few years the number of social welfare professionals doubled; in the field of counseling and clinical social work there was an increase in the number of employed professionals of about 400%. Social work education was reorganized, and from 1970 the former academies of social work (training institutes) were upgraded and became professional universities (*Fachhochschulen*).

The way child maltreatment has emerged as a problem of national and international importance reflects basic changes in the cultural and political interactions of modern societies. Politics as an enactment, as a construction with and through the ever-present media, has changed the character of social problems. Social problems no longer exist as such. They are no longer objective social entities. Modern political and social problems are being produced.

Their reality is a constructed reality depending heavily on the structure of public discourse. Awareness is a media product. The new reality machines indeed invent social problems, establish a certain agenda, and place and eliminate problems within the public discourse. This is how child maltreatment has become an issue.

What we now call child abuse and neglect is a modern construction. As a social problem it has been created; it is not just there, it is a discourse structure that has a dramatic impact on child protective work. Child welfare workers also take part in publicly constructing child abuse and neglect as a social problem. One cannot easily grasp it; it is not just there even if there are, of course, violated and injured kids, disturbed parents, and families in need of services. In order to justly identify it as a "social problem," a public construction of the problem is necessary, which involves societal "fact finding" and "meaning making" (an interpretation of the facts through a complex process of public discourse). Modern cultural industries, by using new paradigms and images, create a new grammar of understanding. Modern child protection movements have become cultural industries, too.

It is important to understand the changing social and political context in which the problem of child abuse and policies for child protection have emerged. Three significant areas of change involve the class structure, political relations, and family structure. As in many other modern societies, there is a marked change in class structures in Germany. (For a discussion of similar developments in France, see Julien, 1995.) This change occurred over the last 10 years, during which the Federal Republic of Germany experienced a dramatic redistribution of income. During this period those in the upper 15% of the income distribution had an increase of 75% of their income, while the income of the lower 20% rose by only 1%. At the same time, for Germany it is characteristic that there has been a concentration of large parts of the population in the middle layers that was accompanied by a dramatic rise in the overall living standards in the postwar period from 1949 to 1965.

In the political arena, basic controversies have emerged concerning the relationship among the state, the administration, and the citizens. With the expansion of the modern welfare state, central government administrations have become much more powerful. This gain in power has not always been matched by increasing political controls from below. This is a crucial point that also affects the social services, raising questions as to whether citizens have a right to participate in decision-making processes and whether the role of centralized government services is balanced by a due respect for regional and nongovernment agencies' interests.

At the same time, there have been marked family changes. As in other developed countries, Germany experienced a remarkable decrease in the number of children. (In some of the new eastern German states, e.g., Laender, the birth rate in the last years has dropped by 50%.) This trend has had consequences for social workers and therapists since fewer children mean fewer demands for professional service. It came as no surprise that the huge increase in services (and not the least in child welfare services) that occurred in the

1970s did not continue in the 1980s. With fewer children to serve, social services had to look for new tasks. The growing interest in child protection in part reflected the search for new needs. New needs were emerging in response to other changes in family life. There was a rising need for out-of-home care as more and more caretakers that traditionally had been available in the family (mostly the mothers, but also grandparents and unmarried uncles and aunts) now left the family for long hours to work or were separated altogether through an increasing rate of divorce. Finally, the dynamics and relational structure of families have generally been influenced by a marked process of individualization in family life, which has led to an increase in aspirations but at the same time has contributed toward greater insecurity in family life. Now people need and have to love one another and that seems to be very difficult. Since we have based our relationships essentially on our feelings, both intimacy and insecurity play a central role in modern family life and have created advantages and disadvantages.

Two other trends have also transformed family life and childhood: gender differentiation and equalization that have promoted the emancipation of women and a change in couple relationships and a change in the prevalent authority structure in a "prefigurative society" that has deeply affected all educational processes. These developments have caused a number of relational dilemmas that have also increased the possibilities of conflict in intimate relationships and of crisis in child-rearing practices. Prefigurative society means that society in principle is now oriented toward the future. It is no longer oriented toward the past. Parents find that their experiences no longer count as much as they did in times when people relied on the experiences of the older generations. Modern parents no longer know "what will be" since everything has changed and is always changing. Modern culture has devalued the experiences of the older generations, and this contributes toward undermining the educational role of both parents and other adults. Postfigurative cultures worshipped the past and relied on tradition. Modern culture is oriented toward the future and thus depends on an openness toward change. To educate the younger generation to be prepared for the future, parents can no longer trust what their parents thought would be helpful. Now they need to anticipate what will be and teach their children flexible concepts and capabilities to cope with new challenges yet unknown. Education in general has become a difficult job, and many parents think it is an impossible job.

All these trends (private and public, societal and political, socioeconomic and relational) not only promote a resurgence of violent crises in family life, but also a growing dependency of families on a wide variety of social services. They also have created a basis for a new and wider interest in child protection and allowed for new formulations of standards of care and education. The development of new standards of care has turned out to be a difficult task since modern culture, particularly in Germany with its historical mix of authoritarian trends and modern openness, has advanced an ambiguous code regarding the use of violence against children and in couple and family relationships. The existing code at the same time encourages and prohibits violent behavior in the private sphere and in educational, medical, and psychiatric institutions (Bernecker & Wolff, 1985).

The new child protection movement reacted to this ambivalent code by drawing the line more clearly so that the use of violence is no longer legitimate. Yet progress in the history of childhood has never been clear-cut. Each generation has been confronted again with the problem of overcoming violence. This historical perspective has oriented the modern child protection movement in Germany, where sociologist and pedagogues, and to a lesser extent medical professionals, played a major role (Bast et al., 1975/1985). The movement developed a contextual and relativist concept of child maltreatment; it came to be understood as a violent social practice and process of interaction embedded in a structure of "societal and systemic violence." The concept of conflict (and not so much of crime) became important: Child abuse is an expression of a conflict in which an attempt is made to maintain a threatened relationship by force. To maltreat a child is basically a helpless and inarticulate attempt to overcome relationship conflicts or a desperate effort to cope with stress and crisis when one is overwhelmed. Social deprivation, poverty, and below-average living conditions increase the risk of child abuse and neglect to a considerable degree (Beiderwieden, Windaus, & Wolff, 1986; Brinckmann & Honig, 1984; Honig, 1982).

This view of the problem is expressed by one of the leading agencies in the field, the Berlin Child Protection Center, founded in 1975. Taking a broad social policy orientation, the center defined child abuse as:

> Not just an isolated violent act of injury of a child. Child abuse embraces the whole system that is constituted by the living conditions and the actions and ommissions that restrict the rights of a child, that endanger his or her development, education and well-being. The discrepancy between these rights and a child's actual living conditions constitutes the totality of child maltreatment. (Kinderschuiz-Zentrum, p. 2)

From a clinical perspective, child maltreatment was broadly defined as a non-accidental, conscious or unconscious act of physical and/or emotional impairment of a child that happens in both families and institutions (e.g., day care centers, schools, foster homes, clinics) that results in injuries, development retardation, and even death and that represents a threat to the well-being of a child and an impairment of a child's right (as outlined in the Child and Youth Welfare Act, 1991).

The Scope of Child Maltreatment

There are reasons to believe that the number of children that could be categorized as maltreated has decreased. This is due in part to a substantial rise in the overall standard of living in Germany since 1945, accompanied by better food, more and better housing facilities, better health and educational services, and in the 1960s and 1970s tremendous expansion in child welfare and counseling services. In addition the authoritarian and brutal "educational" practices that were so typical of Nazi Germany (fully documented by reeducation officers of the Allied armies after 1945) were given up in the course of the postwar period and gave way to nonviolent educational practices.

The real number of maltreated children in Germany however is empirically unknown. This is due to a shortage of representative epidemiological research and to the fact that Germany has no mandatory reporting system. However, since Germany has a broad (state-funded and largely cost-free) system of educational and child welfare and health services that represent a tight-meshed net, most children are regularly seen and monitored. Thus the number of unknown cases of child maltreatment (that need be to "disclosed") is probably smaller than usually claimed by child abuse experts.

The best data available come from both the *Bundeskriminalamt* (the German equivalent of the U.S. Federal Bureau of Investigation) and since 1991 from the Federal Bureau of Statistics. The data from these sources allow an overall estimate of the size of the problem of child abuse and neglect in Germany. Of course police data refer to cases of the most serious forms of child maltreatment. The most striking fact is that the incidence of child abuse and neglect known to the police has remained fairly stable over the years; after 1990 (the year of German unification) the numbers continued to remain the same — they fluctuate between around 25,000 and 33,000 cases per year, which represents a stable rate of 2 children affected per 1,000 minors under the age of 18 years (see Tables 9-1, 9-2, and 9-3).

The data show that nearly half of all cases known to the police represent sexual abuse cases (the local [municipal] and state police play a major role in reporting, investigation, and prosecution). In Germany cases of neglect are rarely reported to the police because neglect is usually not prosecuted; it is generally considered a social problem and not a crime. The data also reveal a decrease in the number and rate of child fatalities related to abuse. Substantially fewer children in Germany die of inflicted injuries than of traffic accidents (in 1994, 431 children were killed and 51,635 were injured in traffic accidents in Germany).

The data available from the child welfare field show that the number of children receiving services (and especially those who were placed out of their families) is three to four times higher than the number of maltreated children known to the police. Since 1991 there are even more data available from enlarged child welfare statistics, which now include reports on child maltreatment. Although a wide definition is used ("child abuse cases include acts where situational, emotional, and physical violence against children is used that have resulted either in physical injuries and/or in life threatening anxiety feelings") (Statistisches Bundesamt, 1995) and there is substantial overlap in the categories of reported cases (number of counseling cases, of cases for which homebuilder services or other individual support programs were used), the new data allow a more realistic assessment of the scope of child maltreatment (see Tables 9-4 to 9-6) (Statistisches Bundesamt, 1995).

In 1992 and 1993 close to 200,000 minors per year were known to the public child welfare agencies. Most of the minors came to the attention of the

Table 9-1. Criminal Offenses Against Children (Number of Victims Under 18) in Federal Republic of Germany, 1982–1993

Offenses	1982[a]	1984	1985	1986	1987	1988	1989	1990	1991	1992	1993
Murder	94	87	68	68	72	65	56	42	60	334	55
Second-degree murder	30	50	41	47	37	42	52	34	42	40	46
Infanticide	28	33	16	21	17	23	25	29	26	18	17
Fatal assault	16	8	16	13	14	13	14	28	17	18	15
Rape [included on next line]	[828]	[780]	[721]	[658]	[676]	[578]	[473]	[531]	[666]	[801]	[885]
Sexual offenses including rape	2,336	2,116	2,000[b]	2,166	1,755	1,800	1,697	1,982	2,295	2,714	2,827
Child sexual abuse	13,067	11,134	11,098	11,848	11,498	13,179	13,680	14,316	14,987	16,381	14,397
Slave trade	15	17	24	7	25	9	17	9	16	29	80
Severe assault/poisoning	9,500	9,403	8,563	9,052	8,462	8,360	8,668	9,600	11,656	12,855	13,149
Maltreatment	1,869	1,579	1,797	1,683	1,528	1,589	1,574	1,664	1,838	1,939	1,949
Neglect	1,025	849	841	825	793	752	764	744	868	1,019	942
Kidnapping	26	9	9	10	6	6	7	6	10	8	9
Hostage taking	22	11	11	14	12	9	19	18	11	20	19
Total	28,028	25,296	24,484	25,754	24,219	25,847	26,573	28,472	31,826	35,375	33,505

The data have been especially compiled for this study by the author.

[a]No victim data are available for 1983. The data from 1990 and after represent all of Germany.

[b]Estimate.

Source: Polizeiliche Krimnalstatistik, Bundesrepublik Deutschland. Bundeskriminalamt. Wiesbaden 1982–1994.

Table 9-2. Victims of All Forms of Abuse Known to the Police, Population Under 18 Years Old, in the Federal Republic of Germany, 1982–1993

Year	Minors Under 18	Abuse Victims	Fatal Abuses
Before unification			
1982	13,317,602	28,028	168
1983 (no data)	12,792,605	–	–
1984	12,266,947	25,296	178
1985	11,830,065	24,484	141
1986	11,527,204	25,754	149
1987	11,233,922	24,219	140
1988	11,233,205	25,847	143
1989	11,410,873	26,573	147
After unification			
1990	15,263,711	28,472	133
1991	15,521,837	31,826	145
1992	15,713,281	35,375	410[a]
1993	15,840,416	33,512	133

[a]The rise in the number of fatal abuses in 1992 is a statistical artifact. Included are cases from other years of the former German Democratic Republic.

services because they had "problems," were referred to the child welfare agencies by other agencies (often day care or medical institutions and schools), or because their parents had sought help. Approximately 100,000 of these children and adolescents were placed in institutional or family foster care (with a rate of 7 children per 1,000 over all the years) (see Table 9-5). Also the number of care orders (which always indicate serious parent-child relationship problems) has climbed slightly from 5,378 in 1983 to 9,277 in 1993, which represents a rise in the rates from 0.42 children per 1,000 minors to 0.59 children per 1,000 minors when parental rights were restricted in some form or another.

The figures show that there is no realistic relation between the incidence of child maltreatment that comes to the attention of social welfare providers and the numbers known to the police. It is obvious that from year to year there seems to be a certain learning process in filling out the statistical forms, and we find a rise in the figures, but the overall reliability of the data is low. Since precise guidelines are lacking, workers tend to rate their cases on merely subjective grounds. From these data it becomes clear that studies that reach the scientific quality of the U.S. National Incidence Studies and that would identify the number of cases known to child welfare agencies using a differen-

Table 9-3. Abuse Victims Under 18 Years Old Per 1,000 Population Known to the Police in the Federal Republic of Germany, 1982–1993

1982	1984	1985	1986	1987	1988	1989	1990	1991	1992	1993
2.10	2.06	2.06	2.23	2.15	2.30	2.32	1.86	2.05	2.25	2.11

Table 9-4. Placements, Adoptions, and Care Orders of Minors Under 18 Years Old, Federal Republic of Germany, 1982–1993

Year	Placements (Institutional and Family Foster Care)	Adoptions	Care Orders
Before unification			
1982	107,588	9,145	5,380
1983	100,947	8,801	5,378
1984	97,048	8,543	5,310
1985	94,075	7,974	6,908
1986	89,696	7,875	6,506
1987	88,409	7,694	6,223
1988	87,604	7,481	5,987
1989	86,962	7,114	6,262
After unification			
1990	104,278	–	–
1991	109,226	7,142	8,756
1992	114,637	8,403	9,160
1993	–	8,687	9,277

Source: Data compiled from Statistisches Bundesamt, Sozialleistungen, Fachserie 13, Jugendhilfe.

tiated definition and controlling the data on a case-by-case basis are much needed in Germany.

In comparison with other countries, Germany (if all data are taken together and on the basis of child welfare statistics), with a child abuse rate of approximately 15 children per 1,000 children under 18 years and a maximum number of about 200,000 cases per year known to public and nongovernment

Table 9-5. Placements in Federal Republic of Germany, 1982–1992

Year	Population Under 18 Years Old	Placements	Rates per 1,000
1982	–	107,588	–
1983	12,792,605	100,947	7.89
1984	12,266,947	97,048	7.91
1985	11,830,065	94,075	7.95
1986	11,527,204	89,696	7.78
1987	11,233,922	88,409	7.86
1988	11,233,205	87,604	7.79
1989	11,410,873	86,962	7.62
1990[a]	15,263,711	104,278	6.83
1991[a]	15,521,837	109,226	7.03
1992[a]	15,713,281	114,637	7.29

[a]East and West after Unification.

Source: Data compiled from Statistisches Bundesamt, Sozialleistungen, Fachserie 13, Jugendhilfe.

Table 9-6. Presenting Problems, Institutional Counseling, Public and Nongovernmental Organization (NGO) Social Services in Federal Republic of Germany, 1991–1993

	Number of Cases		
Presenting Problem	1991	1992	1993
Development problems	18,607	20,574	22,064
Relational problems	26,489	26,065	32,682
Child abuse	851	807	2,317
Child sexual abuse	3,649	5,761	9,416
All cases	154,483	177,482	197,955

Source: Compiled from Statistisches Bundesamt, Sozialleistungen, Fachserie 13, Jugendhilfe.

welfare services, has less than half the substantiated incidence rate of child maltreatment than, for example, the United States. Another difference stands out: While some other child protection systems concentrate on reporting, registering, and prosecuting child abuse cases, Germany, in spite of a long tradition of mixing the policing and social service role of child welfare, since 1949 has concentrated on providing a wide array of child welfare services. These services include individual casework, day care, infant and family health services, and counseling to special child protective services like the child protection centers or special (mostly feminist) agencies concerned exclusively with cases of child sexual abuse. Most of the voluntary welfare programs are financed by local, state, and federal administrations. The services are free for the clients, and they are available in all parts of the country (with typically a two-partite service structure in which communal and voluntary child welfare agencies work together).

The basic child protection system structure is shown in Figure 9-1. Child protection workers legally are required to report only cases of murder and manslaughter to the police, but the police regularly report child abuse cases to the local public child welfare departments. The new Child and Youth Welfare Act (1991) urges all parties concerned to meet in case conferences and develop an open partnership with the families that are served; with involuntary clients, the public child welfare departments quite often fall back on the old practice of intervention and cracking down on families. However the new conceptual orientation of providing an open and universal service and of overcoming the double-mandate structure (acting as a social police force and as a service agency) of child welfare services is in the foreground. The working principles developed in 1992 by a group of social workers in a Berlin child welfare department (in the city of Charlottenburg) stand as an example. They write:

(1) Our work premises shall be characterized by an open, non-bureaucratic atmosphere, a professional counselling setting, and child-friendly arrangements.

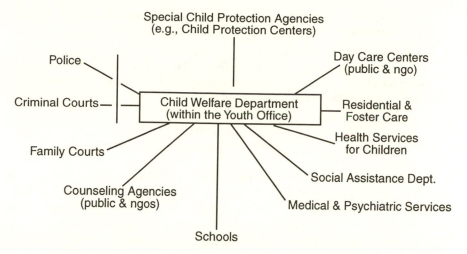

Fig. 9-1. Child protection system structure.

(2) We want to make it clear to our clients that we are interested in children and that we respect their rights.

(3) In our work, we basically offer supportive relationships and provide services; we are not interested in furthering prosecutions, law enforcement, and hunting down perpetrators or in investigating criminal offenses that is the task of other agencies.

(4) We want to work openly and discuss with our clients what we are up to. The family is our informant no. 1. We do not work behind the backs of our clients and guarantee their civil and information rights. We will inform our clients of our methods and the framework of our programs and will give information as to the legal context and consequences of our services.

(5) We provide family based services; our focus is primarily to further the development and well-being of the concerned children. Family support services are more important than measures to separate and place a child outside of his or her family.

(6) We use a bottom-up approach and build on the resources of the family.

(7) Our activities shall not be punitive.

(8) Only if a child is seriously endangered and when there is no co-operation and understanding on the part of the parents shall we involve the family court to protect a child.

(9) We want to work (as much as possible) to contribute towards the de-escalation of conflicts and a calming down of violent behavior and practices.

(10) As a public service agency we want to be a partner with the families and their environments we serve.

(11) We are advocates for children and adolescents in their families and in the wider public.

(12) As state social services we play a role as a co-ordinator in the wider context of various child protection agencies and programs. Working together contributes to the betterment of the services and to an improvement of professional competences and a high quality of work.

Comparing Child Protective Systems — A Conceptual Framework

In order to compare different systems of child protection or to assess child protection in Germany, we need to develop a conceptual framework to help characterize and evaluate the system. In the literature we do not find many studies that use a systemic social science approach. To analyze child protection systems, a multidimensional approach seems to be helpful. The following conceptual analytic dimensions are suggested for child protection systems analysis:

1. The concept of definition: split concepts versus continuum concepts
2. Historical constructions of child abuse and neglect focusing on either the societal pole or the individual pole
3. The strategic orientations of child protection systems characterized as traditional or "new" child protection work
4. The methods used and the services provided within a certain child protection system
5. The structural problems of the service system

If we look at how child maltreatment is defined today in Germany, we find it closely linked to the notion of "violence," which characterizes an action of someone causing harm and implies that something illegal is happening. Violence is strongly associated with the notion of "crime." The German word *Gewalt*, which can be used for the English word violence, however, originally had another connotation meaning "government or power." Yet now the term Gewalt has been transformed and has acquired more the meaning of an illegal destructive interaction or act than of a political and social relation. In the predominant public discourses it is a term that characterizes not so much a social context but rather an individual act.

In other countries, one also finds a marked trend to individualize the problem of child abuse and neglect; the understanding of child abuse as a legal problem is widespread. The fields of law enforcement and medicine have dominated the production of codes that conceptually orient the professional discourse. The practical consequences are enormous: Definitions of child abuse and neglect also determine the practice of child protection shown in Table 9-7.

It is also important to know whether the definition of child abuse and neglect is viewed along a continuum, which implies that child abusers fundamentally are not different from other human beings, that they do not belong

Table 9-7. Professional Codes and Practices

Professional Groups	Code	Practice
Law enforcement	Child abuse and neglect as crime	Prosecution
Medical	Child abuse and neglect as illness or injury	Treatment Healing
Psychologists	Child abuse and neglect as psychopathology or relational problem	Treatment Therapy
Social workers	Child abuse and neglect as a social problem as social harm	Administrative control Casework Support

to another class of "inhuman beings" as is often implied when one talks about child abuse using "split systems" of "them" and "us," of "perpetrators" and of "victims" to characterize protection systems. Understanding child maltreatment as a contextual problem and viewing it along a continuum, we do not question our connectedness with both the abuser and the abused. From this perspective there is no fundamental dividing line between child protectors and abusers. In Germany, the majority of workers tend to have abandoned the more moralistic normative approaches and view child abuse and neglect as a relative phenomenon, somewhere on the line between love on one extreme and murder on the other:

Continuum Approach of CAN

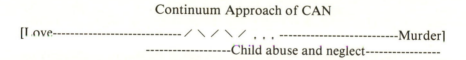

[Love---------------------------- ╱ ╲ ╱ ╲ ╱ . . . --------------------------Murder]
-------------------Child abuse and neglect----------------

Table 9-8 characterizes the focus of child protection systems.[2] Systems that focus on societal or individual poles set different agendas for child protection, determine the width of the field of action and the range of contextuality and of politization of the program, and even imply the use of certain methods (e.g., punitive ones).

Table 9-8. Child Protection Focus

Wide				Narrow
Society_____	Community_____ District	Service_____ Agencies	Family_____	Child/victim Perpetrator
Rights_____				Crimes
Politics_____				Treatment
Commonwealth_____				Individual

The German child protection system strongly leans toward the societal pole, focusing on services and social rights (the left side of Table 9-8), even though currently in the course of the widespread panic about child sexual abuse cases the systemic focus has shifted somewhat toward the other direction, which embodies an individual and crime-oriented approach.

In regard to the strategic orientations (Table 9-9), the German child protection system is again more on the side of a universal, institutional welfare model that allows for choice on the part of the clients, fosters self-help, and has a strong preventive orientation. At the same time the categorical approach periodically reappears (a trend that reappeared with a large number of interventionist social workers entering the professional field following German unification).

Of course, equally important are the methods used in child protection (Table 9-10). They have dramatic consequences: They delimit or broaden the professional fields of action, enable or hinder cooperation, open or close avenues for the clients to seek help themselves, and mount or diminish resistances. Germany's methods and services to deal with child maltreatment still represent a mix; they combine supportive and controlling methods of child protection in spite the widely accepted orientation that is also legally mandated by the progressive 1990 Child and Youth Welfare Act (*Kinder- und Jugendhilfe-Gesetz*). There are a number of structural problems in child protection work. The system, as many child welfare systems elsewhere, is time and again endangered by what Leroy Pelton has called the "double mandate" (Pelton, 1990, p. 24), a mix of support services, casework, and therapy and of punishment and repression.

Basing services on a double-mandate structure undermines the whole child welfare system. It is not working, and it is obscuring the professional identity of the professionals in the health and social services. The German case demonstrates that there is a path to quality management if child protection workers draw a clear line between child protection and law enforcement, between the child welfare services and the police and justice system. Both have their different mandates. If they are mixed up, the human services are seriously undermined.

The German case also reveals another structural problem that has ham-

Table 9-9. Strategic Orientations

Political_____	Nonpolitical
Universal_____	Categorical
Institutional_____	Residual
Social investment_____	Social cost
Choice_____	Coercion
Self-help_____	Expert service

Table 9-10. Methods and Services

Methods			
Active			Reactive
Offer			Registration
Self-referral			Reporting
Nonpunitive			Punitive
Understanding			Blaming
Preventive			Corrective
Building on strength			Controlling deficits

Services			
Support	Compensation	Treatment	Punishment
Education	Aid	Replacement	Control
Day care	Social	Counseling	Fine
School	Assistance	Therapy	Jail
Parents' education	Homemakers	Foster care placements	

pered the efficiency of child protection systems. Very often child welfare and child protective services are markedly class biased. There are different systems and different qualitative standards for well-to-do people, for educated people, and for the poor. Yet the dilemma is, as Richard M. Titmuss (1968) liked to stress: Services especially for the poor tend to be poor services. In such services, most clients are only "looked after." They cannot choose. The services are categorically forced on them. Two totalitarian systems (the Nazi dictatorship and Stalinist Communist state) have taught Germany a lesson of what it means if state welfare services, in order to control deviant and dangerous behaviors, tend to use a highly authoritative approach in cracking down on families. This is not the most effective approach to overcome violent behavior and to cope with maltreatment. Rather it promotes a violent "last-resort" practice that Maud Mannoni, the known French psychiatrist, has called "orientation automatique" — people are reported and automatically driven into the system. Well-to-do citizens would rather call a lawyer to protect their rights than accept a service forced on them as involuntary clients. But in the field of child protection, this is what is often done: Child protection interventionists often ignore civil rights.

Many problems still exist in the structure and practice of child protection services. The following is a list of the problems that continue to challenge child protection efforts in Germany as in many other countries:

1. Double-mandate structure (mixing repression and support and thereby causing a distortion of professional identity)
2. Class-structured services, split services, or both

3. Institutional fixation and traditionalism, which blocks innovation
4. Administrative authoritarianism ("étatisme"), lack of democratic participation
5. Lack of professional consciousness and self-confidence
6. Lack of cooperation and network building
7. Reluctance to control results, costs, and service demands

In many countries the main approach to child protective work is punitive, but in Germany and other European countries child protection workers have devised an alternative to the punitive model. There is a clear dividing line between the old interventionist approach (which relies heavily on prosecution and punishment) and new child protection orientations in the Netherlands, Germany, Belgium, Switzerland, Austria, and Italy, as well as in Scandinavia. Pelton (1990) offers a succinct model of child protective services:

> The public welfare assistance agency does not need informers to find people to whom it can deliver its services. It delivers a highly attractive service — money — for which people come voluntarily and that simultaneously helps achieve the agency's goal, namely, ameliorating the effects of poverty. Similarly, if the public child welfare agency were to dispense services that parents with child welfare problems want and need, without threat or judgement, then parents would seek them out voluntarily; and such services would serve the goal of preserving families and protecting children. (p. 25)

Notes

1. C. P. Gershenson, in his 1990 keynote speech at the 8th International Congress of Child Abuse and Neglect in Hamburg, underlined the fact that in the course of the 19th century, thousands of poor children from England and the European continent were sent to the United States, where they were mainly used as cheap farm hands.

2. I discussed these aspects with Stephen Antler, Ph.D. in Boston, who contributed enormously to clarifying the outlined conceptual orientations.

References

Bast, H., Bernecker, A., Kastien, L., Schmitt, G., & Wolff, R. (Eds.). (1975/1985). *Gewalt gegen Kinder. Kindesmisshandlung und ihre Ursachen* [Violence against children. Child maltreatment and its causes]. Reinbek, Germany: Rowohlt.

Beiderwieden, J., Windaus, E., & Wolff, R. (1986). *Jenseits der Gewalt. Hilfen für mißhandelte Kindert.* Frankfurt, Germany: Stroemfeld, Roter Stern.

Bernecker, A. (1975). *Entwicklung und Probleme des Kinderschutzes in der BRD* [Development and problems of child protection in the Federal Republic of Germany]. Unpublished diploma thesis, Free University Berlin, Institute of Sociology.

Bernecker, A., & Wolff, R. (1985). *Kinder im Familienkonflikt. Verstehen und helfen.* Berlin: Kinderschutz-Zentrum Berlin.

Brinckmann, W., & Honig, M.-S. (Eds.). (1984). *Kinderschutz als sozialpolitische Praxis. Hilfe, Schutz und Kontrolle.* Munich, Germany: Kösel Verlag.

Bunting, M. (1991, July 12). Our kids on the block. *The Guardian,* p. 23.

Gelles, R., & Cornell, C. P. (1983). International perspectives on child abuse. *Child Abuse and Neglect, 7,* 375–386.

Hardiker, P., Exton, K., & Barker, M. (1991). The social policy context of prevention in child care. *British Journal of Social Work, 21,* 341–359.

Honig, M.-S. (Ed.). (1982). *Kindesmißhandlung.* Munich, Germany: Juventa Verlag.

Julien, C. (1995, June). Brève radiographie d'une fracture sociale. Pour une authentique "Pacte Républicain." *Monde diplomatique, 42*495, 16–17.

Kempe, C. H., Silverman, F. N., Steele, B. F., Droegemueller, W., & Silver, H. K. (1962). The battered child syndrome. *Journal of The American Medical Assoc., 18*(1), 17–24.

Kinderschuiz-Zentrum. (1975). Berlin: Plan Und Begruendung, p. 2.

Kuczynski, J. (1969). *Studien zur Geschichte der Lage des arbeitenden Kindes in Deutschland von 1,700 bis zur Gegenwart.* Berlin.

Lorenz, W. (1991). The new German Children and Young People Act. *British Journal of Social Work, 21,* 329–339.

Pelton, L. H. (1990, Fall). Resolving the crisis in child welfare. Simply expanding the present system is not enough. *Public Welfare, 48*(4), 19–25.

Rutschky, K. (1992). *Erregte Aufklarung. Fakten und Fiktionen.* Hamburg, Germany: Klein Verlag.

Rutschky, K., & Wolff, R. (Eds.). (1994). *Handbuch sexueller Mißbrauch.* Hamburg, Germany: Klein Verlag.

Sale, A., & Davies, M. (Eds.). (1990). *Child protection policies and practice in Europe* (Occasional Paper No. 9). London: National Society for the Prevention of Cruelty to Children.

Statistisches Bundesamt: Statistical forms used for Fachserie 13, Jugendhilfe (1995).

Titmuss, R. (1968). *Commitment to welfare.* New York: Pantheon Books.

U.S. Advisory Board on Child Abuse and Neglect Report. (1990, June).

Wittenhagen, U., & Wolff, R. (1980). *Kindesmisshandlung und Kinderschutz. Ein Ueberblick* [Child abuse and child protection. An overview]. Bonn, Germany: BMJFG (Bundesministerium Für Jugend, Familie Und Gesundheit).

Wolff, R. (1996). Kinderschutz. In D. Kreft & J. Mielenz (Eds.), *Wörter buch soziäle arbeit* (4th Ed.). Weinheim, Basel: Beliz.

Zellman, G. L., & Antler, S. (1990). Mandated reporters and CPS. A study of frustration. *Public Welfare, 48,* 30–46.

10

Conclusion

A Comparative Perspective

There are similarities and differences among the policies and practices of the child abuse reporting systems examined in this book. One of the important variations around which the countries were grouped concerns the extent to which their child abuse reporting systems emphasize child protection or family service orientations. These two orientations to practice can be distinguished along several dimensions (see Table 10-1).

First, and perhaps most salient, is how the problem of child abuse is framed. In some systems the act of abuse is perceived foremost as a problem that demands the protection of children from harm by degenerate relatives — the "child-saving" approach as described by Lawrence-Karski (chapter 1). In other systems it is seen as a problem of family conflict/dysfunction stemming from social and psychological difficulties that are responsive to services and public aid. Thus Roelofs and Baartman (chapter 8) note that families reported for abuse are seen as enmeshed in a web of problems that include the parent's psychological and marital problems, the child's problems, communication problems inside the family, and socioeconomic stress. Depending on the nature of their problems, these cases are referred to agencies that provide treatment to the family.

Second, depending on how the problem is framed, the reporting systems tend to operate primarily as a response to family need or as a mechanism of deviance control. Thus preliminary intervention under the child protection systems is more of an investigatory process backed by the legal powers of the state, which stand ever ready to be invoked, in contrast to the therapeutic family needs assessment of the service-oriented systems. "Considering child abuse as a crime or as a result of family dysfunction," Marneffe and Broos (chapter 7) point out, "determines the reactions of society to child maltreatment" (p. 180).

The third distinguishing characteristic follows this observation. That is, representatives of public authority function more in a partnership with parents and even children in service-oriented systems compared to the adversarial relationship characteristic of child protective systems.

Table 10-1. Characteristics of Child Protective and Family Service Orientations

	Child Protection	Family Service
Problem frame	Individual/moralistic	Social/psychological
Preliminary intervention	Legalistic/investigatory	Therapeutic/needs assessment
State-parent relationship	Adversarial	Partnership
Out-of-home placement	Involuntary	Voluntary

Finally, there is a generally high rate of voluntary arrangements with parents in making out-of-home placements under the service-oriented systems. In Denmark, Belgium, and Sweden, for example, 75–90% of out-of-home placements are voluntary. In contrast, the vast majority of out-of-home placements are compelled through the coercive powers of the state in child protective systems.

As noted above, all the countries do not fit neatly into these categories. In England, for example, the central tendency toward a child protective orientation has been modified in recent years as policy initiatives have moved practice away from coercive intrusion into family life. The Children Act 1989, as Berridge (chapter 3) explains, "strikes a good balance among emphasizing themes of partnership with parents, avoiding coercive measures whenever possible, and giving children a stronger voice" (p. 94). Nevertheless, he concludes that child welfare cases too often invoke protective procedures rather than provide welfare. In the Netherlands, the family service orientation is represented by the Confidential Doctor Offices, which receive reports of all types of cases. However, as Roelofs and Baartman note (chapter 8), a more legalistic child protection approach is also present in the Child Care and Protection Board, which receives the most severe cases and often brings these cases to the attention of the courts. In Sweden efforts are under way to modify the family service orientation and to extend protective measures for children.

Recently Canada and the United States have experienced a growing movement toward the "least intrusive" approach to child protection, which emphasizes in-home services and family preservation (Lindsey, 1994a). In the United States, Congress authorized $930 million in 1993 to fund family preservation and community-based family support services over a 5-year period. Still, there are those in the United States who advise caution against separating the investigative and service functions in child protection, pointing to some of the negative consequences that accompanied the separation of financial aid and services in public welfare (Hutchinson, Dattalo, & Rodwell, 1994). Also there is a growing debate about the effectiveness of family preservation services. Initial program evaluations showed little difference between experimental and control groups in terms of preventing out-of-home placements, although these studies have been challenged for methodological weaknesses and research in this area continues (Lindsey, 1994a; Pecora, Fraser, Nelson, McCroskey, & Meezan, 1995).

In examining the characteristics of child protection and family service orientations, there are nuances in the way the problem is framed, even within categories. In Finland, as Pösö points out (chapter 6), the interpretation of the problem is so strongly oriented toward social/psychological aspects of family relations that incidents that might be perceived as child abuse are most often reported and addressed as family conflicts (except for sexual abuse, a point to which I return later). In Germany, as Wolff explains (chapter 9), child abuse is viewed in the broader context as stemming from not only social/psychological difficulties, but related to cultural, political, and gender problems as well.

In some respects the family service orientation favors parents' rights over children's rights, particularly the rights of parents to maintain custody of and on-going relations with their children. In Sweden and Belgium, for example, adoption is almost unheard of and birth parents have the right to continuous contact with their children even when out-of-home placement is required. In Finland out-of-home placements are rare. Yet in other respects children rights are highly advanced in each of these countries, where corporal punishment of children is against the law. The recent revisions proposed in Swedish child welfare legislation noted by Olsson Hort (chapter 4) seek additional safeguards for children by partially limiting parental access to children who are removed from their homes.

Mandatory Versus Nonmandatory Reporting

One of the interesting variations in the legal structure of child abuse reporting systems involves the requirement for mandatory reporting of suspected cases. Of the nine countries, five have mandatory reporting laws under which various designated groups such as doctors, nurses, social workers, police, foster parents, dental hygienists, film developers, and teachers are required to inform the appropriate local child welfare authorities whenever they suspect the likelihood of child abuse. In addition to identifying professionals who work with children specifically, Swift (chapter 2) finds that most of the legislation in Canadian provinces requires reports to be made by " 'anyone' aware of a child in need of protection" (p. 49).

The presence of mandatory reporting laws does not appear to be linked to child protective or family service orientations. Among the family-service-oriented systems, Belgium, the Netherlands, and Germany have no mandatory reporting laws, whereas Denmark, Sweden, and Finland have such laws. In the systems that emphasize child protection, there is mandatory reporting in the United States and Canada, but not in England.

Regarding the British experience, Berridge (chapter 3) notes that mandatory reporting was rejected in England because the built-in channels of communication and professional accountability in local health and social service departments would assure that professionals (e.g., doctors, health visitors, and school nurses) regularly in contact with children would do their duty to protect children. In a similar vein, the absence of mandatory reporting in Belgium, the Netherlands, and Germany might be accounted for by the presence of well-developed and tightly knit social service networks in which children regularly come under professional surveillance of doctors, day care staff, school personnel, and other public service workers. This might explain the need for mandatory reporting in the United States and Canada where local social service provisions are less integrated and well developed, but not in the Nordic countries, which have elaborate social service networks with a high degree of public surveillance of children.

Although mandatory reporting operates in both child protection and family-service-oriented systems, the filing of a report in each of these two systems has somewhat different implications. Reports filed in systems with a protective orientation prompt investigations that are more legalistic and vested with the coercive powers of the state than those filed in systems with a service orientation, which emphasizes therapeutic and voluntary measures.

Reporting and Placement Rates

Efforts by public authorities to collect data on child abuse reporting rates and placements vary in rigor and scope among the nine countries, as do definitions of abuse and types of placement alternatives. The figures presented in the case studies allow only a very rough comparison among the countries, which provides at best a general sense of magnitudes. If we are willing to forego precise discriminations, the figures in Table 10-2 offer broad profiles for comparative purposes that are of heuristic value.

In analyzing reporting rates from different countries it is important to assess the comparability of these data on at least three dimensions: whether the data are child based, thus including all the children subject to a report, or family based, in which case the number of reports cited will usually be smaller than the number of children actually investigated; whether the data include duplicate reports on the same case in one year; and the age limit used to define children for reporting purposes. These dimensions are specified, if known, in Table 10-2.

The child abuse reporting rates shown in Table 10-2 reveal a large degree of variance among regions, ranging from a low of 2 reports per 1,000 children in Finland to 70 per 1,000 in California. (There is also considerable variance within countries as reflected in the figures for the United States and Canada.) In general it appears that the Anglo-American countries with reporting systems oriented toward child protection register much higher rates of reporting than the family-service-oriented systems such as the Netherlands, Finland, and Belgium, for which data are available.

Over the past several years, public attention in most of the countries has increasingly focused on reports of child sexual abuse. This development has been stirred by newspaper and television broadcasts of sensational cases such as the Bolderkar affair in the Netherlands, the Cleveland case in the United Kingdom, and the McMartin Preschool case in California. In Finland, where other forms of child abuse are usually reported as episodes of family conflict, Pösö (chapter 6) notes that "concerns about child sexual abuse are emerging as

Table 10-2. Child Abuse Reporting and Placement Rates, 1992–1993

	Child-Based Reports Per 1,000 Children	Out-of-Home Placements Per 1,000 Children
Netherlands[a] (to age 17)	4.9	5.2
United States	43	
California (to age 18)	70	9.3
England[c] (to age 16)	13.6	1–4
Belgium[d] (to age 17)	2.91	9.0
Finland [e] (to age 17)	−	7.0
Sweden (to age 17)	−	8.5
Canada[f]	−	5.9
Ontario (to age 15)	21	4.9
Denmark (to age 17)	−	10.5
Germany	15	7.3

[a]The report rate for family-based reports was 3.5 per 1,000 children; out-of-home placements do not include court-ordered supervision, under which parents must share authority with a family guardian.

[b]Reporting rates include duplicate reports.

[c]Reporting rates based on extrapolation from eight local authorities. For placement rates, the 1 per 1,000 children figure represents the number of children on child protection registers who are in out-of-home placement; the 4 per 1,000 children figure represents the total number of children in out-of-home placements, most of whom are not recorded on child protection registers.

[d]Rates based on reports to all SOS Enfants and Confidential Doctor Centers. There were also 0.5 per 1,000 children reported to the police (some of whom may also have been reported to the centers).

[e]Out-of-home placement rates for 1987. Estimated reports based on case study and registered cases of abuse and neglect.

[f]Placement rates are for children to age 14 years. Overall placement rate for Canada represents the median rate, ranging from 1.0 to 8.5 per 1,000, for nine jurisdictions.

the most dominant issue for the near future." In Belgium reports of sexual abuse increased by 900% between 1986 and 1992. In the United States advocates claim that one in three young girls will be sexually abused before 18 years of age (Finkelhor, Hotling, Lewis, & Smith, 1990; Russell, 1984), but a critical examination of the research on which their claims are based reveals that these figures are heavily inflated by defining the problem to include everything from attempted petting and threatening kisses to any exploitative contact such as touches on the leg all the way to forced sexual intercourse (Gilbert, 1994). Although the incidence of child sexual abuse in the United States is far from the rate claimed by advocates, it is nevertheless a serious problem; in 1993 there were 140,000 children (or 2.2 per 1,000 children under age 18) substantiated or indicated as victims of child sexual abuse (U.S. Department of Health and Human Services, 1995).

Although not delineated in Table 10-2, the rates at which reports of child abuse are substantiated also vary. In regard to substantiation rates, for comparative purposes it is important to know the base of reported cases (all reports, only those investigated, etc.) against which the rates are calculated and how substantiation is interpreted (i.e., clear evidence of abuse, enough suspicion of abuse to reach a second or third level of screening, etc.). In the

United States, 39% of reported cases were substantiated compared to, for example, an 85% substantiation rate in the Netherlands. However the Dutch calculate substantiation relative to reports investigated. Only 55% of the cases reported in the Netherlands were investigated; the remaining 45% were deemed in need only of advice rather than investigation. Thus in relation to the total number of cases reported in the Netherlands, 47% were substantiated, which is much closer to the U.S. rate.

In Ontario, Canada, the substantiation rate was 28% with an additional 31% of the child abuse reports classified as "suspected," which suggests that although evidence was not found, one could not rule out the occurrence of abuse. In England a study of eight local authorities showed that 24% of all cases reported reached the third level of screening (interagency child protection conference) and only 16% were retained in the system after the child protection conference. The experiences in these countries suggest that while overall rates vary, a significant proportion, 50% or more, of child abuse reports are not substantiated.

What happens when reports of child abuse are substantiated? The responses to child abuse include offers of advice, psychological counseling, day care services, and material assistance, as well as court-ordered supervision, under which parents must share responsibility for their children with a family guardian, and out-of-home placement of children, which may be voluntary or involuntary. Involuntary removal of children from their home is usually reserved for cases that are most threatening to the child's well-being.

The data on out-of-home placement rates in Table 10-2 make for interesting comparisons to the reporting rates on two accounts. First, varying from a low of 1 to 4 per 1,000 children (depending on whether one counts only those in out-of-home placements who were on child protection registers or all children in out-of-home placements) in England to a high of 10.5 per 1,000 children in Denmark, the range of out-of-home placement rates is much narrower than the range of reporting rates. Second, there is no apparent link between placement rates and the orientation of reporting systems. The United States, with a child protective orientation, and Denmark, with a family service orientation, register the highest out-of-home placement rates, while the lowest placement rates appear in family-service-oriented Netherlands and child-protective-oriented England. Although the differences are small, Finland, Sweden, and Belgium have higher rates than Canada.

However, an examination of what these numbers represent in terms of the types of placements made and the extent to which they are involuntary suggests some operational patterns that do reflect the different orientations of reporting systems. Denmark, Sweden, Belgium, and Finland, for example, are the family-service-oriented systems with the highest out-of-home placement rates, but in each of these countries the vast majority of placements, from 75 to 90%, are voluntary. In the countries with child-oriented systems, most out-of-home placements are involuntary. Regarding the nature of placements, as Pruzan (chapter 5) points out, Denmark's relatively high out-of-home placement rates include stays in boarding or continuation schools, placements on a ship, and lodging that allows adolescents to live independently away from their parents. (Out-of-home placement rates in the United States would no doubt climb precipitously if publicly subsidized units were available for adolescents having difficulties at home.) The fact that the out-of-home placement rates per 1,000 children are higher than the child abuse reporting rates in, for example, the Netherlands, Finland, and Belgium suggests that a large proportion of these placements may be addressing problems other than child abuse, such as delinquent behavior, parent-child conflicts, and handicaps.

Divergent Trends

With child abuse reporting rates increasing significantly in most of the countries, one might expect a concomitant rise in out-of-home placement rates. The more problems uncovered, the more children to be removed from dangerous conditions at home. It is somewhat paradoxical therefore to find a declining rate of out-of-home placements in almost every country, with the notable exception of the United States. (In California, for example, out-of-home placements rose from 5.7 to 9.3 per 1,000 children between 1986 and 1991.)

Why have out-of-home placement rates diminished even as reports of abuse are increasing? There are a number of plausible explanations that might be offered. First, out-of-home placements are very costly. In recent years these costs have become more difficult to finance because of increasing fiscal pressures on the welfare systems in North America and western Europe, where public expenditures are being stretched to meet the rising needs of aging populations. Second, beyond the economics of placement, as Roelofs and Baartman (chapter 8) and Berridge (chapter 3) suggest, there has been mounting evidence about the negative developmental consequences for children of disrupting parent-child relationships. At the same time, Berridge (chapter 3) and Olsson Hort (chapter 4) note growing concerns in England and Sweden, respectively, about state intrusion into the private lives of families, prompting efforts to constrain the powers and role of the state vis-à-vis parental rights. It has also been suggested that demographic shifts such as lower marriage rates and particularly the increasing proportion of women working outside the home have reduced the pool of potential foster care providers, placing practical limits on the possibilities for out-of-home placements.

In addition, the lower rates of out-of-home placements per 1,000 children may reflect not so much that fewer children are being placed in out-of-home care in recent years as that those being placed are staying there for shorter periods, resulting in higher termination rates each year, which appears to be the case in Sweden.

To varying extents, these economic, psychological, political, demographic, and social factors help to explain the decreasing rates of out-of-home placement, but they do not directly address the issue of why these placement rates have declined in the face of rising reports of abuse. On this point we might speculate that the increased reporting rates represent more a heightened sensitivity to the less severe and less threatening forms of child abuse than a vast detection of highly dangerous cases of abuse.

This heightened sensitivity is reflected, for example, in the Finnish and Swedish laws against corporal punishment of children and in broad legislative definitions of abuse that have shifted, as Pösö (chapter 6) notes, "from specific concerns about abusive behavior to more comprehensive (and vaguer) concerns for ensuring the child's health and development" (p. 148). In the Netherlands, over 40% of all substantiated reports involve "emotional abuse and/or neglect," a vague concept that embraces, as Roelofs and Baartman (chapter 8) suggest, "all situations not beneficial to the development and well-being of the child" (p. 197). Swift (chapter 2) indicates that emotional abuse is increasingly being substantiated in Canada. Similarly, in Belgium, Marneffe and Broos (chapter 7) explain that emotional or psychological abuse refers to detrimental treatment, which includes verbal harassment, criticism, belittlement, withdrawal, and rejection of a child.

Finally, in making cross-national comparisons of reporting rates and placement trends it is important to bear in mind several broader factors about the national contexts in which the child abuse reporting systems are embedded. To what extent do the incidence of poverty and drug abuse and the accessibility of public provisions such as day care, home health visitors, and family supplements contribute to the reported rates of abuse and the need for out-of-home placements?

According to Lawrence-Karski (chapter 1), the high rate of involuntary out-of-home placements in California is associated with poverty and drug abuse. More generally, both Lindsey (1994b) and Pelton (1989) have argued that many of the children who come to the attention of child protective services in the United States are victims of poverty-related neglect or inadequate care. Canada and the United States have the highest rates of children in poverty and the highest rates of child abuse reports and involuntary placements. It is possible that in comparing a country with relatively high levels of poverty, drug abuse, and involuntary out-of-home placements with a country where rates of poverty and drug abuse are low and involuntary out-of-home placements are rare, we are to some degree dealing with different types of problems under the general rubric of child abuse. That is, for example, families that voluntarily seek assistance from the Confidential Doctor Centers in Belgium and the Netherlands might have more in common with many American families who voluntarily receive counseling and family therapy from private practitioners than with families who come under investigation from public child protective service agencies.

Comparative analysis of the nine countries surveyed in this book illustrates alternative perceptions of child abuse and varied arrangements designed to address this problem. The analysis indicates that while the number of reports has generally increased, the rate of out-of-home placements has declined (except in the United States) and in many countries a significant proportion of child abuse reports is not substantiated. While focusing on details of programs and policies, comparative analysis inevitably draws our attention to broader societal conditions that may influence the scope of the problem and the character of the public response. Although the analysis does not yield firm conclusions about how best to design systems of intervention that accurately identify and effectively treat child abuse, it deepens our understanding of this difficult problem and opens new avenues of thought and action for policy makers to explore.

References

Finkelhor, D., Hotling, G., Lewis, I., & Smith, C. (1990). Child abuse in a national survey of adult men and women: Prevalence, characteristics, and risk factors. *Child Abuse and Neglect, 14*(1), 19–28.

Gilbert, N. (1994). Miscounting social ills. *Society, 31*(3), 18–26.

Hutchinson, E., Dattalo, P., & Rodwell, M. (1994). Reorganizing child protective services: Protecting children and providing family support. *Children and Youth Services Review, 16*(5/6), 295–308.

Lindsey, D. (Ed.). (1994a). Family preservation and child protection: Striking a balance [Special issue]. *Children and Youth Services Review, 16*(5/6).

Lindsey, D. (1994b). *The welfare of children.* New York: Oxford University Press.

Pecora, P., Fraser, M., Nelson, K., McCroskey, J., & Meezan, W. (1995). *Evaluating family based services.* New York: Aldine De Gruyter.

Pelton, L. (1989). *For reasons of poverty: A critical analysis of the public child welfare system in the United States.* New York: Praeger.

Russell, D. (1984). *Sexual exploitation: Rape, child sexual abuse, and workplace harassment.* Beverly Hills, CA: Sage Publications.

U.S. Department of Health and Human Services. (1995). *Child maltreatment 1993: Reports from states to the National Center on Child Abuse and Neglect.* Washington, DC: Government Printing Office.

Author Index

Subject Index